Recognizing Textual Entailment

Models and Applications

Synthesis Lectures on Human Language Technologies

Editor
Graeme Hirst, *University of Toronto*

Synthesis Lectures on Human Language Technologies is edited by Graeme Hirst of the University of Toronto. The series consists of 50- to 150-page monographs on topics relating to natural language processing, computational linguistics, information retrieval, and spoken language understanding. Emphasis is on important new techniques, on new applications, and on topics that combine two or more HLT subfields.

Recognizing Textual Entailment: Models and Applications
Ido Dagan, Dan Roth, Mark Sammons, and Fabio Massimo Zanzotto
2013

Web Corpus Construction
Roland Schäfer and Felix Bildhauer
2013

Semi-Supervised Learning and Domain Adaptation in Natural Language Processing
Anders Søgaard
2013

Linguistic Fundamentals for Natural Language Processing: 100 Essentials from Morphology and Syntax
Emily M. Bender
2013

Semantic Relations Between Nominals
Vivi Nastase, Preslav Nakov, Diarmuid Ó Séaghdha, and Stan Szpakowicz
2013

Computational Modeling of Narrative
Inderjeet Mani
2012

Natural Language Processing for Historical Texts
Michael Piotrowski
2012

Introduction to Chinese Natural Language Processing
Kam-Fai Wong, Wenjie Li, Ruifeng Xu, and Zheng-sheng Zhang
2009

Introduction to Linguistic Annotation and Text Analytics
Graham Wilcock
2009

Dependency Parsing
Sandra Kübler, Ryan McDonald, and Joakim Nivre
2009

Statistical Language Models for Information Retrieval
ChengXiang Zhai
2008

Recognizing Textual Entailment: Models and Applications

Ido Dagan, Dan Roth, Mark Sammons, and Fabio Massimo Zanzotto

ISBN: 978-3-031-01023-1   paperback
ISBN: 978-3-031-02151-0   ebook

DOI 10.1007/978-3-031-02151-0

A Publication in the Springer series
SYNTHESIS LECTURES ON HUMAN LANGUAGE TECHNOLOGIES

Lecture #23
Series Editor: Graeme Hirst, *University of Toronto*
Series ISSN
Synthesis Lectures on Human Language Technologies
Print 1947-4040   Electronic 1947-4059

Recognizing Textual Entailment

Models and Applications

Ido Dagan
Bar-Ilan University, Israel

Dan Roth
University of Illinois, Urbana, IL

Mark Sammons
University of Illinois, Urbana, IL

Fabio Massimo Zanzotto
University of Rome "Tor Vergata," Italy

SYNTHESIS LECTURES ON HUMAN LANGUAGE TECHNOLOGIES #23

ABSTRACT

In the last few years, a number of NLP researchers have developed and participated in the task of Recognizing Textual Entailment (RTE). This task encapsulates Natural Language Understanding capabilities within a very simple interface: recognizing when the meaning of a text snippet is contained in the meaning of a second piece of text. This simple abstraction of an exceedingly complex problem has broad appeal partly because it can be conceived also as a component in other NLP applications, from Machine Translation to Semantic Search to Information Extraction. It also avoids commitment to any specific meaning representation and reasoning framework, broadening its appeal within the research community. This level of abstraction also facilitates evaluation, a crucial component of any technological advancement program. This book explains the RTE task formulation adopted by the NLP research community, and gives a clear overview of research in this area. It draws out commonalities in this research, detailing the intuitions behind dominant approaches and their theoretical underpinnings. This book has been written with a wide audience in mind, but is intended to inform all readers about the state of the art in this fascinating field, to give a clear understanding of the principles underlying RTE research to date, and to highlight the short- and long-term research goals that will advance this technology.

KEYWORDS

natural language processing, textual entailment, textual inference, knowledge acquisition, machine learning

Contents

List of Figures

List of Tables

Preface

In the last few years, a number of NLP researchers have developed and participated in the task of Recognizing Textual Entailment (RTE). This task encapsulates Natural Language Understanding capabilities within a very simple interface: recognizing when the meaning of a text snippet is contained in the meaning of a second piece of text. This simple abstraction of an exceedingly complex problem has broad appeal partly because it can be conceived also as a component in other NLP applications, from Machine Translation to Semantic Search to Information Extraction. It also avoids commitment to any specific meaning representation and reasoning framework, broadening its appeal within the research community. This level of abstraction also facilitates evaluation, a crucial component of any technological advancement program. This book explains the RTE task formulation adopted by the NLP research community and gives an overview of research in this area. It draws out commonalities in this research, detailing the intuitions behind dominant approaches and their theoretical underpinnings.

Chapter 1 provides the context for textual entailment research. It describes the motivation and rationale for the entailment recognition task and specifies its scope and positioning. The chapter further reviews the utility of entailment recognition in various NLP applications and describes in detail the evaluation methodologies used for RTE. Chapter 2 focuses on the intuitive model underlying RTE systems developed to date, and describes a generic architecture to which those systems conform. It describes limitations of the naive approach and motivates the more detailed discussion that follows. Chapter 3 describes Machine Learning techniques applied to the RTE task, and fleshes out the theoretical basis of the various models developed for RTE. Chapter 4 surveys some specific RTE systems, describing them in terms of the framework developed in the preceding chapters in order to facilitate comparison. Chapter 5 addresses the problem of the "knowledge acquisition bottleneck," i.e., the problem of acquiring the background knowledge needed for broad textual inference, surveying research in this area. Chapter 6 concludes the book with a short exploration of open research questions in this area.

This book has been written with a wide audience in mind, but is intended to inform all readers about the state of the art in this fascinating field, to give a clear understanding of the principles underlying RTE research to date, and to highlight the short- and long-term research goals that will advance this technology.

Ido Dagan, Dan Roth, Mark Sammons, and Fabio Massimo Zanzotto
May 2013

Acknowledgments

The authors are indebted to the publisher, Mike Morgan, and editor, Graeme Hirst, for their hard work in coordinating this project, and for their patience. We thank the three anonymous reviewers for their thorough reviews and insightful suggestions that helped us significantly improve the book. We thank Jonathan Berant and Eyal Shnarch for contributing input to the chapter on Knowledge Acquisition. We are grateful to the colleagues who were intensively involved in establishing and organizing the Recognizing Textual Entailment (RTE) challenges, including Oren Glickman, Bernardo Magnini, Luisa Bentivogli, Danilo Giampiccolo, Hoa Trang Dang, Lucy Vanderwende, Bill Dolan, and Peter Clark, as well as the PASCAL Network of Excellence, NIST, and CELCT for funding the challenges and Michele Sebag from PASCAL for her continuous support. We also thank students and colleagues whose joint work contributed ideas and perspectives that found their way into this book: Lorenzo Dell'Arciprete, Maayan Zhitomirsky-Geffet, Idan Szpektor, Roy Bar-Haim, Shachar Mirkin, Jonathan Berant, Eyal Shnarch, Asher Stern, Lili Kotlerman, Jacob Goldberger, Sebastian Pado, Marco Pennacchiotti, Alessandro Moschitti, V.G. Vinod Vydiswaran, Vasin Punyakanok, Rodrigo de Salvo Braz, Vivek Srikumar, Ming-Wei Chang, Dan Goldwasser, Roxana Girju, and other members of the Cognitive Computation Group at Illinois that helped this effort directly or indirectly. We thank the substantial support of the EXCITEMENT project to RTE research and infrastructure, under the European Community's Seventh Framework Programme (FP7/2007-2013), grant agreement no. 287923, and to other research sponsors that have funded our RTE-related work: Boeing; the U.S. government via ARDA, DHS, the DARPA Machine Reading program, and the DARPA Deep Exploration and Filtering of Text program; the Israel Science Foundation; the Israeli Ministry of Science, Technology and Space; and the collaboration project of FBK-irst, University of Haifa, and Bar-Ilan University.

Ido thanks Taly, his wife, for endless patience and support along the years, without which his Textual Entailment endeavor would not have been possible, as well as Yuval, Ori, and Inbal for accommodating the long hours spent on this book. He also thanks his students at the Natural Language Processing Lab for their dedication, and the great atmosphere they created along the joint effort.

Dan thanks his wife, Michal, for her love and support, and Noam, Edo, and Ella for their love and for reminding him what really matters. He also thanks his students and colleagues in the Cognitive Computation Group for their hard work over the years and for making it all possible.

Mark thanks Lauren, Alex, and Teddy for their enduring support and understanding, and his colleagues and research partners in the Cognitive Computation Group for their hard work on numerous RTE-related projects.

Fabio thanks Emanuela Bizzarri for her supportive help during these years used to develop, collect, and write the ideas in this book.

Ido Dagan, Dan Roth, Mark Sammons, and Fabio Massimo Zanzotto
May 2013

CHAPTER 1

Textual Entailment

1.1 MOTIVATION AND RATIONALE

Inference is generally perceived as the process by which new consequents are concluded from given information. For example, the Merriam-Webster online dictionary[1] defines the first sense of *infer* as "to derive as a conclusion from facts or premises". Somewhat more technically, *inference* is defined as "the act of passing from one proposition, statement, or judgment considered as true to another whose truth is believed to follow from that of the former".

Moving to the realm of Natural Language Processing (NLP), we can analogically perceive inference over information stated in human language. Such inference can be defined as the process of concluding the truth of a *textual* statement based on (the truth of) another given piece of text. This language-oriented view on inference was captured by the *textual entailment* paradigm, originally proposed by Dagan and Glickman in 2004 [74] and subsequently established through the series of benchmarks known as the *PASCAL Recognising Textual Entailment (RTE) Challenges* [76].[2]

While capturing a generic notion of inference over texts, the introduction of entailment recognition as a computational task was particularly motivated by its overarching potential for NLP applications. For example, consider a Question Answering (QA) scenario, addressing the question "*Who painted 'The Scream'?*". In order to provide the answer "Edvard Munch", based on the text snippet "*Norway's most famous painting, 'The Scream' by Edvard Munch,…*", the QA system needs to validate that the hypothesized answer statement "Edvard Munch painted 'The Scream'." is indeed *entailed* (inferred) by the given text.

As argued in the textual entailment literature (e.g. [73]), despite the fact that such similar semantic inference needs arise across numerous applications, research and technology practices have been largely scattered. Typically, complete inference mechanisms are developed separately, and quite independently, within each application area. General purpose resources and tools, on the other hand, exist only for some specific semantic phenomena. These include knowledge resources of lexical-semantic information, either created manually, most notably WordNet [90] and FrameNet [92], or extracted statistically from corpora, such as distributional similarity thesauri [141] and inference rules for predicates [143], or created from semi-structured web resources like Wikipedia [230]. With respect to computational processing modules, just a few individual seman-

---

[1]http://www.merriam-webster.com
[2]At the time of writing, RTE 7 was underway. See http://www.nist.gov/tac/2011/RTE/index.html.

tic sub-tasks have matured to provide publicly available tools, notably Named Entity Recognition [214], Semantic Role Labeling [44], and Word Sense Disambiguation [270].

With generic components covering only specific semantic phenomena, building a complete inference mechanism within an NLP application typically involves somewhat ad-hoc assembly of a subset of such components along with additional targeted developments. These practices vary largely across application areas, where researchers in one area might not be sufficiently aware of relevant methods developed in the context of another application. To a large extent, this fragmented state of affairs was caused by the lack of a generic framework that captures the inference needs of different applications in a unifying manner. This situation might be contrasted, for example, with the state of affairs in syntactic processing, where a clear application-independent task is commonly accepted, which is in turn investigated by a coherent community.

Establishing such a unifying framework for applied semantic inference was exactly the goal of the textual entailment paradigm. The motivation for focusing on this particular task was the observation that many semantic inference needs in NLP can be cast in terms of textual entailment. Following our example above, question answering systems have to recognize that a candidate text passage indeed entails the hypothesized answer. Similar entailment inferences would be needed for an Information Extraction (IE) system, such as for recognizing that the pair "Munch; The Scream" is a valid extraction instance for the "painter of" relation. Within Information Retrieval, the combination of semantic concepts and relations in certain queries should be entailed from relevant retrieved documents, such as for the query "Scandinavian paintings".

As elaborated later in this chapter, such reductions from various application inferences to the entailment task were exercised in both constructed benchmarks and actual application evaluations. In the PASCAL RTE Challenges entailment test cases were created from data corresponding to several applications (see Table 1.1). The CLEF Answer Validation Exercise (AVE)[3] focused on validating the output of actual QA systems through entailment recognition [190], following the scenario exemplified above. A number of works tested the utility of textual entailment technology as inference components within different applications, including question answering [109], unsupervised information extraction [207], text summarization [110], machine translation [168], machine translation evaluation [183], and intelligent tutoring [181].

As described throughout this book, textual entailment research has led so far to the development of appealing inference algorithms, components, and knowledge resources, and yielded a fairly good understanding of a range of problems and methods. Overall, the promise behind the textual entailment paradigm is that it can provide a complete inference process under a single core task, while bundling many inference components and knowledge resources that may be hidden from the end application. The ultimate goal of the field is thus to provide packaged entailment-based "inference engines", which different applications can leverage as embedded technology. Recently, it was proposed to extend this rationale to *Cross-lingual Textual Entailment*, where the goal is to recognize that a text in one language entails a text in another language [159]. Fulfilling

---

[3]http://nlp.uned.es/clef-qa/ave/

this more ambitious goal may further bring the benefits of generic entailment technology to the realm of cross-lingual applications.

1.2   THE RECOGNIZING TEXTUAL ENTAILMENT TASK

The Recognizing Textual Entailment (RTE) task, as defined by Dagan, et al., and established in the RTE challenges [76], is formulated as follows:

Definition 1.1   *Textual entailment* is defined as a **directional** relationship between pairs of text expressions, denoted by T (the entailing "Text") and H (the entailed "Hypothesis"). We say that T entails H if humans reading T would typically infer that H is most likely true.

As noted by Dagan, et al. [76], this definition is based on common human understanding of language, much like the definition of any other language understanding task. Accordingly, it enables the creation of gold-standard evaluation data sets for the task, where humans can judge whether the entailment relation holds for given *Text-Hypothesis* pairs (as elaborated in Section 1.4). This setting is analogous to the creation of gold standards for other text understanding applications like QA and IE, where human annotators need to judge whether the target answer or relation can indeed be inferred from a candidate text. The distinguishing characteristic of the textual entailment task is that it captures textual inference in a generic, application-independent manner. This allows research to focus on core inference issues, while making the results applicable across application areas.

Similar to other semantic annotation tasks, such as those mentioned above, the RTE judgment criterion has some fuzziness with respect to "what a person would typically infer", particularly in boundary cases. However, the various RTE annotation efforts have shown that sufficiently consistent human judgments can be obtained, allowing research progress on this task.

1.2.1   THE SCOPE OF TEXTUAL ENTAILMENT

Table 1.1 shows examples of Text-Hypothesis pairs from the RTE-2 benchmark [8],[4] along with the name of the application from which each pair was drawn and the corresponding entailment annotation. As can be seen from the examples, the textual entailment relation corresponds to a rather broad notion of inference over text expressions. Some entailment cases correspond to the general perception of inference as deriving *new* information from premises, based on reasoning. For example, in pairs 294 and 387 of Table 1.1 the assertions in the hypotheses are derived through general world knowledge, by which "presidents are citizens of their countries" and "people work in their offices". Of course, any type of reasoning may be involved in inferring new information, for example logical reasoning, which yields the non-entailment judgment in pair 110 based on negation, or numerical reasoning, by which we may conclude that "103" entails "more than a

---

[4]http://www.pascal-network.org/Challenges/RTE2

hundred" (e.g. *"The dealer sold 103 cars"* entails *"The dealer sold more than a hundred cars"*). Another type of inference of new information corresponds to consequences of events, where the Hypothesis describes a (most likely) consequent of an event described in the Text[5].

In other textual entailment cases the Hypothesis may not represent new information relative to the Text but rather a *generalization* of some information in it. For example, in pair 415 the Text discusses "slowing down or halting" the disease, which entails the more general statement in the Hypothesis about "treating" the disease. Further, in other cases the statement in the Hypothesis may be *equivalent* to a statement in the Text, while being expressed in different terms. In the simplest case this might correspond to synonym substitution, such as replacing "buy" with "purchase", but in other cases the difference may involve more complex paraphrases. Altogether, we see that textual entailment does not pertain only to the derivation of *new* information through reasoning, but also captures the *variability* of language expression, by which the same information may be stated in many different ways, or at different levels of abstraction. Clearly, both types of inferences are needed for language understanding applications. For example, an answer to a question may be stated explicitly in a text that just phrases it in different terms, or may only be implied from a text through "extra-linguistic" reasoning. While the boundary between such intra- and extra-linguistic inferences is often vague, textual entailment models should cover both types of inference, possibly without making an explicit distinction between them.

It should be emphasized at this point that, in the general case, textual entailment, like logical entailment, is a *directional* relation. Symmetric inference pertains only to the case of *equivalence*, corresponding to bi-directional entailment, in which both text expressions entail each other. Crucially, the directionality of entailment fits the nature of semantic inferences in text understanding applications, which are typically directional as well. Referring to our example 415 again, a query or question about drugs that *treat* Alzheimer's disease should clearly retrieve statements about drugs that *halt* the disease, as well as drugs that *slow it down* or *relieve* its symptoms. On the other hand, a more strict question about *halting* Alzheimer's should not retrieve all mentions of *treatments* for the disease, since these might refer to other levels of treatment. This desired behavior directly corresponds to the fact that *halting* a disease entails *treating* it while entailment does not hold in the opposite direction, in this case because the latter statement is a generalization of the former. As an example for directional inference stemming from world-knowledge reasoning consider an information extraction system that needs to construct a historical database about married couples. In this case, information about a couple getting *divorced* should extract a tuple for the *marriage* relation, because getting divorced entails getting married, historically. On the other hand, if the task is constructing a database of *divorces* then it should not be populated based on instances of *marriages*, because entailment does not hold in this direction.

It is worth comparing the definition and scope of textual entailment to two related notions in NLP research, namely *text similarity* and *paraphrasing*. Text similarity is typically a rather vague

---

[5]The terminology of RTE is overloaded. We use text [span] to describe generic sentences, paragraphs, or portions of same, and Text to refer to the larger component of an entailment pair.

Table 1.1: Examples of Text-Hypothesis pairs, taken from the RTE-2 development set, along with the application (Task) from which they were derived and the human annotation of whether the pair satisfies the entailment relation or not (Judgment). SUM=summarization; IR=information retrieval; IE=information extraction; QA=question answering. See Section 1.4 for the data-set generation methodology

ID	Text	Hypothesis	Task	Judgment
77	Google and NASA announced a working agreement, Wednesday, that could result in the Internet giant building a complex of up to 1 million square feet on NASA-owned property, adjacent to Moffett Field, near Mountain View.	Google may build a campus on NASA property.	SUM	YES
110	Drew Walker, NHS Tayside's public health director, said: "It is important to stress that this is not a confirmed case of rabies."	A case of rabies was confirmed.	IR	NO
294	Meanwhile, in an exclusive interview with a TIME journalist, the first one-on-one session given to a Western print publication since his election as president of Iran earlier this year, Ahmadinejad attacked the "threat" to bring the issue of Iran's nuclear activity to the UN Security Council by the US, France, Britain and Germany.	Ahmadinejad is a citizen of Iran.	IE	YES
387	About two weeks before the trial started, I was in Shapiro's office in Century City.	Shapiro works in Century City.	QA	YES
415	The drugs that slow down or halt Alzheimer's disease work best the earlier you administer them.	Alzheimer's disease is treated using drugs.	IR	YES
691	Arabic, for example, is used densely across North Africa and from the Eastern Mediterranean to the Philippines, as the key language of the Arab world and the primary vehicle of Islam.	Arabic is the primary language of the Philippines.	QA	NO

notion, which refers to some similarity in text meaning but is not related directly to inference. Texts like "monkeys like bananas" and "monkeys like mangoes" would be typically considered similar, but neither can be inferred from the other. The notion of paraphrasing also lacks a clear definition, but it is more closely related to inference since it generally refers to equivalence of meaning. Thus, under a more strict interpretation, the paraphrasing relation between a pair of expressions may be perceived as textual *equivalence*, that is *bi-directional textual entailment*. Under more loose interpretations, the paraphrasing literature often covers cases of limited *generalization* (abstraction), which map to (uni-)directional entailment, as well as cases of almost-complete, yet *partial*, entailment, where each of the expressions strictly entails most of the information stated in the other, but not all of it (possibly omitting some less central information). A survey covering both paraphrasing and entailment methods is provided in [4].

Finally, from a procedural point of view, textual entailment systems were typically applied so far in *recognition* mode, where a $T - H$ pair is given as input and the system needs to classify whether entailment holds for the pair or not. However, since textual entailment is a relation between pairs of texts, it can also be applied in search and generation modes. In *search* mode, the system is given a Hypothesis and a corpus, and needs to find all text fragments in the corpus that entail the hypothesis. Initial explorations of this mode were reported by Bar-Haim et al. [9] and Roth et al. [210]. The search mode also inspired the design of the RTE-5 Pilot Search Task and the subsequent main task of RTE-6 and RTE-7 (see Section 1.4). In *generation* mode, the entailment system is given a text and needs to generate statements which are entailed by the text. This mode has not been explored much yet, but it served as a component for generating entailed sentences, termed "commitments", to support entailment recognition in [117]. Future exploration of this mode may be promising. Particularly, the architecture of transformation-based entailment systems is built around generating consequents from the text and thus lends itself for implementing the entailment generation mode (see Section 4.3). Applying this mode would further relate the entailment framework to the lines of research on paraphrase generation and text-to-text generation.[6]

1.2.2   THE ROLE OF BACKGROUND KNOWLEDGE

As explained above, the definition of the textual entailment recognition task, like that of any other text understanding task, refers to human understanding of language. Such definition necessarily assumes common background knowledge, on which the (human) entailment judgment relies. In accordance with the scope of textual entailment inference (Section 1.2.1), this knowledge should cover both extra-linguistic world knowledge, such as mentioned above for pairs 294 and 387, as well as knowledge of the language itself.[7] Accordingly, entailment systems need to possess substantial amounts of such common world and language knowledge, aiming to mimic the same

---

[6]See for example the Workshop on Monolingual Text-To-Text Generation: https://sites.google.com/site/texttotext2011/

[7]See Section 1.4 for some detail on the scope of knowledge assumed when judging entailment pairs, and corresponding inter-annotator agreement.

amount of knowledge which is assumed for human judgment of entailment. As described later in this book, knowledge acquisition is indeed a major issue in textual entailment research.

The specification of the RTE task also requires that the Text be an essential part of the reasoning for inferring the truth of the Hypothesis. That is, the assumed background knowledge may be used to *augment* the information represented by the Text, in order to entail the Hypothesis. However, we are not allowed to assume background knowledge that entails the hypothesis on its own. For example, consider the Text "*The U.S. citizens elected their new president Obama.*" We can say that this Text entails the Hypothesis "*Obama was born in the U.S.*", based on the assumed common knowledge "U.S. presidents should be naturally born in the U.S.", since this knowledge and the Text *together* imply the Hypothesis. However, we may not conclude that this Text entails the Hypothesis "*The U.S. presidents were born in the U.S.*" based on the same background knowledge. This is because in the latter case the assumed background knowledge suffices to entail the Hypothesis on its own.

This last requirement may be captured in more precise terms by refining the definition of textual entailment in the following spirit. We may say that a text T entails a hypothesis H if there *exists* some background knowledge K such that T and K *together* entail H while K alone does not. In fact, this requirement has implications not only on gold standard annotation guidelines but also on the intended methodology by which textual entailment systems are expected to assess entailment. Systems should validate that information from the given text T is indeed necessary for inferring H, but they should not assess the truth of H only based on some external knowledge resource, such as Wikipedia. Notice that this requirement is implied also in common evaluations of text understanding applications, for which we may want to use embedded entailment systems. In QA and IE, for example, an answer or extraction are typically attributed to concrete text passages, and are considered correct only if they can indeed be inferred from the identified passage.

1.2.3 TEXTUAL ENTAILMENT VERSUS LINGUISTIC NOTION OF ENTAILMENT

The applied-oriented notion of textual entailment is related, of course, to a classical logic-based notion of entailment in linguistics. A common definition of entailment in formal semantics [53] specifies that a Text T entails another text H (hypothesis, in our terminology) if H is true in *every* circumstance (*possible world*) in which T is true. For example, in pair 415 of Table 1.1 the Text strictly implies that Alzheimer's disease is being treated using drugs (literally H), thus matching the classical notion of entailment. However, the textual entailment definition allows for cases in which the truth of the hypothesis is highly plausible ("most likely true"), for most practical purposes, rather than certain. For example, the truth of H in pair 387 may be considered slightly uncertain: there might be a circumstance, at least hypothetically, by which the office in Century City belongs to Shapiro but he is not actually working there. Still, this pair was annotated as YES, which seems to match the practical inference that would typically be expected in an applied scenario. In our case, pair 387 was constructed from a QA instance, and we would indeed expect

> **Text:** The purchase of Houston-based LexCorp by BMI for \$2Bn prompted widespread sell-offs by traders as they sought to minimize exposure. LexCorp had been an employee-owned concern since 2008.
>
> **Hyp** 1: BMI acquired an American company.
> **Hyp** 2: BMI bought employee-owned LexCorp for \$3.4Bn.
> **Hyp** 3: BMI is an employee-owned concern.

Figure 1.1: Representative RTE examples, including contradiction.

a question answering system to provide the answer "Century City" for the question "Where does Shapiro work?", based on the given text.

Another, rather theoretical, difference between textual entailment and the classical notion of entailment pertains to the case in which H is a tautology, that is, it is true in every possible circumstance. According to the formal linguistic definition, such H would be entailed from any T. As specified above (Section 1.2.2), for textual entailment to hold we require that the Text would be essential for inferring the truth of H.

Glickman et al. [104] presented a first attempt to define a coherent probabilistic notion of textual entailment which captures these differences between textual and logical entailment. Roughly speaking, their definition regards T as *probabilistically* entailing H if it *increases* the prior probability of H to be true, where the prior may be interpreted as considering background knowledge alone. It thus allows the truth of H to be uncertain given T, and excludes entailment of an H whose prior probability to be true is 1. For another discussion of the relation between textual entailment and some classical linguistic notions, such as presupposition and implicature, see [259].

Despite these differences, textual entailment follows the same goal as traditional notions of entailment, of capturing inference relations between statements. In both cases the entailment relation is *directional*, where a more specific statement entails a more general one, but not vice versa (unless the two are equivalent). Here, the notion of *specific* versus *general* may be interpreted through the classical definition of entailment quoted above, where the set of circumstances in which the entailing statement is true should be a subset of the corresponding set for the entailed statement. As explained above, in textual entailment inclusion is not strictly required, but circumstances in which T is true while H is not should be rather unlikely.

1.2.4   EXTENDING ENTAILMENT RECOGNITION WITH CONTRADICTION DETECTION

The task of recognizing whether entailment holds for a given $T - H$ pair or not constitutes a two-way classification task. In Figure 1.1, the Text entails Hyp 1, but not Hyp 2, or Hyp 3.

The three-way RTE task introduces the concept of contradiction. We define contradiction in entailment based on de Marneffe, et al. [81]:

Definition 1.2   The Hypothesis H of an entailment pair contradicts the Text T if a human reader would say that H is highly unlikely to be true given the information described in T.

The three-way RTE task requires that systems label each entailment pair as either *Entailed*, *Contradicted*, or *Unknown*—i.e., either T entails H, or H contradicts T, or it is unknown whether H is true given T. In Figure 1.1, the Text T entails Hypothesis 1; Hypothesis 2 contradicts T; and the truth value of Hypothesis 3 is unknown given the information in T. As described in Section 1.4, the RTE-4 and RTE-5 benchmarks included both the two-way and the three-way classification tasks. Wang and Zhang [250] address the sub-task of identifying *text relatedness*, which holds when the Text either entails or contradicts the Hypothesis; otherwise, the Text and Hypothesis are considered unrelated.

1.2.5   THE CHALLENGE AND OPPORTUNITY OF RTE

It is illuminating to trace the inference steps that seem necessary for informed classification of the three entailment pairs in Figure 1.1.

To recognize that Hypothesis 1 is entailed by the Text, a human reader must recognize that 1) "company" in the Hypothesis can match "LexCorp", based on either background knowledge, or on named entity recognition, or on identifying the coreference relation between "LexCorp" and "concern" and the lexical knowledge that "concern" implies "company", and that 2) "based in Houston" implies "American". She must also 3) identify the nominalized relation "purchase", and 4) determine that "A purchased by B" implies "B acquires A".

To recognize that Hypothesis 2 contradicts the Text, similar steps are required, with the difference that the reader must infer that because the stated purchase price is different in the Text and Hypothesis, but with high probability refers to the same transaction, Hypothesis 2 contradicts the Text.

Hypothesis 3 consists entirely of words from the Text, but asserts a relation that cannot be discerned from the Text, and so its label is "Unknown".

This trace illustrates that fully solving the RTE problem seems to a large extent "NLP complete": a reliable and complete model for RTE would require solving many types of NLP problems, as well as additional inference problems investigated in Artificial Intelligence. Indeed, some of the steps needed for RTE relate to tasks that are commonly addressed by the NLP/Computational Linguistics community, such as Named Entity recognition (recognizing that LexCorp and BMI are companies), Co-reference resolution (different mentions of LexCorp refer to the same underlying entity), Semantic Role Labeling (BMI did the buying, not LexCorp), inference-rule acquisition (the entailment relationship between purchasing and acquiring, with proper argument mapping) and context-sensitive inference (knowing that acquisition is synonymous to purchase only when acquiring goods, but not for acquiring knowledge, which partly corresponds to disambiguating between two senses of acquisition). Other relevant tasks have not yet been well-developed in isolation, though some of them may be related to recognized problem definitions, such as modeling monotonicity [151] and bridging references [166]. Even harder may be textual inference steps that require applying understanding of the world to identify cause-effect relations and abstraction over multiple statements to a general principle. And so on.

Of course, actual entailment systems are expected to identify more accurately some of the "easier" phenomena, while heuristically "guessing" otherwise, just like many other language technologies. Taking this rationale to something of an extreme, it might be hypothesized that rather shallow methods, and particularly lexical ones, would perform well for RTE, similar to other experience in NLP of lexical models often being hard to beat (e.g., in statistical machine translation and language modeling). Yet, considering the examples in Figure 1.1 it should be evident that the Text can be made lexically very dissimilar to Hypothesis 1 while maintaining the Entailment relation, and that conversely, the lexical overlap between the Text and Hypothesis 2 can be made very high, while maintaining the Contradiction relation. This intuition is borne out by the results of the RTE challenges, which show that lexical similarity-based systems indeed provide rather high baselines, but are eventually outperformed by systems that use more structured analysis.

As described throughout this book, a range of relevant language processing and inference tasks has already been incorporated and addressed in RTE systems. Other relevant phenomena and tasks were identified in several insightful data analysis investigations, including statistical analysis of the frequency of various phenomena, which may guide future research priorities [11, 60, 98, 166, 243]. The challenge of RTE research is thus to gradually tackle additional and harder entailment phenomena, by focusing on broad coverage of generic inference problems. The corresponding opportunity is that as RTE engines address successfully a richer array of phenomena it would become more beneficial for application developers to utilize them as embedded technology, saving the need to tackle these inference problems explicitly within each application. Initial benefits in this spirit were reported for various applications, as described in the next section.[8]

1.3   APPLICATIONS OF TEXTUAL ENTAILMENT SOLUTIONS

This section describes how several works have cast the inference needs of individual applications in terms of textual entailment, and then utilized entailment technology to improve end-application performance.

1.3.1   QUESTION ANSWERING

In **Question Answering**, entailment recognition can be employed to validate or re-rank candidate answers retrieved by the QA system. The reduction of the answer validation problem to textual en-

---

[8]Information on various types of textual entailment resources is available at http://aclweb.org/aclwiki/index.php?title=Textual_Entailment_Resource_Pool.

tailment is based on the following observation: a candidate answer should be considered correct if and only if the corresponding hypothesized answer statement is entailed by the candidate passage from which the answer was retrieved. Consider again the question *"Who painted 'The Scream'?"*, illustrated at the beginning of this chapter. Initially, this question is transformed to an affirmative-form hypothesis template, with a place-holder variable for the expected answer: "[ANSWER] painted 'The Scream'." Next, when retrieving the candidate answer "Edvard Munch" from the text passage *"Norway's most famous painting, 'The Scream' by Edvard Munch,…"*, this answer instantiates the place-holder variable to form the concrete Hypothesis "Edvard Munch painted 'The Scream'.". This Hypothesis can now be given to an RTE system along with the corresponding text passage, to check whether entailment indeed holds for the pair or not. In case of a correct answer, as in this example, the RTE system is expected to confirm that entailment holds, thus validating the hypothesized answer. For an incorrect candidate answer the RTE system is expected to recognize that entailment does not hold for the pair, allowing to filter out this candidate.

Harabagiu and Hickl [109] followed this methodology to apply an RTE-based solution to re-rank candidate answers of their question answering system. While the top candidate answer proposed by that system may not be correct, in many cases the correct answer is in the set of returned candidates. They then used an RTE system to assess each candidate answer. Their system first applied a rule-based implementation to transform the input question into an affirmative-statement template, creating an entailment pair for each candidate answer as illustrated above. The RTE system is then applied to each pair in turn, moving candidates corresponding to entailing pairs to the top of the list. Their study showed that including the Textual Entailment component improved system accuracy from 30.6% to 42.7%.

Celikyilmaz, et al. [45] transform the query in a similar way to Harabagiu and Hickl, and then employ an entailment recognition system to compute entailment scores for pairs of questions and candidate answer passages. In particular, they address the typical problem of having rather small data sets of labeled gold-standard entailment pairs that can be used for training. They thus use a semi-supervised graph-based method to propagate labels to un-annotated pairs, which enabled them to improve generalization performance over state-of-the-art QA models.

Textual entailment was used for another variant of the question answering setting in the QALL-ME system [91], which addresses the task of **Question Answering from a Structured Database**. Here, an RTE engine is used for question interpretation, that is, for mapping between a natural language question and a (structured) query to the database. This is done by specifying, for each possible database query pattern, a "prototypical" natural language question pattern, for example *"Where can I see the movie [MOVIE]?"*. Then, given a user question, the system looks for a prototypical question pattern that is entailed by the user question, under a matching variable instantiation. In our example, the question *Which cinemas show the movie Dreamgirls tonight?* entails the prototypical pattern given above, when instantiating *[MOVIE]* with *Dreamgirls*. Then, the system triggers the database query to which this pattern is mapped, with the corresponding variable instantiation.

It should be pointed out that the main interface to the RTE engine constitutes the prototypical natural language patterns. Once these have been specified, the QALL-ME system may leverage any RTE engine to address the difficult problem of identifying possible question variants, regardless of the underlying implementation of the RTE system. Indeed, the QALL-ME project experimented with a range of RTE approaches, of different complexity levels.

1.3.2   RELATION EXTRACTION

With respect to inference needs, the task of **Relation Extraction (RE)** is largely analogous to (factoid) question answering. In both cases, it is required to extract textual elements, typically arguments of predicates, which satisfy a given proposition. In RE, the task is to identify text mentions of a given target semantic relation (e.g. *product-announcements*), and identify their arguments (e.g. *announcing-company* and *announced-product*). In the standard supervised setting for RE, the target relation is effectively defined by an input training corpus, which is annotated with relation mentions and their corresponding arguments and is used to train supervised learning algorithms. In **unsupervised Relation Extraction**, on the other hand, no labeled training is given. Instead, the input may include a simple textual template that specifies the predicate and the arguments to extract, possibly with type restrictions on the arguments. In our example, the input specification may be given by the template X *announce* Y, with type restrictions specifying that X should be a company and Y a product type. In this unsupervised scenario the generic textual entailment setup can be of use, where the goal is to find texts that entail instantiations of the target template, which is considered as the Hypothesis.

This approach was applied by Romano et al. [207] to the task of extracting mentions of protein interactions in bio-medical abstracts. The input target template was defined as X *interacts with* Y, while the arguments were restricted to mentions of proteins. The entailment technology employed included automatically learned entailment rules, such as X *bind to* $Y \rightarrow X$ *interacts with* Y and X *form complex with* $Y \rightarrow X$ *interacts with* Y (see Section 3.2), and manually written rules covering generic syntactic variations, including passive voice, relative clauses, appositions, conjunctions, and other variations (see Section 2.3.3). For each text sentence, the system checked whether it entailed the input target template under some instantiation of the variables by protein names appearing in the text. For example, the text "…**iCdi1**, a human G1 and S phase protein phosphatase that associates with **Cdk2**, …" entails the input template under the instantiation of X and Y with the two bolded protein names. The entailment can be recognized in this case using the entailment rule X *associate with* $Y \rightarrow X$ *interacts with* Y and the generic syntactic rule which identifies the apposition structure. Their results, while not matching supervised performance, showed useful performance for an unsupervised domain-independent setting and assessed a potential high coverage of automatic acquisition of entailment-rules.

Bar-Haim et al. [9] applied a similar approach for RE to evaluate their entailment system, extracting nine different relations from a large corpus. To address the need of efficiently finding relevant relation mentions in the corpus they incorporated a "backward inference" phase, which included query expansion and search over the corpus. For each target predicate, a query was formed which included the given target predicate as well as all predicates that were known to entail it, according to their set of entailment rules (e.g., for the above example the query would include *interact*, *bind to*, and *form complex with*). A similar search approach was investigated by Roth et al. [210] for their focused textual entailment approach, SERR (Scalable Entailment Relation Recognition).

The above RE experiments introduced two novel extensions to the textual entailment setting. The first is the use of *template hypotheses*, that is, hypotheses including variable slots, which should be instantiated by some elements in the entailing text. Supporting template hypotheses enables utilizing entailment systems for the actual extraction step in various applications, rather than just for validating entailments for already extracted elements, as was done in the question answering settings described above. As illustrated for the protein-interaction example, the variable instantiations obtained from the text through entailment recognition specify the extracted information elements (e.g. the protein names). The second extension is applying entailment recognition in search mode, in which all texts that entail a given Hypothesis are searched for in a corpus.[9] Taken together, these two extensions suggest the potential for using generic RTE technology in ad-hoc information seeking applications, such as question answering or "on-the-fly" information extraction.

1.3.3 TEXT SUMMARIZATION

In text summarization, and particularly in **Multi-document Summarization (MDS)**, textual entailment is relevant for several types of inferences. This was exemplified by Harabagiu et al. [110]. They utilized their textual entailment system [119] to combine six different summarization strategies, by selecting the best summary amongst the six candidates in each individual case. The entailment assessments were employed for two key tasks. First, they used entailment judgments between all pairs of sentences appearing in distinct summaries to measure their semantic overlap. Based on these measures they identified the *Semantic Content Units (SCUs)* of these summaries, which are "atomic" propositions that represent common content across the summaries. In a subsequent step, they utilized the entailment engine to assess how well summary sentences matched the identified SCUs, and considered this assessment when computing the final score for each summary. Their evaluation showed that this entailment-based summary selection method selected the most responsive summary amongst the six candidates in 86% of the cases. This accuracy is notable since the different summarization strategies often produced summaries of quite similar quality, while the overall best strategy produced the most responsive summary in only 34% of the cases. The authors conclude that this was considered a particularly encouraging result, as it suggests that SCU creation using textual entailment is sufficiently discriminative to identify differences even among sets of similarly responsive summaries.

---

[9]A related search mode was introduced in the pilot task of the RTE-5 challenge and then adapted with some modifications in the RTE-6 and RTE-7 challenges, as described in Section 1.4.2.

The work of Harabagiu et al. demonstrates two typical tasks within automatic summarization which inherently require entailment inference: identifying semantic overlap between sentences and ensuring that summaries are indeed entailed by important text content (see also the summarization-oriented evaluations of RTE described in Section 1.4). Naturally, these tasks have been regularly addressed by summarization systems, but typically using rather shallow lexical matching methods. Harabagiu et al., on the other hand, leveraged an extensive high-performing entailment system that they had available. We may conjecture that having extensive entailment engines publicly available would facilitate improved inference across summarization systems, and similarly across application areas.

1.3.4   ADDITIONAL APPLICATIONS

The need to assess semantic overlap between pairs of sentences also arises in other applications. Within the growing area of NLP for education, **Answer Assessment** for open questions (to be distinguished from multiple-choice questions) involves comparing student answers to a recorded reference answer. From an inference point of view, we would like to check whether the student answer fully entails the reference answer, or whether a contradiction exists. Such entailment-based approach was taken by Nielsen et al. [181] and by Sukkarieh and Stoyanchev [231]. Similar to the notion of SCU in summarization, the student and reference answers were first decomposed to atomic propositions, termed *facets* [181] or *concepts* [231]. Then, the entailment (or contradiction) relationships between these propositions were determined and used for scoring the student answer.

A similar scenario arises in **Machine Translation (MT) Evaluation**. Here we need to compare the translation produced by the machine translation system to the reference translation produced by a professional translator (in analogy to the student and reference answers in intelligent tutoring). The dominant similarity metrics used for such evaluations are n-gram-based; while these measures have reasonable correlation with human judgments, they are far from perfect since they do not account for many lexical and structural variations which may preserve the same meaning. From an entailment perspective, the task is to determine whether the system and reference translations are *equivalent*, that is, whether the entailment relation holds in *both* directions; missing information in the system translation means that it does not entail the reference, while spurious information would mean that the reference does not entail the system translation.[10] Following this perspective, Padó, et al. [183] applied the Stanford Entailment Recognizer to pairs of system and reference translations, adapted to the translation evaluation setting and training data. By employing this entailment engine they could leverage a range of available entailment recognition features, such as considering lexical variability and alignment score, modality, polarity, tense mismatches, semantic relations, entity and date compatibility, and others. As their results show, this approach yielded better correlation with human judgments than surface matching-based metrics.

---

[10]Notice that evaluating the fluency or linguistic quality of the translation is a separate issue.

The utility of *generating entailments*, rather than recognizing them, was exemplified in **Machine Translation (MT)** (for the translation task itself, to be distinguished from the *MT evaluation* task described above). The utility of generating entailments for MT may not be surprising, since translation is itself is concerned with generating semantically equivalent sentences, albeit in a different language. Callison-Burch et al. [40] identified the utility of generating semantic equivalences *within* the source language, taking a paraphrasing approach, which enriches the space of "starting points" to be translated. Potentially, a paraphrase for the original source sentence may be easier to translate, while consolidating the outcomes of equivalent source variants may yield a more reliable translation. In their work, Callison-Burch et al. [40] used paraphrases that were acquired from parallel bilingual corpora, but the general paraphrasing approach may utilize other paraphrasing resources as well, including monolingual ones.

Mirkin, et al. [168] took this rationale a step further, while using entailment to tackle the translation of unknown terms. When running into relatively rare terms, or when translating from a language with scarce linguistic resources, certain source terms may not appear in the phrase table used by the MT system. Mirkin, et al. address this problem by applying lexical substitutions to unknown terms in the source sentence, before it gets translated, in order to generate an entailed sentence. The generated sentence may be either semantically equivalent to the source sentence, when unknown terms are replaced by their WordNet synonyms, or may represent a more general meaning, when the substitute is a broader term (hypernym, as a case of directional entailment). The latter case is justified in "fallback" situations: if we cannot find a known synonym for the unknown term then we may better get along with a somewhat broader term that would still preserve much of the original meaning. For example, if *skyscraper* is unknown to the translation system then we may translate *building* instead, and still obtain a reasonable, though not perfect, translation. Their results showed that allowing for directional-entailment substitutions increases the coverage of unknown terms by as much as 50% over allowing only synonym substitutions (a la the paraphrase approach). The percentage of correct translations (precision), on the other hand, drops only by few percentage points.

An interesting and quite innovative application for textual entailment was introduced in the SemEval-2010 Shared Task of **Parser Evaluation using Textual Entailments** (PETE) [258].[11] The main idea of this task was to evaluate whether a parse of a sentence is correct or not by examining the validity of some entailed consequents that can be deduced based on that parse. Consider the following example, taken from the shared task announcement. A correct parse of the sentence "*The man with the hat was tired.*" would identify "man" as the subject of "was tired". Hence, based on the correct parse it should be very easy to recognize that the sentence "*The man was tired.*" is a valid entailment from the original sentence. On the other hand, an incorrect parse that identifies "hat" as the subject of "was tired," would suggest that the "*The hat was tired.*" is entailed by the original text, which is of course false. This way, it should be possible to distinguish correct parses from incorrect ones by testing whether they yield true or false entailments.

---

[11]http://pete.yuret.com

Accordingly, the PETE data set included sentences to be parsed by the parser under evaluation, along with valid entailments that can be easily recognized from the correct parse as well as non-entailed sentences that would likely be recognized (wrongly) as entailments based on incorrect parses. Participating systems are expected to utilize a parser under evaluation and use its output to predict which sentences are indeed entailed. A more accurate parser is thus expected to enable better recognition of these entailments. As the PETE organizers present, they leveraged the entailment recognition methodology to achieve several novel goals, including: to focus parser evaluation on semantically relevant phenomena; to introduce a parser evaluation scheme that is independent of any particular parsing formalism, thus enabling cross-formalism parser evaluation; to introduce a targeted textual entailment task focused on a single linguistic competence (namely parsing).

To summarize, different modes of textual entailment inference were found useful in a broad range of applications. Information seeking applications, such as question answering and information extraction, can utilize entailment recognition to *validate* that their candidate hypothesized answers, or extractions can indeed be inferred from the text. In a more involved setting, an entailment system can be used to actually *identify* the sought information elements, by tracing variable instantiations for template hypotheses. Assessing the overlap in meaning between given pairs of sentences is useful in several settings, including summarization, answer assessment, and MT evaluation. Finally, *generating entailments* was found useful for machine translation, and may have potential utility for other text-to-text generation settings.[12]

In most of the works reviewed above the authors utilized relatively elaborate entailment systems, which were at their disposal, in order to improve the end application. As textual entailment research gradually improves, and better entailment engines and platforms become publicly available, we may expect increased use of such approaches for various applications.

1.4   TEXTUAL ENTAILMENT EVALUATION

The primary framework for evaluating textual entailment systems has been the series of the PASCAL Recognizing Textual Entailment (RTE) Challenges [8, 19, 20, 21, 76, 101, 102]. These challenges served as a major driving factor for research in this field since its introduction in 2004. The challenges were sponsored by the European PASCAL and PASCAL-2 Networks of Excellence,[13] and since RTE-4 in 2008 became a track in the Text Analysis Conference (TAC) evaluation campaign, organized by the U.S. National Institute of Standards and Technology (NIST). The next two sub-sections provide an overview of these RTE challenges, followed by two subsections that survey additional evaluation efforts and future directions for entailment evaluation.

---

[12]As exemplified in the proceedings of the the Workshop on Monolingual Text-To-Text Generation: http://aclweb.org/anthology-new/W/W11/W11-1600.pdf.

[13]http://www.pascal-network.org/

1.4.1   RTE-1 THROUGH RTE-5

The RTE datasets were designed following the rationale exemplified in the previous section, by which entailment recognition captures semantic inference needs of many applications. In each of the first five challenges, the Text-Hypothesis pairs were collected from several application scenarios, reflecting the way by which the corresponding application could utilize an automated entailment judgment. The main application scenarios utilized throughout these five challenges included Question Answering, Relation Extraction (as a subtype of Information Extraction), Information Retrieval, and Summarization. The exact methodology for creating the Text-Hypothesis pairs has evolved and changed somewhat throughout the years, but mostly followed a consistent setting, which we summarize next (see the organizers' paper of each of the challenges for further detail, or [73] for a detailed overview of the prototypical RTE-2 methodology). Table 1.1 illustrates typical examples from RTE-2, drawn from news sources texts.

The creation of Text-Hypothesis pairs for the **Question Answering** (QA) scenario was based on the reduction methodology described in Section 1.3 for this application, assessing that a candidate answer is indeed entailed by the corresponding text passage. The annotators took samples of questions, often from available QA benchmarks such as TREC-QA and QA@CLEF, along with candidate answers for these questions which were retrieved by actual QA systems. For each candidate answer a Hypothesis was created by transforming the question into an affirmative-form template, into which the candidate answer was plugged (such as the Hypothesis "Edvard Munch painted 'The Scream'." illustrated in the previous section). The corresponding retrieved passage, from which the candidate answer was extracted, was taken as the Text. As explained earlier, correct answers of the QA system yield positive entailment pairs while incorrect answers yield negative pairs.

The creation of Text-Hypothesis pairs for the **Relation Extraction** scenario was based on the reduction methodology described in Section 1.3 for that application, aiming to assess that an extracted relation is indeed entailed from the corresponding text. The annotators utilized various target relations, some of them taken from known Information Extraction (IE) benchmarks while others were specified by the annotators as typical target relations for various news domains. First, for each target relation a template was created that corresponded to a prototypical textual statement expressing the relation, such as *X works for Y*. Then, the annotators considered texts in which a candidate instance of the relation was identified and used them to construct Text-Hypothesis pairs. For each candidate Text, a Hypothesis was formed by substituting the argument variables in the relation template with the actual argument mentions extracted from that Text. For example, for the Text "Gates founded Microsoft ..." the corresponding Hypothesis would be "Gates works for Microsoft" (ignoring tense aspects), formed by instantiating the above template with the arguments extracted from the Text. For some of the Text-Hypothesis pairs in the datasets the candidate texts and relation mentions were identified by actual IE systems, while in other cases the annotators simulated manually a typical behavior of IE systems. As with the QA examples, correct relation extractions yield positive Text-Hypothesis pairs while incorrect extractions yield negative pairs.

The creation of Text-Hypothesis pairs for the **Multi-document Summarization** scenario simulated the need to recognize redundant information in clusters of news documents to be summarized. Annotators were given output of multi-document summarization systems, including the document clusters and the summaries generated for them. They then picked sentence pairs with high lexical overlap, which were thus suspected for entailment, where at least one of the sentences was taken from the summary. As often only sub-parts of sentences entail each other, the annotators were allowed to remove some sentence parts, creating positive and negative Text-Hypothesis pairs of similar sentence structures.

Finally, in the **Information Retrieval** (IR) setting the hypotheses were constructed as propositional IR queries that specified some statement, for example "Google goes public". These hypotheses were adapted from standard IR evaluation datasets, including TREC and CLEF. Candidate entailing texts were selected from documents retrieved for these queries by a web search engine. In this setting it is assumed that relevant documents should entail the given Hypothesis.

When judging entailment for each Text-Hypothesis pair, the annotators were asked to follow the standard textual entailment definition, as presented earlier in this chapter, while assuming "typical" background knowledge of an educated person reading the news. Each example went through a cross-annotation process, which typically yielded reasonable agreement levels, relative to similar text-understanding annotation tasks. Controversial examples were usually removed, yielding highly consensual annotations. For example, in RTE-2 the average agreement on a sample of the test set was 89.2%, with average Kappa level of 0.78, which corresponds to "substantial agreement" [42]. In RTE-1 a couple of participating teams performed partial re-annotations which showed agreement levels of between 91% and 96%. In later RTE rounds reconciliation processes were introduced, to better address cases where disagreements were due to misunderstandings, which further improved judgment quality. Independent support for the achievable consensus in RTE annotations was provided by Snow et al. [226], who utilized non-expert Amazon Mechanical Turk annotators[14] to annotate examples from the RTE-1 dataset. When employing seven annotators per example and calibrating their annotations with a bias correction model they achieved 90% accuracy relative to the RTE-1 gold standard. This result is particularly encouraging as it shows that RTE annotations can be produced easily by individual researchers through crowd-sourcing, rather than solely by professionally organized evaluation campaigns.

All datasets for RTE-1 through RTE-5, except RTE-4, have separate development and test sets, each having between 600 and 800 entailment pairs; RTE-4 has a single component of 1,000 pairs. All datasets are balanced, with approximately 50% having *Entailed* and 50% *Not Entailed* labels, yielding a convenient 0.5 performance for a random-classification baseline. In RTE-4 and RTE-5, the *Not Entailed* examples were further divided into two categories: *Un-*

---

[14]http://mturk.com

known and *Contradicted* (35% and 15% of total examples respectively), introducing an evaluation for the three-way RTE classification task which involves contradiction detection.

Another aspect that evolved over the years is the length of the Text component in the entailment pairs. While in the first rounds the Text consisted of one or two sentences, substantially longer texts were introduced starting in RTE-4. This incorporated discourse effects, such as co-reference resolution, into the entailment decision. As described in the next sub-section, the impact of discourse became more prominent in the settings of RTE-6 and RTE-7.

The main task in the RTE challenges was considered as *classification*—determining the entailment judgment for each test pair. The evaluation criterion for this task was *accuracy*—the percentage of correctly classified pairs. A secondary optional task was *ranking* the pairs, according to their entailment confidence, which was evaluated using the *Average Precision* measure [246]. Following the introduction of the three-way classification setup, Bergmair [26] proposed several modifications to the evaluation criteria, and particularly a mutual-information based evaluation metric that accounts for class imbalance in the dataset.

1.4.2   RTE-6 AND RTE-7

The first five RTE challenges provided effective evaluation datasets that triggered substantial research activity on textual entailment. However, from an evaluation methodology perspective, the dataset creation process described in the previous subsection suffered from the following problem: the distribution of entailment examples within these datasets did not correspond to any "natural" distribution of entailment cases in a concrete setting. Despite the fact that many of the entailment pairs were based on the output of actual NLP applications, the subset of examples which were eventually included in the datasets was determined manually by the annotators, and was artificially balanced to fit the 50-50% split between positive and negative examples.

To address this concern, a new dataset creation methodology was devised as a pilot task in RTE-5, and was then slightly modified to become the main task in RTE-6 and RTE-7 [19, 20]. The primary rationale behind this approach was to create a faithful set of entailment pairs that represents the distribution of entailment decisions relevant for a concrete application over a concrete test collection. The entailment scenario chosen for these challenges was based on datasets taken from Multi-Document Summarization (MDS) evaluations conducted in another track of the Text Analysis Conference (TAC).

In the text summarization evaluation, the summarization systems were given clusters of documents, each corresponding to a particular topic (such as global warming and mining accidents in China), and were required to produce a short summary for each cluster. In the *update summarization* task, the produced summary is supposed to include only information from the document cluster which is novel relative to an earlier known cluster about the same topic. The RTE task was designed to identify repeated versus novel information in the document clusters, mimicking this need within summarization systems.

Specifically, the hypotheses for the RTE task consisted of sentences, or snippets of sentences, which appeared in the document cluster and were included in automatically-generated extractive summaries (produced by systems that participated in the original summarization benchmark). The RTE goal was then to identify the sentences in the corresponding document cluster which entail each hypothesis. For each given Hypothesis, the challenge organizers first extracted candidate entailing sentences from the document cluster by the following process: the Hypothesis was issued as a search query to a standard search engine and then the top retrieved sentences were taken as candidate entailing texts. The search engine was thus used as a preliminary "filter" that identifies sentences with some prior likelihood to entail the Hypothesis, based on lexical overlap. The retrieval threshold was set such that, on average, about 90% of the actually entailing sentences in the document cluster would be included amongst the retrieved candidate sentences. This process created multiple Text-Hypothesis pairs for each hypothesis. These pairs were judged for entailment by human annotators, to create the gold standard, and were given to the participating RTE systems for entailment classification.

A particular property which was specified for this setting regarded a *discourse-sensitive* definition of entailment. When judging whether the meaning of the Text sentence entails the Hypothesis, that meaning was interpreted while considering available information from the complete discourse. That is, the interpretation of the Text sentence could assume knowledge of all explicit and implicit references pertaining to that sentence available in the broader discourse. For example, the Hypothesis could mention a location that is not mentioned explicitly in the Text, but is assumed to be part of the interpreted meaning of the Text through a co-reference or bridging relation. This setting gives rise to extensive integration of discourse information into semantic inference, as was clearly demonstrated by Mirkin at al. [166].

In this objective setting of selecting the candidate Texts for each Hypothesis, only a small fraction of the Texts actually entail the Hypothesis (few percentage points). This reflects a natural distribution by which most texts in a given corpus would not entail any particular Hypothesis. Accordingly, the evaluation measure for the RTE systems was chosen to be F_1, the harmonic mean of Recall and Precision. Systems are thus expected to recognize a substantial number of the entailing Texts without introducing a substantial number of false positives, in analogy to information retrieval evaluation. An additional *novelty detection* subtask was introduced in the RTE challenge, which simulates more directly the needs of the update summarization task mentioned above. In this task a Hypothesis was considered novel if no entailing sentences were found for it, and the RTE systems were measured by their success in identifying the novel hypotheses.

An additional pilot *KBP Validation* task was included in RTE-6 and RTE-7. This RTE task was based on the Slot Filling task of the Knowledge Base Population (KBP) track in the Text Analysis Conference. The Slot Filling task largely corresponds to a traditional relation extraction task, formulated as automatically filling slots in Wikipedia Information Boxes (Info Boxes). The KBP Validation task for the entailment systems was then phrased in the spirit of the reductions described in the previous subsection for the Relation Extraction task: hypotheses corresponded to pre-specified templates for each type of slot, which were instantiated by the candidate extractions made by the original KBP (information extraction) systems. The corresponding Text for each such Hypothesis was the (full) document from which the KBP extraction was made. By judging whether entailment holds for each pair the RTE system essentially validates whether the extraction proposed by the KBP system is correct or not. The RTE system performance for this task was measured using Micro-Averaged Precision, Recall, and F-measure.

Altogether, the RTE-6 and RTE-7 campaigns marked an attempt to obtain generic RTE datasets, that is, datasets whose format follows the generic RTE Text-Hypothesis setting, which represents more faithfully the expected entailment inferences within particular applications. Under this methodology, each RTE dataset is based on a particular dataset of a single application and is constructed based on the output of actual systems performing the original application task. Furthermore, the RTE dataset covers all instances of the original application dataset and thus corresponds to a "real" distribution of entailment cases and phenomena in a particular setting. Future entailment benchmarks may pursue this methodological scheme for additional applications and datasets.

1.4.3 OTHER EVALUATIONS OF TEXTUAL ENTAILMENT TECHNOLOGY

While the main tasks of the RTE Challenges attracted most attention in the research community, several other important evaluation efforts for entailment systems and components were reported.

The CLEF Answer Validation Exercise (AVE), conducted in 2006, 2007, and 2008, has a similar structure and rationale as other generic RTE datasets, while focusing on the Question Answering (QA) setting [190, 191, 205, 206]. Their starting point was the reformulation of the Answer Validation task as a Recognizing Textual Entailment problem, under the assumption that hypotheses can be automatically generated by instantiating hypothesis patterns with the QA systems' answers. This setting follows the entailment reduction for QA validation described in Section 1.3, where the Text part corresponds to the text passage from which the answer was extracted, while aiming to automate the hypothesis generation process. The AVE datasets were created based on datasets of the CLEF QA track, using answers of QA systems that participated in that track. Datasets were generated for multiple languages involved in the CLEF QA evaluation, including Basque, Bulgarian, German, English, Spanish, French, Italian, Dutch, Portuguese, Romanian, and Greek. Another evaluation campaign which included the core entailment recognition task was EVALITA 2009, which was concerned with evaluating various NLP technologies for the Italian language on a range of problems, including RTE. [15]

Another evaluation mode for entailment technology was exhibited in works applying entailment technology to the Relation Extraction task, as described in Section 1.3. As explained there, these works utilized generic entailment technology for the actual extraction of the sought relation arguments, rather than just for validating extractions made by systems targeted for this application. The key idea in these evaluations was the use of *template hypotheses*; that is, hypotheses

---

[15]http://www.evalita.it/2009

which include variables, whose instantiation during the entailment recognition process identi-fies the target relation arguments to be extracted. Bar-Haim et al. [9] utilized this methodology to evaluate a complete entailment recognition system, while in [207, 233, 235] this setting was used to evaluate the effectiveness of specific modules within an entailment architecture, including knowledge resources of entailment rules and models for validating rule applicability in context. Pursuing this methodology in future work seems attractive, as it will enable investigating the util-ity of generic textual entailment technology as part of the core extraction processes in applications such as information extraction and question answering. Such evaluation settings may complement the prior standard evaluation settings for RTE, in which entailment technology was used in the context of validating extractions made by other systems or for assessing semantic overlap between sentences.

An important assessment activity started in RTE-5, which incorporates *ablation tests* of the participating systems. Each group was asked to submit several additional runs of their sys-tem, where in each run a single component was removed (ablated) from the system, be it either a knowledge resource or a processing module. This enables identifying the net impact of each component on overall system performance, and may reveal those components of a complex RTE system that contributed most to its performance. The detailed impact figures for all components in all systems have been published under the RTE Knowledge Resources web page[16] and were summarized in the organizers' paper for each challenge. Of course, the impact of a certain com-ponent may vary from one system to another, due to differences in the way in which the resource is utilized or its interplay with other system components. However, the ablation tests data do provide an overall reference point for the success in leveraging various components within RTE systems, which correlates to some extent with overall resource utility. Further discussion of these ablation tests with respect to knowledge resources appears in Chapter 5.

1.4.4   FUTURE DIRECTIONS FOR ENTAILMENT EVALUATION

The past evaluation activities reported above were instrumental to initiate and advance textual entailment research in the last seven years. However, substantial development of additional eval-uation methodologies and datasets is needed in order to advance this field further and to bring it to maturity. In the spirit illustrated earlier, such novel datasets may be created either within or-ganized benchmarks or by individual research projects, possibly leveraging crowd sourced labor, while aiming to make them publicly available to facilitate research advancement.

One obvious extension would be following the direction taken in RTE-6 and RTE-7 (Section 1.4.2), of deriving generic RTE datasets from complete datasets of end-application tasks, while covering all entailment inferences needed for the application. For example, additional datasets of this sort may be created from available benchmark data for Question Answering, In-formation Extraction, Machine Translation evaluation, and automatic Answer Assessment, in the spirit of the reductions described in Section 1.3. Additional efforts may be made to have some

---

[16]http://aclweb.org/aclwiki/index.php?title=RTE_Knowledge_Resources

datasets involving *template hypotheses*, including variables that need to be instantiated (extracted) from the Text during the entailment recognition process.

There is an important aspect of entailment research which has remained largely unaddressed in existing evaluation methodologies. Being a very complex phenomenon, entailment modeling requires the development and integration of many different modules that address different entailment phenomena, as discussed in Section 1.2.5 (consider, for example, the modeling of modality, or temporal inference, or nominalizations, as such specific phenomena). When developing such specific modules and embedding them in a complete entailment system, researchers need to evaluate their quality by the net impact on overall system performance. However, since so many inference phenomena are involved in entailment inference, the frequency of each individual phenomenon in a generic RTE dataset is typically low. Consequently, it becomes impossible to reliably assess the quality of a new targeted module using these datasets. Indeed, so far the generic RTE datasets were used mostly to evaluate the quality of complete RTE architectures rather than for individual inference modules.

This concern has been troubling the RTE research community for some time. A potential solution may be the creation of specialized datasets, which are biased to include a large number of entailment examples that exhibit a particular phenomenon, as was advocated in several publications [18, 212]. For example, we may form a dataset in which a temporal expression appears in every hypothesis, and would thus be suitable for evaluating the impact of temporal inference modules. To a notable extent, the experiments reported in [233, 235] exhibit a successful case of specialized evaluations. These works dealt with the application of entailment rules (inference rules) that involve a single predicate, such as *X walk* → *X move*. The impact of rule application was measured on a specialized dataset that was derived from the ACE event detection dataset, where each (template) hypothesis involved only a single predicate. Thus, improved applications of entailment rules for these individual predicates had a direct impact on overall performance in a substantial number of cases. On the other hand, it was typically much more difficult to measure the impact of such entailment rules through ablation tests over generic RTE datasets, where the hypotheses are typically more complex and entailment recognition involves subtle interaction of multiple modules. Overall, further efforts are expected to construct specialized datasets for various entailment phenomena, which will enable research to focus on the development of individual inference components. One such effort has been initiated under the DARPA *Deep Exploration and Filtering of Text (DEFT)* program, a broad research initiative that addresses many Natural Language Processing and textual inference challenges, including RTE. The program will produce as one of its specialized data sets an entailment corpus in which inference phenomena required to determine the labels of entailment pairs are annotated, using a scheme related to that outlined by [212]; this corpus, together with a corpus of standard entailment examples, is expected to be released by late 2013.

An interesting aspect of entailment recognition mechanisms was evaluated in a pilot test within the RTE-3 challenge. In this pilot task, systems were asked to provide justifications for the system's decisions, explaining how entailment was assessed for a given Text-Hypothesis pair. The goal of providing justifications was to explore how eventual users of entailment systems can understand the system's decisions, aiming to increase user trust and to allow further analysis of system behavior. Participating systems were allowed to decide on the type of explanations they provided while the quality and clarity of the provided justifications was assessed by human judgments. This pilot task was not pursued further in later benchmarks, partly due to the difficulty in objectively assessing the quality of the justifications provided by various systems. However, this issue does seem important and relevant for RTE research, and may be worth pursuing in future work.

Finally, the ultimate test for generic entailment technology would be in assessing its contribution to end user applications, as well as to other NLP tasks. Initial evaluations that showed such positive impacts were described in Section 1.3. Further, evaluations of some other tasks clearly refer to inference needs, such as the ongoing benchmark on Question Answering for Machine Reading (QA4MRE) which is positioned as an evolution of QA, RTE and Answer Validation evaluations.[17] Broad proliferation of entailment modules and engines across applications is likely to be a longer process, in analogy to the increased use of parsing technology as it gradually matured. This process would much depend on entailment engines becoming publicly available, and portable. Once this is realized, it will facilitate evaluating their impact on various applications, and comparing it with performances on generic RTE datasets.

[17]http://celct.fbk.eu/QA4MRE/

CHAPTER 2

Architectures and Approaches

Recognizing Textual Entailment (RTE) is a complex task, and RTE systems themselves tend to be complex as a result. This chapter gives an overview of different approaches that have been developed so far by the RTE community, and lays out a generic architecture which will help to situate our descriptions and analysis of different aspects of RTE systems and approaches.

We first motivate a general model of the RTE process based on an intuitive view of the problem: representing the meanings of the Text T and Hypothesis H, and determining whether or not the representation of H's meaning is contained in the representation of T's meaning (Section 2.1).

We next outline several general approaches to RTE using representations of different sophistication (Section 2.2), viewing them from the perspective of our intuitive model. We start with the conceptually simplest approach (Section 2.2.1), then describe more complex ones (Section 2.2.2). We then describe dominant approaches to inference (Section 2.3). Our intent in these sections is to give a broad overview of approaches to RTE; work describing individual systems implementing these approaches is covered in more detail in Chapter 4.

Having surveyed the most popular RTE representations and decision models, we outline a generic RTE architecture in Section 2.4 that is sufficiently general to map intelligibly to a broad range of actual RTE system implementations. This will provide a conceptual framework that can encompass descriptions of a broad range of existing work in RTE, and which will allow the reader to readily place the main topics of this book in context; it abstracts away the difficulties of system engineering, allowing us to focus on aspects of RTE system design that inform research in this area.

The chapter finishes with an assessment of the fundamental design problems uncovered by these different approaches (Section 2.5), to provide a grounded context for the discussion of machine learning approaches to RTE in Chapter 3 and of knowledge acquisition in Chapter 5.

2.1 AN INTUITIVE MODEL FOR RTE

Consider the Textual Entailment example shown in Figure 2.1. From a human perspective, it seems straightforward to determine that this example should be labeled "entails." But how should an automated system make this prediction? Given that RTE is fundamentally a Natural Language Understanding task, one approach would be to represent the meanings of the Text and Hypothesis of the example using some canonical meaning representation, and to determine whether the meaning of the Hypothesis is contained in the meaning of the Text.

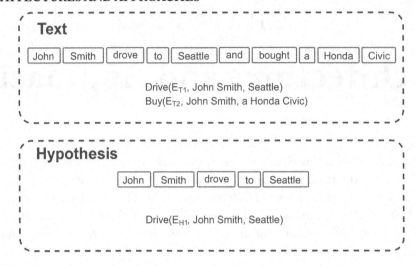

Figure 2.1: Sample entailment pair with notional meaning representation.

Those familiar with research into formal semantics and other areas relating to automated reasoning for natural language will know that the design of a suitable meaning representation is vexed; but for now, suppose an appropriate representation has been agreed upon, and that it is of the form presented in Figure 2.1. The predicate names are assumed to map to corresponding semantic definitions. Each predicate has some number of arguments that, in this simple example, are identifiers corresponding to entities represented in the example text. Some identifiers are grounded—i.e., they refer to specific entities ("Seattle" and "John Smith"), or to type entities ("Honda Civic"), or to variables (the E_{XN} identifiers can be thought of as variables that represent events themselves—i.e., the Text predicates refer to a Drive event and a Buy event).

Given this representation, it is straightforward to unify the Hypothesis with the Text (by requiring that E_{T1} and E_{H1} refer to the same event), and to therefore conclude that the Text entails the Hypothesis. Similarly, it is straightforward to determine for the example in Figure 2.2 that the meaning of the Hypothesis does not correspond to any part of the meaning of the Text.

However, it is (presently) unrealistic to expect a self-contained system to automatically derive a well-formed meaning representation from arbitrary, well-formed natural language text, even assuming a suitable representation has been designed. The Natural Language Processing research community acknowledges these difficulties, and focuses instead on representations that can be (more or less) reliably induced from text, and on "reasoning" with such representations, whether using hand-crafted decision functions (rules) or statistical inference based on characteristics of the represented text. This pragmatic approach sacrifices adequacy of meaning representation with the hope of achieving reliable, if partial, success in predicting the relevant semantic characteristics—for RTE, predicting the labels of entailment pairs. In the following section, we

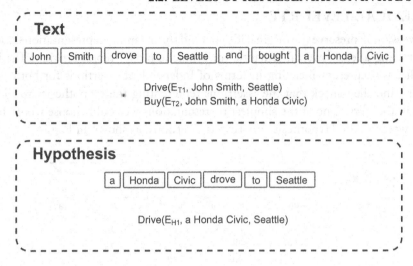

Figure 2.2: Sample non-entailing entailment pair with notional meaning representation.

survey general approaches to RTE based on different levels of representation, and the resources deployed to overcome limitations associated with those representations.

2.2   LEVELS OF REPRESENTATION IN RTE SYSTEMS

We have argued in Chapter 1 that RTE is a complex task requiring some approximation of Natural Language Understanding on the part of automated systems in order to perform well on arbitrary inputs. Nonetheless, there is a trade-off in NLP technology that identifies underlying syntactic and (shallow) semantic structure in free text between the complexity of the induced representation and the accuracy of that representation. Part-of-Speech tagging, for example, has a reported accuracy of around 97%F1, while syntactic parsing performance has leveled off at around 92%F1. Semantic Role Labeling performance is significantly lower. This trade-off, combined with the success of keyword-based approaches to tasks such as Information Retrieval, invites the following questions: might a simple representation, possibly combined with good lexical semantic language resources, be a better basis for an RTE system than a more complex representation that has more innate errors? If the performance of a simple system is not sufficiently good, and we entertain more complex representations, what approaches might address the limitations of the simple systems in a robust way?

   In the rest of this section, we describe variations in architecture based on the choice of representation and decision model.

2.2.1   LEXICAL-LEVEL RTE

Suppose we want to preserve the original idea behind the meaning-representation-based approach above, but using a less powerful semantic (or syntactic proxy) representation. The basic model requires that we represent meaning in terms of independent assertions for both the Text and Hypothesis, and then check that the assertions representing the Hypothesis are all matched by assertions in the Text. One of the simplest representations we could choose would be to use the individual words in the Hypothesis and Text as assertions, as shown in Figure 2.3.

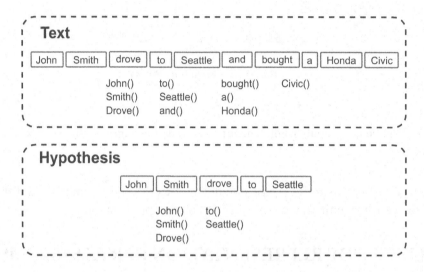

Figure 2.3: Sample entailing entailment pair with pure lexical meaning representation.

For the example shown, the process works: every assertion in the representation of the Hypothesis (here, each assertion corresponds to an individual word) is contained in the representation of the Text, resulting in the prediction that the Text entails the Hypothesis. Of course, this impoverished representation will lead to errors in examples like that in Figure 2.4: the assertions representing the Hypothesis are still a subset of the assertions representing the Text, but the resulting prediction is incorrect: the structure of the Hypothesis and Text sentences encodes aspects of underlying meaning that cannot be captured by the purely lexical representation.

It is easy to come up with other examples where the pure lexical model fails: for example, suppose the Hypothesis in Figure 2.3 had the word "went" instead of "drove." A human reader will almost certainly assign the label "entailment" to this example, but our pure lexical model will predict "non-entailment." It is also easy to propose remedies for such limitations: we could use a resource like WordNet or VerbNet to capture some valid word substitutions such as "went" for "drove." It is not difficult, however, to propose new examples where such resources fail by leading to an incorrect system prediction, or by lack of coverage. On the other hand, this approach is

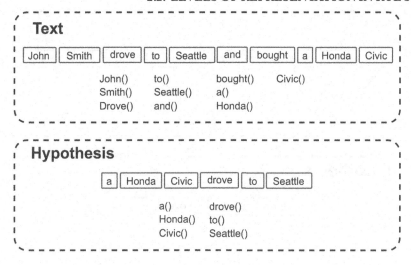

Figure 2.4: Sample non-entailing entailment pair with pure lexical meaning representation.

low-cost (in terms of development), and might be expected to achieve partial success in RTE on a non-adversarial set of examples.

The actual implementation of pure lexical RTE systems tends to frame the model not in terms of assertions in the Hypothesis being a subset of the assertions representing the Text, but in terms of alignment, as shown in Figure 2.5: the decision function considers each word in the Hypothesis and finds the "best" match in the Text. Standard refinements include a fixed list of "uninformative" words that are effectively ignored (function words like prepositions and determiners; punctuation; and possibly auxiliary verbs like "be" and "have"); stemming or lemmatizating the words in the Text and Hypothesis (to abstract away from verbal/gerundive/nominal forms of the same word, for example); and using a lexical resource such as WordNet or VerbNet to determine the relative similarity of candidate matching words. Lexical systems of this kind (for example, [1]) have achieved modest success in RTE evaluations, forming a strong baseline to which more complex systems can be compared.

2.2.2   STRUCTURED REPRESENTATIONS FOR RTE

Based on the examples shown above, it is logical to seek a more complex representation that captures, at some level, the structure underlying the words in the Text and Hypothesis. Syntactic constituency and dependency parsers (e.g., [157], [132], [194], [106]) have been developed by the NLP community that achieve respectable performance on well-formed text. These parsers give information about the grouping of words (phrase boundaries; which adjective modifies which noun; "heads" of phrases), and hierarchical structure (nesting of verb structures in text; which prepositional phrase modifies which noun or verb). Syntactic structure plausibly provides impor-

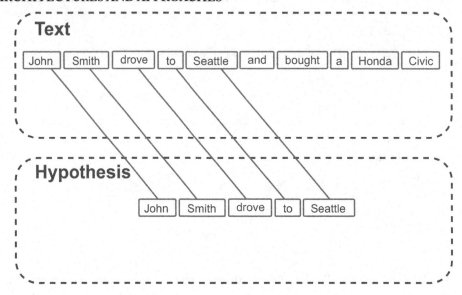

Figure 2.5: Sample entailing entailment pair with lexical alignment.

tant cues to the underlying meaning of text, and so a number of RTE systems have used syntactic constituency or dependency structure to represent the Text and Hypothesis. Figure 2.6 shows a syntactic constituency representation of the running TE example.

A more abstract representation of the structure of text is that of Semantic Role Labeling (SRL), based either on the formalism underlying PropBank [131], or on that underlying FrameNet [5]. This is a coarser representation than syntactic structure, providing grouping of words into "arguments" (an argument being a textual descriptor in a sentence that could represent an entity such as a person or place, or manner of behavior, or location or time of an event, for example) and "predicates" (a predicate being a verb or noun representing an event or the state of some entity). In addition, these formalisms assign labels to the roles the arguments take with respect to the predicate to which they are attached. This additional abstraction is potentially helpful, because it removes purely syntactic distinctions between certain representations such as passive vs. active voice, and makes more immediate connections between arguments and predicates. For example, compare the semantic role representation in Figure 2.7 with the syntactic parse structure in Figure 2.6: in the latter, the word "John" is intuitively an argument of the predicate represented by the verb "drove," but the two words are separated by a sequence of dependency edges. Given the expressiveness of the dependency representation, it should be evident that there are many possible sequences of edges that could represent such a connection, and many other sequences that do not. It has so far proven very hard to directly handle such equivalences and distinctions in a general way when working with a syntactic representation. In addition, the SRL representation

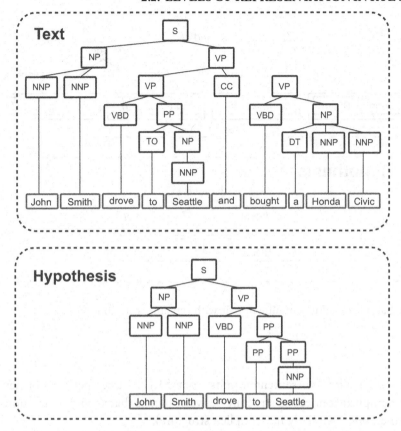

Figure 2.6: Sample entailing entailment pair with syntactic parse annotation.

directly captures modal and negation modifiers of predicates, which can be useful in distinguishing between otherwise similar Text and Hypothesis structures. Naturally, there is an associated cost: the accuracy of Semantic Role Labeling systems is lower, on average, than syntactic parsers. Nevertheless, some RTE systems have used the SRL representation instead of, or in addition to, a syntactic representation; and some add more links, representing other relations, between word or phrase or argument constituents from either the syntactic or SRL representation.

Whichever structured representation is used, the question of determining the equivalence or non-equivalence of the meanings of the Hypothesis and Text must be addressed. Since syntactic parses of sentences are monolithic, it is not straightforward to discern individual assertions. The simplest approach is to assume that the Hypothesis will always be a short sentence, and that its parse tree represents a single assertion. If the Text contains the same structure (i.e, dependency edges and words in the example in Figure 2.6), the system will predict "entails" and otherwise it will predict "not entails." (Note that although the SRL representation is at some level naturally

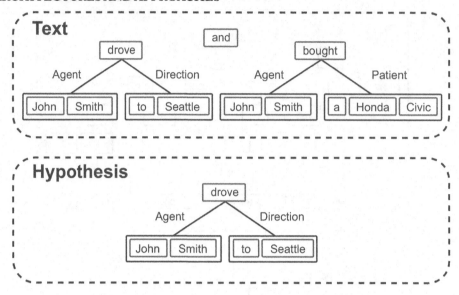

Figure 2.7: Sample entailing entailment pair with semantic role annotation.

segmented into smaller, sub-sentential units—one SRL "frame" per verb or deverbal noun—there is often implicit connecting structure between frames that should be accounted for, and the arguments themselves similarly have implicit structure).

However, that the structure of the Hypothesis in Figure 2.6 is **not** identical to the corresponding part of the Text syntactic parse tree, due to the embedding of the "drove" verb phrase in a larger verb phrase containing the conjunction of the "drove" and "bought" verb phrases. And just as with the pure lexical examples in Section 2.2.1, it is possible to generate many variations of a simple Hypothesis like the one in Figure 2.6 that should still be entailed by the Text sentence, and which have different syntactic parse structure; see, for example, Figure 2.8, which has lexical and syntactic structures that are quite different from the hypothesis in Figure 2.6, and yet retains approximately the same meaning.

Whichever representation is chosen—and many more can be invented, based on combining and/or augmenting the representations discussed so far—there is clearly a need for a principled mechanism to determine which distortions of lexico-syntactic/predicate-argument structure yield valid alternations of the same underlying meaning, in order to assess whether a given Hypothesis is entailed by a given Text. The next section discusses, in broad terms, popular approaches in RTE research to date.

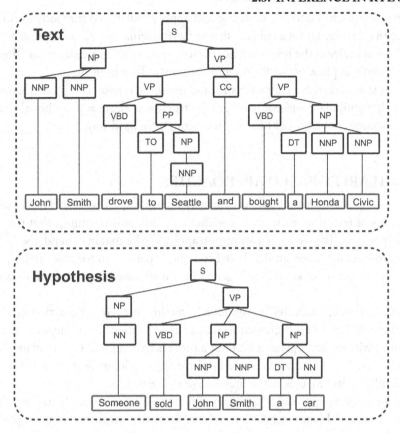

Figure 2.8: Entailing entailment pair with rephrased Hypothesis, with syntactic parse annotation.

2.3   INFERENCE IN RTE SYSTEMS

Several common strands have emerged in the decision processes embodied by RTE systems. Similarity-based approaches are rooted in the assumption that a Hypothesis with "similar" content to the Text is more likely to be entailed by that Text than a Hypothesis with "less similar" content. Similarity measures may use external knowledge resources like lexical taxonomies in an effort to improve recall while maintaining precision.

Alignment-focused approaches try to refine the simple similarity models to account for discontinuities in the relation between similarity and entailment that can be attributed to structural semantic phenomena such as modality and negation. Local similarity measures are combined into a global similarity function, which is used to determine the most "useful" alignment for determining entailment, possibly using a separate decision function.

Stricter approaches attempt to define and apply proof-based methods to RTE. In most if not all cases, the representation used falls short of a true semantic representation but still captures some structure underlying the text, such as syntactic or semantic role structure. These approaches use lexical symbols in place of predicates and constants. They may either choose a formal logical representation to encode these characteristics and use some version of a proof-theoretic approach, or may directly manipulate and compare graph structures. These approaches also allow external knowledge resources to be brought to bear in a straightforward way.

2.3.1   SIMILARITY-BASED APPROACHES

The concept of similarity is nebulous. As shown by Figure 2.2, a Text and Hypothesis that are very similar in terms of lexical items may have sufficiently different meanings that the Text does not entail the Hypothesis. The working assumption appears to be that in general, the "entails" relation is *more likely* to hold for more similar Text/Hypothesis pairs than for less similar pairs, although the underlying definition of similarity is generally not specified beyond defining a mathematical function.

In RTE research, similarity is grounded in the linguistic representation used, but the similarity function itself may be a highly customized (hand-crafted) heuristic, or a standard measure of edit distance within that representation, or a process that augments a standard similarity measure with additional tests that apply some intuitive rules to identify cues for non-entailment for otherwise similar content (such as the presence of a negation).

Lexical similarity approaches are exemplified by [1], and typically measure lexical overlap between the Text and Hypothesis. More robust similarity measures than simple stemming of words—similarity measures that account for synonymy or hyponymy, using a resource such as WordNet, for example—bring world knowledge to bear on the RTE task.

Syntactic similarity approaches are based on tree edit distance, using syntactic dependency parses of the Text and Hypothesis. The work of [158] extends the basic edit distance approach by allowing lexical similarity resources to be used when computing the similarity of dependency tree nodes, while [116] introduce more complex edit operations that violate the standard locality assumptions, but which accommodate some syntactic alternations that cannot be expressed in the standard tree edit distance model.

One significant challenge in such approaches is that of lexical ambiguity: many words are homomorphic or polysemous, and a human reader relies on context to determine which meaning of a given word is intended. Word sense disambiguation is itself a challenging, very much open problem in NLP (performance of a state-of-the-art knowledge-based system [178] is 83.2% for identifying coarse-grained senses across all words), and for similarity-driven approaches to achieve strong performance in RTE, progress must be made in this area too.

2.3.2   ALIGNMENT-FOCUSED APPROACHES

Alignment-focused RTE approaches seek to refine the simple similarity approach by defining a meaningful way of determining local similarities between parts of the Hypothesis and parts of the Text, selecting a subset of pairs of these parts to identify the most relevant sections of the Text for determining entailment, and using the resulting alignment as the basis of a decision function for determining the entailment label. Typically, such alignments are selected via search of the space of all possible alignments (possibly constrained via heuristics), using a scoring function to represent the "quality" of the alignment.

The role of alignment varies across systems: in some, it is a proxy for entailment, and in such cases the alignment scoring function must account for semantic constructions such as negation and modality. In others, the goal is to factor out local cues that strongly affect similarity (such as negation of a verb) for a later decision stage: these cues play no role in determining the "best" alignment, and the resulting alignment guides the later stages of the system in determining which such cues are relevant to the entailment decision. While some successful systems use a hand-coded heuristic function for alignment (such as [123]), some work (notably [78]) has focused on learning alignment separately from determining entailment.

2.3.3   "PROOF THEORETIC" RTE

Given the kinds of inference indicated in Section 1.2.5 in Chapter 1, it seems natural to seek to model a process of explanation of RTE example labels. This intuition underlies a number of RTE systems, but is generally instantiated in one of two ways: either as a classical formal model that uses predicate calculus and well-established theorem-proving techniques, or as a model that more explicitly works at the level of linguistic structures such as parse trees, and which explores a search space of modifications to those structures according to a set of rules analogous to assertions in a predicate calculus. The two appear to be isomorphic, but in practice different approaches are used in tandem with these two representations to handle the inevitable problems arising from trying to represent the meaning of sentences; of acquiring and representing the knowledge needed to make inferences; and of making the process robust to errors in the induced representation of the Text and Hypothesis, and inconsistencies and gaps in the knowledge resources used.

Formal Logic Approaches

Formal proof-theoretic models encode facts in a Knowledge Base using a formal representation such as Propositional or First-Order Logic, and apply rules of inference to determine the set of facts that can be derived from the Knowledge Base. This expansion of the knowledge base may be directed by a target proposition (or query).

In RTE, such systems must derive the logical representation of the Text and Hypothesis from an almost certainly imperfect syntactic or shallow semantic representation generated by NLP tools. The logical representation is usually based on the lexical forms rather than canonical predicates. These characteristics introduce significant problems for standard proof-theoretic approaches, as the resulting proof process may be neither sound nor complete.

Two examples of logic-based approaches for textual inference are those of Hobbs et al. [120] and Moldovan et al. [169]. Hobbs et al. use an abductive approach to reasoning, essentially finding a minimum cost proof whose steps involve the assumption of missing knowledge that would allow a mapping between representations to be made via a chain of inference steps. Moldovan et al. describe a deductive system that depends on rules that to some extent replicate this abductive process—that is, they specify rules that allow certain types of unmatched elements in the Text or Hypothesis to be dropped. These rules are specified in advance, but their costs may be learned from RTE example data.

In the entailment setting, the Knowledge Base must contain rules that represent the (subset of) human knowledge required to perform inference over the domain of interest. Just as crucially, it also requires a module that maps from the plain text representation of the entailment pair to the corresponding formal representation. This will allow the system to (temporarily) add the formal statements encoding the Text to the knowledge base, while the encoded Hypothesis will be used to direct the search for entailment or contradiction.

Proof by entailment uses operations such as modus ponens to derive new assertions from existing ones. Rules are represented as implications, and when an antecedent of a rule matches an assertion in the set representing the current state of belief about the world (in RTE, this is based on the Text of an entailment pair), the variables of the assertion and the rule antecedent are unified and the consequent is added to the state of belief as a new assertion. This process is exemplified in Figure 2.9. If at any stage the Hypothesis can be unified with the current state of belief, the Text can be judged to entail the Hypothesis. The sequence of unifications constitutes a proof of entailment. If all possible non-trivial extensions of the state of belief have been generated and the Hypothesis has not been reproduced, it is inferred that the Text does not entail the Hypothesis.

An alternative method, proof by refutation, adds the negated form of the hypothesis to the current state of belief, and represents all implications as disjunctions (with the negated antecedent as one term and the consequent as the other). It searches for the empty clause by seeking clauses with a matching predicate, but where one is negated and the other is not. The corresponding clauses can be unified by dropping this predicate. If the empty clause is derived, a contradiction has been found, and the sequence of operations used to reach the empty clause constitutes a proof of entailment (because the *negated* form of the hypothesis was used). If at some stage of the search for the empty clause the application of the operators does not change the working knowledge base, refutation has failed, and it may be assumed that the Hypothesis is not entailed by the Text. An example of proof by refutation is shown in Figure 2.10.

There are other proof strategies, but these approaches are illustrative. The corresponding RTE system diagram is shown in Figure 2.11.

A number of RTE systems, such as [3, 16, 33, 201], have used theorem-proving as their conceptual basis. These systems derive a logical form from the natural language entailment pair us-

Text: John bought a Jeep.

Hyp: John owns a car.

World Knowledge:
1. ∀ X Jeep(X) → car(X)
(a Jeep is a car)
2. ∀ X,Y buy(X,Y) → own(X,Y)
(if X buys Y, then X owns Y)

Proof: Initial state of belief (Text):
∃ A,B John(A) ∧ Jeep(B) ∧ buy(A,B)
(John bought a Jeep)

Target assertion:
∃ C,D John(C) ∧ car(D) ∧ own(C,D)

1. apply rule 1 with Text clause "Jeep(B)":
Jeep(B) → car(B)

State of belief is now:
∃ A,B John(A) ∧ car(B) ∧ buy(A,B)

2. apply rule 2 with Text clause "buy(A,B)":
buy(A,B) → own(A,B)

State of belief is now:
∃ A,B John(A) ∧ car(B) ∧ own(A,B)

State of belief entails target by substitution of variables, therefore T entails H.

Figure 2.9: Example of the proof process using Modus Ponens.

ing a syntactic parser to extract predicate-argument or dependency structures. The system knowledge bases are populated with rules of three main types: rules designed to encode linguistic decompositions and equivalences based on syntactic structure (e.g., apposition); rules encoding world knowledge; and rules expressing lexical mappings, usually derived from WordNet [90].

One of the more carefully theorized approaches is that of [201], which induces a Horn clause representation of a syntactic dependency annotation of the entailment pair text. Each node

Text: John bought a Jeep.
Hyp: John owns a car.
World Knowledge:
1. ∀ X ¬ Jeep(X) ∨ car(X)
(a Jeep is a car)
2. ∀ X,Y ¬ buy(X,Y) ∨ own(X,Y)
(if X buys Y, then X owns Y)

Proof: Initial state of belief (Text and negated Hypothesis):
∃ A,B John(A) ∧ Jeep(B) ∧ buy(A,B)
(John bought a Jeep)
∀ C,D ¬ John(C) ∨ ¬ car(D) ∨ own(C,D)
(noone called John owns any car)
Target assertion:
(empty clause)
1. resolve left hand term of rule 1 with Text clause "Jeep(B)": State of belief is now:
·∃ A,B John(A) ∧ car(B) ∧ buy(A,B)
∀ C,D ¬ John(C) ∨ ¬ car(D) ∨ own(C,D)

2. resolve left hand term of rule 2 with Text clause "buy(A,B)"
State of belief is now:
∃ A,B John(A) ∧ car(B) ∧ own(A,B)
∀ C,D ¬ John(C) ∨ ¬ car(D) ∨ ¬ own(C,D)

3. resolve John(A) and *neg* John(C) by binding variables C and A;
State of belief is now:
∃ A,B car(B) ∧ own(A,B)
∀ A,D ¬ car(D) ∨ ¬ own(C,D)

4. Resolve car(B) and *neg* car(D) by binding variables B and D;
State of belief is now:
∃ A,B own(A,B)
∀ A,B *neg* own(C,D)

5. Resolve own(A,B) and *neg* own(A,B);
State of belief is now:
{}

We have derived the empty clause, therefore T entails H.

Figure 2.10: Example of the proof process using Refutation.

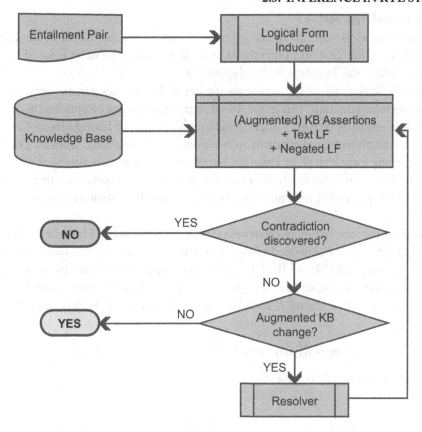

Figure 2.11: Block diagram for an RTE system based around a (refutation resolution-based) Theorem Prover.

of the parse tree is converted to a logical term, and is assigned a unique constant. Edges are represented by sharing arguments between terms corresponding to the linked nodes. The resolution process uses unit resolution refutation to derive a proof for each entailment example. This approach is complete and runs in polynomial time. However, relaxations were required to improve robustness and thus enable the system performance to be competitive with other, less formal approaches (see Chapter 4, Section 4.2.2).

Systems that maintained a strict adherence to the proof-theoretic model, like [16], proved brittle; the more successful systems relaxed the model to overcome inevitable limitations due to knowledge coverage and to errors in the transformation from natural language to the logical form. Typical relaxations are described in Chapter 4, Section 4.2, which describes selected RTE approaches based on formal logical methods.

Transformational Approaches

Transformational approaches focus on generating valid alternative forms of the initial induced representations of the Text and Hypothesis, and determining via some form of sub-graph isomorphism whether the Text entails the Hypothesis.

Many RTE systems use syntactic constituency or dependency parse structures as the basis of their meaning representation. This graph-based representation can be enriched with other knowledge resources—such as Named Entity boundaries and types, or boundaries and links representing predicates, arguments, and semantic roles—possibly creating more arbitrary graph structures. Mappings between equivalent or entailing linguistic structures can also be directly encoded in terms of graph structure: for example, a rule for transforming passive to active constructions, or appositive to explicit verbal structures, or expressing causality relations between verb-argument structures.

These approaches first induce a representation of the Text and Hypothesis, $I(T)$ and $I(H)$, and apply a set of rules, R, encoded in the same formalism. These rules may be acquired from a resource like VerbOcean [54] or DIRT [142], or they may be hand-coded by the system designers.

For example, let assume that the interpretation function is a constituency-based syntactic interpreter I_{synt} and that the set R contains rules describing passivization, such as the rule:

$$\rho_1 = \boxed{X} \text{ has been } \boxed{V}\,\boxed{Z} \text{ by } \boxed{Y} \;\rightarrow\; \boxed{Y}\,\boxed{V}\,\boxed{X}\,\boxed{Z}$$

This rule can be graphically represented as follows:

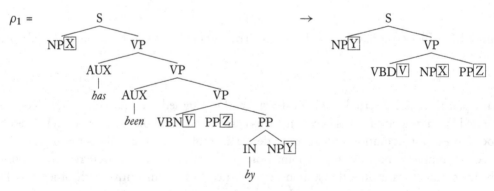

Suppose we need to determine whether or not the following entailment holds:

$T_2 \Rightarrow ? H_2$	
T_2	"Overture has been sold to Google by Yahoo."
H_2	"Yahoo sold Overture to Google."

The first step is to interpret T_2 and H_2 with respect to the linguistic interpretation function I_{synt}. The resulting interpretations are:

$I_{synt}(T_2)=$

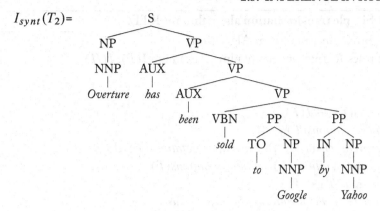

and

$I_{synt}(H_2)=$

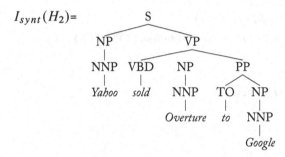

We can apply the rule ρ_1 and thereby discover that the text T_2 entails the hypothesis H_2 as the application of the rule transforms the first syntactic structure to that in the second.

The approach just described can be applied to more general graph-based representations. Given a representation of the entailment pair, $I(T)$ and $I(H)$, and a set of rules R encoded using the same formalism, the method is outlined in Algorithm 1.

This naïve algorithm reproduces the basic logic-based theorem-proving approach described in Section 2.3.3: rules are applied to the existing representations $I(T)$ of the Text of the entailment pair, by checking if the rule head matches (entails) some part of the graph $I(T)$. If so, the body of the rule is used to replace part of the original representation to create a new representation: the subtrees in the original $I(T)$ structure bound to the rule variables are attached to the corresponding positions in the new parse tree. This new representation is then compared to $I(H)$, the interpretation of the Hypothesis; if the hypothesis is subsumed, there exists a valid sequence of operations (a proof) that links the Text to the Hypothesis. The process terminates either when a proof is found, or when the rule applications have been exhausted—no new representations of the Text can be generated.

Braz et al. [34] provide a model-theoretic justification of this approach: when a rule is applied to the entailment pair Text, the augmented representation makes explicit one possible

---

Algorithm 1 Simple transformation algorithm for RTE.

Graph Transformation Entailment Algorithm

Input: set of rules R, Interpreted entailment example $I(T), I(H)$

    $Interpretations(T) \leftarrow I(T)$
    $PreviousInterpretations(T) \leftarrow \emptyset$
    while $Interpretations(T) \neq PreviousInterpretations(T)$ **do**
      $PreviousInterpretations(T) \leftarrow Interpretations(T)$
      $Interpretations(T) \leftarrow \emptyset$
      for all $i(T) \in PreviousInterpretations(T)$ **do**
        for all rule $r = h \Rightarrow b \in R$ **do**
          if $i(T) \subseteq h$ **then**
            $i'(T) \leftarrow APPLY(i(T), r)$
            $Interpretations(T) \leftarrow Intepretations(T) \cup i'(T)$
          end if
        end for
        if $i'(T) \subseteq I(H)$ **then**
          RETURN "true"
        end if
      end for
    end while
    RETURN "false"

(valid) interpretation of that Text (ideally, in a way that makes the Text more closely resemble the Hypothesis). If any such representation of the Text is subsumed by the Hypothesis (that is, the Hypothesis is isomorphic to a subgraph of the Text), the Text entails the Hypothesis.

One implementation that closely follows this model is that of Bar-Haim et al. [9] (see Chapter 4, Section 4.3.2), which uses syntactic structure as the basis for both the Interpretation I of the entailment pair, and to encode rules that express syntactic equivalences. Hand-coded rules are used to abstract over a range of syntactic alternations, including conjunctive, passive-active, and genitive structures, as well as nominalized (deverbal) and factive constructions. These rules pair two syntax tree fragments with placeholders representing subtrees that remain unchanged in the transformation. As distinct from the naïve algorithm 1, rather than generate explicitly a new representation for each rule application, a single graph is maintained that encodes all such rule applications.

An alternative way of using the transformation rules described above is to incorporate them directly into the graph subsumption step that determines whether $I(T) \subseteq I(H)$, if the rules and graph structure are suitably encoded. The simplest example is typified by Adams [1], whose RTE system uses a WordNet-based similarity metric to compute similarity scores between pairs of tokens drawn from the Hypothesis and Text of each entailment example. In its simplest form, such a metric might return a boolean value indicating whether a mapping exists between two words—knowledge which could be expressed instead as a set of rules between pairs of words that are linked by some relation in WordNet. For example, WordNet contains the terms "jeep" and "car," and relates them via a hypernymy/hyponymy link. This link can be interpreted as a rule that indicates that the word "jeep" entails the word "car." (In the actual metric developed in [1], the value returned is a real value $\in [0, 1]$, interpretable as a probability that an entailment relation holds between that pair of words.) This approach can be extended to larger linguistic structures, as in Mehdad et al. [158], whose system computes a tree edit distance based on syntactic dependency trees, but using costs for individual edits based on lexical mapping resources; Sammons et al. [213] describe an RTE system in which mappings between predicate-argument structures are encapsulated in a similarity metric.

2.3.4 HYBRID APPROACHES

Hybrid approaches are also possible, and in fact could be said to dominate the RTE landscape. Most systems incorporate some element of alignment, one or more measures of local and/or global similarity, and some criterion for the quality of the alignment of the representations of the Text and Hypothesis. Transformation rules, or their equivalent, may be incorporated in the form of specialized modules that decorate or modify the representation of the Text and Hypothesis with additional relations rather than as part of an incremental search (e.g., [125]); and many proof-theoretic systems use a final feature extraction and classification stage (for example, [32]), or an alignment and heuristic scoring function (such as [10]), as a back-off model to overcome the limitations of knowledge resources in terms of coverage and precision. Still others use machine learning techniques to compare entailment pairs aligned with a heuristic similarity function to tie intra-pair similarity patterns to inter-pair label matches (e.g., [262]). Chapter 4 describes a number of specific representative systems, and indicates within the system descriptions when a hybrid strategy is used.

2.4 A CONCEPTUAL ARCHITECTURE FOR RTE SYSTEMS

The previous sections of this chapter have surveyed popular representations and reasoning processes used by RTE researchers. We now present an abstract architecture that generalizes over these different approaches.

The different approaches share the following basis. First, a linguistic representation model, i.e., a lexical, a syntactic, or a semantic model, is chosen. Each Text-Hypotheses pair is first represented in terms of this linguistic model (preprocessing). Next, a decision function is applied to determine whether or not the Hypothesis can be derived from the Text. As indicated in previous sections in this chapter, this decision function may involve algorithmic augmentation of the representation of the Text and Hypothesis using rules (enrichment); computations of similarity between constituents of the Text and Hypothesis (candidate alignment generation); selection of a subset of similar constituents (alignment selection); and a final decision component that predicts the entailment label based on the outputs of these previous stages (classification).

Slightly more formally, we define a skeleton of an RTE system with a linguistic interpretation[1] function I and a "semantic containment" function $\models (I(T), I(H))$. Given a Text-Hypothesis pair (T, H), the prototypical RTE system will:

1. interpret T and H producing $I(T)$ and $I(H)$;

2. determine whether $I(H)$ is "semantically contained" in $I(T)$.

There are many different representations that can be entertained for $I()$, and many different models to capture the notion of "semantic containment;" the function $\models (I(T), I(H))$ could be a similarity measure, or a machine-learned classifier, or a derivation based on formal axioms and a set of logical statements about the relevant background knowledge needed to recognize entailment. Entailment pairs are processed either one at a time or as a batch; for simplicity, we describe the process per pair. We describe the system in terms of its *evaluation* (which corresponds to the behavior of a deployed RTE system); protocols for training RTE systems are discussed with reference to specific implementations in Chapter 4.

Figure 2.12 shows three versions of an abstract RTE architecture: each has the same underlying steps (described next), but each handles different subsets of steps in combination, based on the underlying design philosophy. We first describe the underlying architecture components, then the three different models of decision-making described by approaches 1–3.

2.4.1 PREPROCESSING

We assume that as the first step in the RTE process, the system applies a suite of annotators to the entailment pair to induce its representation. While the list of resources is open-ended, typical resources include: sentence and word segmentation (identify sentence boundaries, word and punctuation tokens); lemmatization (identify the roots of each word); part-of-speech (POS) tagging; syntactic dependency or constituency parsing; named entity recognition; co-reference resolution; semantic role labeling. These different resources are applied to the text of the entailment pair to induce the representation used by later stages of the RTE system.

2.4.2 ENRICHMENT

We use the term *enrichment*, as distinct from *preprocessing*, to refer to resources that operate on an Interpretation to either transform or to augment that Interpretation, usually by applying Entailment Rules (as described in Section 2.3.3). Such resources are generally not prepackaged,

---

[1]We use the term "interpretation" even though the resulting representation is not a true semantic meaning representation, but an approximation that typically abstracts away some linguistic structure and morphology, leaving lexical entries as predicate names in place of canonical meanings.

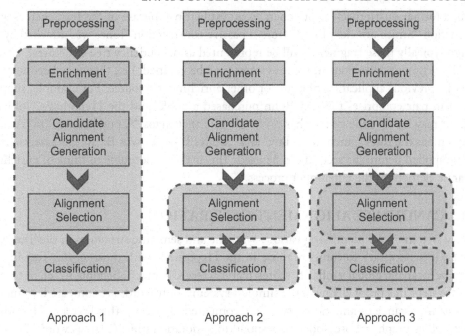

Figure 2.12: Block diagram for generic RTE framework, with Machine Learning applied to different aspects of the entailment process. Each Approach contains the same underlying conceptual steps, but combines or links a different subset of these steps. Approach 1 uses a decision function that combines all but the first step. Approach 2 uses two decision functions: one to determine the alignment between $I(H)$ and $I(T)$, and a second to determine entailment based on this alignment. Approach 3 uses a joint decision process to maximize alignment quality for each possible entailment label before selecting the best label.

i.e., do not have a programmatic interface, as distinct from the types of resources applied during preprocessing. Enrichment resources generally serve one of two functions: to abstract over some text/annotation patterns by mapping them to a closed set of structures; or to augment the existing annotation by recognizing implicit content in the input text/annotation and making it explicit as new structure.

An example of abstraction would be to represent modifiers of verbs such as "failed to" in the sentence "Attackers failed to enter the building," or "said that" in the sentence "John said that Mary lied," by using an attribute in the verb or relation node in the corresponding predicate-argument structure. For the second example, an enrichment resource might mark the embedded predicate "lied" in the phrase "Mary lied" with an attribute indicating uncertainty.

An example of augmentation is the case where a rule makes implicit content of the underlying text more explicit—such as generating a predicate "is" for an appositive structure like "Mike

Smith, a former quarterback"—or generates an explicit paraphrase of the text, such as an active construction "Smith attacked Jones" from a passive construction "Jones was attacked by Smith" (though typically these fragments will be represented as dependency tree structures).

Enrichment operations in some systems may be chained, i.e., they may become valid because of a previous application of a rule or other enrichment resource. For example, suppose the entailment pair comprises the text "John purchased a book" and the Hypothesis "John owns a book." It may be that the system has no single rule that maps "A purchases B" to "A owns B," but that it has the rules "purchase → buy" and "A buys B → A owns B;" in this case, the first rule must be applied before the second can be used. This makes it desirable to think of enrichment as a separate element of the entailment process.

2.4.3 CANDIDATE ALIGNMENT GENERATION

In many systems, after identifying various syntactic and semantic structures in the Text and Hypothesis, it is necessary to compare those in the Hypothesis with those in the Text in order to determine local and global similarity scores/features (see Chapter 3, Section 3.2.2), or to compute scores for steps in a proof chain. In the simplest systems, only words are compared. In more complex systems, a range of annotation types are compared. Typically, the Text and Hypothesis are represented as graphs whose nodes correspond to annotation units (such as words, Named Entities, parse sub-trees, SRL verb arguments), and whose edges correspond to connections within an annotation type (e.g., connecting different mentions of a single entity via co-reference edges, or linking words in a dependency tree with typed dependency edges).

Then, the constituents in the Hypothesis are linked to those in the Text based on some measure of similarity (possibly simply identity), to form a graph distinct from the Text and Hypothesis structures. This similarity graph may be used independently of the representations of the Text and Hypothesis as the basis of a model for determining entailment.

2.4.4 ALIGNMENT SELECTION

The intuition behind the alignment selection stage, made explicit by de Marneffe, et al. [81], is that only a relatively small portion of the Text is relevant to the Hypothesis. The goal of alignment is to identify that relevant portion and thereby simplify the inference step. The formal model for this component is described in Chapter 3, Section 3.2.

Many RTE systems have an explicit alignment step; others have an integrated alignment/inference process. In general, alignments map each constituent in the Hypothesis to a single constituent in the Text. This is a heuristic based on the observation that the Hypothesis tends to be much shorter than the Text, and that in positive entailment examples, a human reader can often generate a "piecewise" explanation of the Hypothesis using portions of the Text.

Most RTE systems first integrate all constituents into a single graph structure and align each constituent in this representation. Others perform an alignment using only words, and in the inference step analyze the structure of linguistic annotations that corresponds to the aligned words, or perform multiple alignments for different groups of annotations, and in the inference step compare the different alignments to discern cues for entailment/non-entailment.

2.4.5 CLASSIFICATION

All RTE systems must use a decision component to label each entailment pair. This may be identity/strict subsumption—perhaps using a theorem-prover over a logical representation induced from the entailment pair and the analysis from the preprocessing step. The decision component might instead be a relatively simple measure of overlap plus a threshold (such as that described in Chapter 3, Section 6), or it may be significantly more complex—for example, extracting features from the alignment graph and applying a machine-learned classifier to determine the final label (Chapter 3, Section 3.3).

2.4.6 MAIN DECISION-MAKING APPROACHES

The architecture depicted in Figure 2.12 is an abstraction; actual systems may ignore or merge steps depending on their requirements. The three versions of RTE architectures indicated by Approaches 1, 2, and 3 in the diagram represent typical system designs as seen in the RTE challenges described in Chapter 1, and differ in the way their entailment decision functions are specified.

Approach 1 merges the steps after the Interpretation of the entailment pair is induced: for example, a maximal match approach that searches exhaustively or greedily through possible embeddings of $I(H)$ in $I(T)$ essentially considers many graphs/alignments over these representations, and possibly, many different enriched versions of $I(H)$ and $I(T)$, and may stop as soon as a sufficiently good match is found. The lexical approach described in Section 2.2.1 exemplifies this approach, having a no-op enrichment step.

Approach 2 has a fixed enrichment and candidate alignment generation step, but uses two decision functions: one determines the alignment of $I(H)$ to $I(T)$ that will be used as the basis of the classification decision, and the other determines the entailment label considering that alignment and the representations $I(H)$ and $I(T)$. Such systems may be referred to as having "two-stage" architectures: the first stage determines the best possible alignment (according to one set of criteria), and the classification step uses only this best alignment as the basis of its decision.

Approach 3 also has two separate decision functions for the alignment and classification steps, but performs joint inference over the two steps. Typically, this means that there is some measure of alignment *quality*, and the best decision is made based on a combination of alignment quality and classification confidence, so many alignments are considered.

2.5 EMERGENT CHALLENGES

Regarding the most pressing problems in developing RTE systems, two main themes emerge from the RTE literature: the need for background knowledge to enable robust performance, and the need to accommodate noise arising from a range of sources—limitations in the expressiveness of the chosen representation; errors in the representation arising from limitations of the tools used to induce it from the underlying text (including resolution of ambiguity of words and expressions); errors due to missing knowledge; and errors arising from other decision elements in the system.

2.5.1   KNOWLEDGE ACQUISITION BOTTLENECK: ACQUIRING RULES

While the rule-based model described in Section 2.3.3 is intuitive, a number of limitations become apparent when implementing a rule-based system. Common to all knowledge-based systems is the difficulty of acquiring the background knowledge required to determine entailment. Most systems use hand-crafted rules in the representation required by the Interpretation model they use (such as Horn clauses or syntactic dependency fragments). Numerous RTE systems have used the DIRT rule collection [144], which is a large but noisy database of paraphrases expressed in terms of paths through dependency trees. Some have used VerbOcean [54], which characterizes semantic relations between verbs. Still more use WordNet [90]. When there are many rules, this may itself create problems for system developers; for example, Bos et al. [33] did not simply create a static knowledge base containing all rules they would use, but generated lexical mapping rules from WordNet "on demand," presumably for efficiency. The consensus of the community is that existing knowledge resources are not adequate for the RTE task, and the research area of Knowledge Acquisition remains very active (see Chapter 5).

Problems remain with the graph-expansion-based approach: if rules are not completely reliable and unambiguous, their application may introduce errors. This risk increases with the "chaining" of rules (subsequent application of a rule to a newly introduced structure that was itself the result of a previous rule application). Also, the problem of dealing with large sets of rules, such as those derived from WordNet in [94] remains: simply adding them as rules in the naïve approach above tends to greatly increase running time in each round of rule applications. This also greatly increases the probability of chaining, which blows up the space of represented meanings and may itself lead to "loops" in rule chains, complicating the task of detecting when a rule application truly results in a new instantiation of the original text. Finally, the rule representation may be relatively inefficient in terms of space if all such lexical mappings are encoded the same way as the syntactic rules. Alignment-based approaches, on the other hand, effectively prevent the chaining of rules, which is a problem if multiple rule applications to the same parts of $I(T)$ and $I(H)$ are required to complete the inference chain needed to determine the entailment label.

2.5.2   NOISE-TOLERANT RTE ARCHITECTURES

NLP components make errors, and RTE systems typically combine many components. Errors may be made at every stage of the conceptual architecture described in Section 2.4, including in the specification or automatic acquisition of rules for enrichment, and this tends to make deterministic decision processes very brittle. To address the problems that arise from these errors, it is natural to apply Machine Learning methods to provide robustness. While there are many specific RTE system architectures, there are many overlapping areas of functionality in which learning may be applied.

Machine learning is already applied in many NLP tools that are used in the preprocessing stage, but since these are widely treated as black boxes by the RTE community, this will be out of scope for our discussion of RTE. But machine learning has been applied to the problem of alignment and to designing decision functions for RTE systems, and even to the learning of entailment rules or of weights for such rules. Chapter 3 deals in depth with the different ways learning has been applied to these aspects of the RTE task, and Chapter 4 describes the role of machine learning in specific systems.

CHAPTER 3

Alignment, Classification, and Learning

Chapter 2 sketches a framework for building textual entailment recognition systems. This chapter outlines the role Machine Learning can play within this framework, based on approaches described in the research literature to date and, in particular, strives to answer the question: how do we characterize and induce a decision function in an RTE system?

Machine Learning techniques are being applied extensively in tools used in the preprocessing steps of RTE systems. In this section, however, we focus on the use of machine learning in other parts of the RTE system. Specifically, we focus on the use of machine learning methods in supporting the final textual entailment decision. Like many other natural language tasks, in most cases, the final TE decision function is machine learning based; the reason is that many factors contribute to this decision and all hide a lot of uncertainty emerging from earlier stages of the process, preventing us from coming up with a deterministic "rule" that can be used reliably in the final decision. The machine learning based decision is designed to account for uncertainties emerging from:

1. **Errors in the interpretation stage.** All NLP tools, such as syntactic parsers and semantic role labelers, are imprecise, making errors as they induce their representation of the underlying text.

2. **Knowledge gaps.** There are inevitably incorrect and missing pieces of knowledge incorporated in various stages of the process. These could be due to inherent underspecification and ambiguities in the natural language representation used, lack of coverage of knowledge resources, or other knowledge engineering or acquisition inaccuracies.

3. **The complexity of the decision space.** The number of possible combinations of component decisions used to make the global entailment decision for a given entailment pair may grow exponentially with the length of the input data. Machine learning methods allow us to abstract over this huge space and collapse large sets of observations and intermediate decisions into a smaller space, weigh the factors based on their relative contributions in earlier experiences, and guide the decision.

3.1   AN ABSTRACT SCHEME FOR TEXTUAL ENTAILMENT DECISIONS

The first and simplest case of entailment is when the hypothesis H is expressed directly in the text T. This may be a trivial case but it motivates a simple but interesting baseline approach. The basic idea is to check if the hypothesis H is a part of the text T. The simplest of these approaches is *token level similarity*, one example of which counts the tokens in common between the Text and the Hypothesis. This simplistic model can be used to describe the rationale of the three key components of the architecture presented in Chapter 2: *candidate alignment generation, alignment,* and *classification.*

To determine whether T implies H using token-based similarity, we use the following running example:

$T_3 \Rightarrow H_3$	
T_3	*"The **seven refineries located** in **Lake Charles** appear to be the ones hardest hit by the water and wind that accompanied **Rita**."*
H_3	*"**Rita** caused damages to **seven refineries located** in **Lake Charles**"*

We can compute an indicator of how well T covers H and then decide whether or not the value of the indicator is sufficient to predict that T entails H. One possible indicator for token-based similarity is the token coverage of H by T, which can be defined as the ratio between the number of tokens in common between T and H, and the number of tokens in H. Focusing on the content words (i.e., skipping classical stopwords such as determiners and prepositions), this token coverage or token-based similarity is $6/8 = 0.75$ (see words in bold). This value may be considered to be relatively high. If we have somehow determined a threshold value for the token coverage of 0.7, we will predict that T_3 entails H_3 as the actual value is above the threshold.

Of course, this is a very simplistic approach; it does not even take into account semantic similarities between words when estimating the similarity between H and T (e.g., between *water* and *lake*). [86] provides an example of a better, still lexical, approach to this problem, and Chapter 2 discusses it in the context of approaches to RTE. Nevertheless, we can use this simple example to illustrate the steps one may need to go through on the way to a TE decision.

- **Candidate Alignment Generation** First, we looked at the text T and the hypothesis H to search for similar tokens. To do this, we compared each token or phrase in H with each token or phrase in T to determine whether or not they are similar. *Lake Charles* in *T* and *Lake Charles* in *H* are identical, so would get the highest similarity score, but *water* in *T* and *Lake Charles* in *H* might also be given a high score if one has an appropriate matching resource. The outcome of this step is a list of potential *anchors* where an anchor represents a link between a token in T and a token in H, associated with a similarity score (which could be a binary score—0 for "no match" or 1 for "match").

- **Alignment** Second, we selected an *alignment* between T and H by choosing, for each token in H, the best corresponding element in T—in this case, we did it greedily based on the link with the highest similarity score. The outcome of this step is the list of best *anchors*.

- **Classification** Third, we made a final decision as a *classification*: given the set of *anchors*, we computed a set of features representing the aligned pair $\langle T, H \rangle$—in this case, the classification could be as simple as averaging the similarity scores assigned to the edge features—and then assigned a final class to the pair $\langle T, H \rangle$ by comparing the resulting value of the average similarity to a threshold.

These components are clearly interdependent: the first is useful for the second; the first and the second are useful for the third.

For simplicity, we have presented a simple example where candidate alignment generation, alignment, and classification were the *only* steps used. In general, these three steps will follow a *preprocessing* and an *enrichment* step. The system then aligns enriched representations of Text and Hypothesis (such as syntactic parses), extracts features based on this alignment, and learns a classification model that is based on the enriched representations and the alignment. Moreover, full-symbolic approaches like the *proof theoretic approaches* (see Section 2.3.3) and *transformational graph-based approaches* (see Section 2.3.3) can be presented this way too, in terms of alignment and classification. In proof theoretic approaches, the alignment is the final unification between the transformed and enriched Text and the Hypothesis, and the classification is the final logical decision. In *transformational graph-based approaches* (see the last *if* of Algorithm 1 in Section 2.3.3), the alignment is the final matching $i'(T) \subseteq \mathcal{I}(H)$ (i.e., a subgraph isomorphism) and the classification is determined based on the value of this matching.

So what does this approach tell us about a way to think about a decision function for Textual Entailment? We can't easily represent the true meaning of the Text and Hypothesis in an abstract formalism, so we look for more manageable, local evidence of similarity by comparing tokens (e.g., words): if we can find a good alignment between most elements of H and elements of T, we have more evidence that T entails H than if the alignment covers only a few elements in H. In our previous example the alignment was very simple: greedily connect similar words. However, we can use a more sophisticated representation (connect similar phrases, or clauses, or verb/argument structures, etc.) and/or a more sophisticated alignment function (prefer alignments of lexical elements where the aligned words in H are linked by syntactic structure similar to the syntactic structure linking their aligned words in T.) We can also develop a global view of alignment. The key concept is that this decision function is modeled in terms of **similarities between H and T.**

Because we can't rely on our representation or our alignment function to be perfect, in our example, we used a threshold value between 0 and 1 to determine what is "similar enough." When our alignment yielded a similarity value higher than that threshold, our decision function predicted the label "entails." The implication is that we may want to use relaxed matching (using machine learning or deterministic procedures) in reaching the final decision; the reason is that the preprocessing step may make mistakes and the alignment may be erroneous. We will need an approach that can abstract over the fine details of the representation and thus could strike a balance between precision (only predicting "entails" when we are very sure) and recall (predicting "entails" for more examples).

3.2 GENERATING CANDITATES AND SELECTING ALIGNMENTS

Candidate Alignment Generation and *Alignment* are basic steps for RTE systems. This section introduces these two steps more formally by describing their underlying goals, and framing them as an optimization problem.

3.2.1 ANCHORS: LINKING TEXTS AND HYPOTHESES

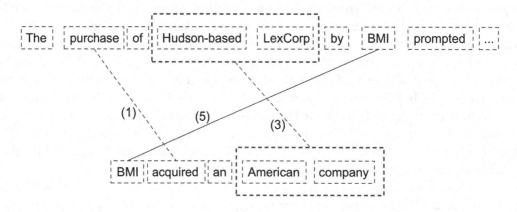

Figure 3.1: An alignment of an entailment pair, where edges represent "similar" or "compatible" terms.

To give a clearer sense of the role of candidate alignment generation and alignment, we use the Text and the Hypothesis *Hyp 1* of Figure 1.1 as a running example.

As discussed earlier in Section 3.1 and illustrated in Figure 3.1, an RTE system needs to recognize a set of links between parts of the Text and parts of the Hypothesis. In this case, we expect three *anchors* linking *T* and *H* as follows: (1,*purchase,acquired*), (3,*Hudson–based LexCorp, American company*), and (5,*BMI,BMI*). There are several ways to infer these links and one way to do so is to make use of the following entailment rules, the first of which describes the lexical behavior of *purchase* and *acquire* and the second, an underspecified rule that describes the nominalization of a verb.

- ρ_4 = purchase of $\boxed{X}$ by $\boxed{Y}$ $\rightarrow$ $\boxed{Y}$ acquired $\boxed{X}$

- ρ_5 = $\boxed{Z\text{:Noun}}$ of $\boxed{X}$ by $\boxed{Y}$ $\rightarrow$ $\boxed{Y}$ $\boxed{Z\text{:Verb}}$ $\boxed{X}$

In order to apply one of these rules to the example, variables $\boxed{X}$, $\boxed{Y}$, and $\boxed{Z}$ should be unified to actual tokens in the sentence, and this may also require additional information such as *syntactic classes* and *semantic interpretations*.

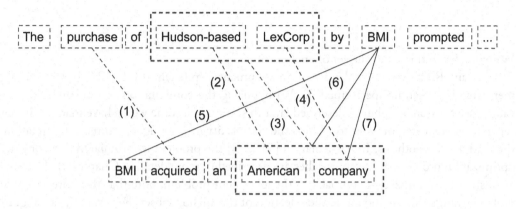

Figure 3.2: Candidate Alignment Generation: linking similar edges for an entailment pair.

Finding the best anchors shown in Figure 3.2 is not straightforward as this task typically involves lexical knowledge and world knowledge. In this example, it is important to determine that *Hudson-based LexCorp* is anchored to *American company* and *purchase* is anchored to *acquired*, but the anchor selection process needs to search among more possibilities. For example, the token *BMI* can be potentially linked to *BMI*, *American company*, and *company* generating the anchors (5,*BMI,BMI*), (6,*BMI,American company*), and (7,*BMI,company*). The same applies to (3,*Hudson-based LexCorp,American company*) that can be alternatively represented as (2,*Hudson-based,American*) and (4,*LexCorp,company*). How does one devise an approach that chooses the right anchors?

We can define the set of anchors to be the set of the best potential matches for each component. This discussion indicates that it is useful to split the anchor selection process to two parts:

- *Candidate Alignment Generation*, where one generates all the potential *anchors* between Texts and Hypotheses

- *Alignment*, where the best *anchors* are selected.

The *Candidate Alignment Generation* step finds the correspondences that map the text T and the hypothesis H by taking into account token matching, lexical resources, and similarity functions and can rely on multiple preprocessing tools in supporting it. The result of the process is a set of potential *anchors*:

$$PA = \{(T_i, H_j) | T_i \text{ is a part of } T \text{ and } H_i \text{ is a part of } H\}$$

The *Alignment* step then selects the best subset of this set of edges. Here, one hopes that the "best" alignment means the alignment that supports the most reliable entailment decision for a given pair. The result of the alignment process is a set of pairs, called the set of best *anchors A*:

$$A \subseteq PA$$

We will refer to this set as the set of anchors.

Many RTE systems make use of an alignment step (such as [78, 127, 149]). This alignment step is sometimes performed implicitly during the computation of the similarity feature values (see Section 3.4), but as described later in section 3.5, some works have made alignment a separate, explicit step in order to address the complexity of aligning structured interpretations of the Text and Hypothesis. In particular, in [51, 213] the problem is formulated as a constrained optimization problem (these approaches are described in more detail in Chapter 4). To motivate a constrained optimization approach to the alignment problem, note that there are several natural constraints that should guide the selection of the anchor subset. For example, an alignment $A \subseteq PA$ is usually constrained to include exactly one similarity edge linked to each component in the Hypothesis (see Figure 3.1). In this formulation, one can consider the set of anchors A along with the text T and the hypothesis H as a bipartite graph. A is the set of *similarity edges* linking structural component nodes in T to those in H; if all possible pairwise component comparisons are made, this will be a complete bipartite graph between the components of the Hypothesis and the components of the Text.

Note that the notion of "best alignment" does not directly yield the label of the entailment pair; that decision depends on characteristics of the resulting alignment. Given perfect interpretation and matching functions, it might be possible to label a pair as "entailing" only if all components of H are aligned with components of T with sufficiently high score. However, in reality, the chosen decision function must accommodate noisy interpretation and imperfect matching functions. Moreover, alignment does not deal with issues of negation, polarity, and modality and these need to be handled by a subsequent step that makes use of the alignment results. This process may also be required to handle additional labels of the RTE question, such as the contradiction label.

It is worth noticing that H is typically smaller than T, so parts of T will not align with H. And, in many cases, there will be parts of H that do not align. These parts cannot be directly used in the entailment decision that relies on similarity detection but can be important for other kinds of features as described in Section. 3.4.4.

3.2.2 FORMALIZING CANDIDATE ALIGNMENT GENERATION AND ALIGNMENT

As described earlier, almost all textual entailment approaches can be abstracted to include a candidate alignment generation and alignment process. Designing the candidate alignment generation and alignment processes in the form described above requires, respectively, the following functions:

- The *Candidate Alignment Generation* phase needs similarity/matching functions $s(T_i, H_j)$ that compare components H_j of $\mathcal{I}(H)$ with components T_i of $\mathcal{I}(T)$. Note that these components could themselves be structured, such as parse subtrees connecting a group of words.

- The *Alignment* phase needs a global similarity/matching function $G(\{(T_i, H_j)\})$ that compares complete alignments of $\mathcal{I}(H)$ with $\mathcal{I}(T)$ in order to identify the "best" one.

More formally, the alignment task can be formulated as a constrained optimization problem. Its result is a set of *anchors* as previously described. In the following sections we will describe the functions $s(T_i, H_j)$, the constraints on the search space $\mathcal{C}$ of the optimization, and, finally, the global function $G(\{(T_i, H_j)\})$.

Similarity Functions for Candidate Alignment Generation

Functions $s(T_i, H_j)$ are specialized similarity functions that model component-level decisions as scores; without loss of generality, we assume they return a score in the range $[0, 1]$, with 1 being the strongest match (e.g., "buy a car" and "buy a car"), 0 indicating irrelevance (e.g., "car" and "soldier"). These functions may also return, in addition, a label indicating contradiction for pairs of components that are highly incompatible (e.g., "rise" and "fall") to facilitate selecting the most *relevant* matching components of T for their counterparts in H. Note that these functions might be trivial, returning 1 only if the components are identical and 0 otherwise, but they might also refer to sophisticated ontologies [223], or appeal to similarity heuristics [86] or learned classifiers [85]. There may also be different functions for different types of components (e.g., individual words, Named Entities, syntactic parse subtrees).

The motivating example exhibits the need for constraints on the search space that serve to eliminate some of the mappings from H to T. These constraints are expressed via the set $\mathcal{C}$, which comprises valid subsets of pairs of components (H_i, T_j), each pair representing an edge from component H_i to component T_j. The simplest constraint requires that each token in H must be included at most once in the set of components H_j that is mapped to the set T_i, but many others can be added.

Optimization for Alignment

Given these definitions for similarity functions and constraints, we can define the global alignment objective function $G(\{(T_i, H_j)\})$. In the more complex alignment formulations, in addition to the functions $s(T_i, H_j)$, there may be an additional function intended to quantify the "quality" of a global alignment; this can be represented as an additional term in the objective function, $Q(\{(T_i, H_j)\})$. This function might, for example, give a higher score to alignments in which components in T that are mapped to H are more closely grouped together. The function $G(\{(T_i, H_j)\})$ should also account for asymmetries between entailment pairs: some pairs have longer Texts and/or Hypotheses, which will tend to result in more candidate anchors. This can be addressed via the normalization term, $N(H, T, I)$, which adjusts the value according to characteristics of T, H, and the indicator function $\mathcal{I}$. The global alignment objective function is then:

$$G(\{(H_i, T_j)\}) = \frac{Q(\{(H_i, T_j)\}) + \sum\limits_{(H_i, T_j)} S(H_i, T_j)}{N(T, H, I)} \tag{3.1}$$

The maximization problem along with the resulting anchors A is defined as follows:

$$A = \underset{\{(H_i, T_j)\} \in \mathcal{C}}{\arg\max} \; G(\{(H_i, T_j)\}) \tag{3.2}$$

This formulation provides a useful way to characterize different approaches to modeling RTE; paradigms for feature specification and selection depend on characterizing the similarities between (parts of) the Text and the Hypothesis in an entailment pair, and then on distinguishing the *ways* alignments of pairs with a given label differ from alignments of pairs with different labels.

Within the alignment formulation itself, systems vary in the representation $\mathcal{I}(\cdot)$ used to specify the components of H and T, and in the similarity function(s) $s(H_i, T_j)$ used to compare them. There is also some work on *learning* similarity functions (see Section 3.5.2) using aligned pairs.

Given some definition of the "best" alignment, a number of different approaches have been taken to compare aligned T-H pairs and to support the final entailment decision. The following sections describe the representations, similarity functions, and algorithms used to determine alignments and the way machine learning techniques are applied to the task of making the final entailment decision given a set of aligned T-H pairs.

3.3 CLASSIFIERS, FEATURE SPACES, AND MACHINE LEARNING

Classification is a natural component of textual entailment recognition and it is the last component of the generic architecture. Given a pair $x = \langle T, H \rangle$, the classifier is asked to decide whether it belongs to the class of *entailment cases* or to the class of *non-entailment cases* (or, similarly, to one of three classes: *entailment*, *non-entailment*, and *contradiction*). Namely, we seek a classification function

$$C : X \rightarrow Y$$

where an input instance $x = \langle T, H \rangle$ is represented in a feature space generated by the previous analysis steps. The definition of the *feature space* in which we represent the pair x is the key challenge faced by the machine learning step. We denote the feature space $F = F_1 \times \ldots \times F_n$, where each F_i is an observable feature. We often think of F as a subset of $\{0, 1\}^n$, where the features are all Boolean or, in general, as a subset of R^n. The feature space, and thus the representation of the pair x in it: $\mathcal{F}(x) = (f_1, ..., f_n)$, will depend on the preprocessing step discussed earlier and the alignment between the Text and Hypothesis in $x = \langle T, H \rangle$.

Conceptually, one can think of at least two possibilities for building the classification function C: a manual definition or using machine learning techniques. Both approaches are used in RTE but the second is more widespread due to reasons discussed earlier. A manual definition of the classification will be designed to exploit the representation $\mathcal{F}(x)$. In a supervised machine learning approach, on the other hand, the developer will choose the family of hypotheses that can be learned (these could be linear functions of F, decision trees over F, etc.) and then use a set $Train \subset X \times Y$ of annotated examples (pairs of examples and their labels) as a way to *learn* a classification function in this class. This learned function can then be used to determine the label of a new, previously unobserved instance $x = \langle T, H \rangle$. The success of this learning process largely depends on the ability to represent x in a good feature space F, that supports an appropriate level of abstraction over the surface level representation of x.

The following sections introduce different classes of feature spaces. In Section 3.4 we introduce the types of features one can expect to extract given preprocessing of x via the notions of *similarity* and rewrite rules. In Section 3.4.4 we introduce the equivalent notion of *kernels* and discuss the construction of kernels for RTE applications.

3.4 SIMILARITY FEATURE SPACES

Similarity feature spaces aim to capture the intuition that the text T implies the hypothesis H if an excerpt of the text T is "similar" to the hypothesis H. There are two major ways of computing the similarity:

- *Coverage*: the similarity is based on the coverage of H with respect to T.

- *Longest common subsequence (LCS)*: the similarity is based on the size of the longest common subsequence between T and H.

The *coverage* similarity generally considers sentences as bags of independent elements, e.g., bag-of-words, bag-of-synsets, or bag-of-syntactic-dependencies. The *longest common subsequence* similarity instead considers sentences as sequences of elements. Different interpretation levels give rise to different possible feature representations from this class of feature spaces. We review here features that correspond to the classical interpretation levels: token level, syntax, and semantics.

3.4.1 TOKEN-LEVEL SIMILARITY FEATURES

This level generates the simplest features for textual entailment recognition. Nevertheless, these are often very effective features since they are generally not affected by errors in preprocessing. For brevity, we will call the representation of instance x after preprocessing, the interpretation $\mathcal{I}$ of x. To illustrate the different features we use the following example:

$T_6 \Rightarrow H_6$	
T_6	"*The seven refineries located in Lake Charles appear to be the ones hardest hit by the water and wind that accompanied Rita.*"
H_6	"*Rita caused damages to seven refineries located in Lake Charles*"

Lexical Overlap

The simplest token level *coverage* feature is the lexical overlap (L): the percentage of content words of the hypothesis H that are in the Text. In general, content words are nouns, adjectives, verbs, and adverbs. We can define the lexical overlap (L) as follows:

$$\overline{s_l}(T, H) = \frac{|W_H \cap W_T|}{|W_H|} \tag{3.3}$$

where W_H and W_T are respectively the content words of H and of T. The value of this fraction depends on the tokenization, i.e., on the interpretation function $\mathcal{I}$, and it makes use of a component similarity function in the implicit alignment process; the simplest version of this function could be $s(w_i, w_j) = 1$ if $w_i = w_j$ and $s(w_i, w_j) = 0$ otherwise.

In the above example, if we assume that tokens are those character sequences with no spaces, the lexical overlap is $\overline{s_l}(T_6, H_6) = \frac{6}{8} = 0.75$. However, if we assume that proper names are single tokens, the lexical overlap changes, i.e., $\overline{s_l}(T_6, H_6) = \frac{5}{7} = 0.714$.

Lexical overlap is often used as a baseline model for the RTE challenges, although typically a more sophisticated component similarity function is used (see [86]).

Weighted Lexical Overlap

A more complex token level *coverage* feature is the weighted lexical overlap (WL) (e.g., [66]). The principle is the same but each token has an external weight such as the inverse document frequency of the words over a large external corpus such as Wikipedia. The weighted lexical overlap (wl) is defined as follows:

$$\overline{s_{wl}}(T, H) = \frac{\sum_{w \in W_H \cap W_T} \omega_w}{\sum_{w \in W_H} \omega_w} \tag{3.4}$$

where ω_w is the weight for the token w. As before, this feature uses a component similarity function.

The weights play an important role here. For example, if the weight is the inverse document frequency of the word in a corpus, proper names will have a higher weight since proper names are less frequent than other words. Thus, they will have a very important role in the overall sum to the extent that the $\overline{s_{wl}}$ can in some cases be completely determined by the proper names (or their absence) in the hypothesis H.

Weighted Similarity-based Lexical Overlap

Finally, the more complete token level *coverage* feature is the weighted lexical similarity (WLS), which relaxes the matching constraint. Two words w_1 and w_2 are related if they are similar according to a component similarity function $s(w_1, w_2)$ which ranges between 0 and 1. As mentioned earlier, multiple similarity functions $s(w_1, w_2)$ can be used [66, 86, 262], which range from Levenshtein distance (which is useful for spelling correction and to assign similarity values between nouns and their adjectival forms, e.g., Jamaica vs. Jamaican), to WordNet-based distances, to named entity distance functions. The weighted lexical similarity (WLS) is then defined as follows:

$$\overline{s_{wls}}(T, H) = \frac{\sum_{(w_t, w_h) \in A} \omega_{w_h} s(w_t, w_h)}{\sum_{w \in W_H} \omega_w} \tag{3.5}$$

Going back to the previous example $\langle T_6, H_6 \rangle$, we will use a weight 1 for every word and a similarity function s based on the Jiang&Conrath (J&C) distance [126] that uses WordNet [162]. According to this measure, the verbs *hit* and *cause* are related with $s(hit, cause) = 0.089$. Then, the weighted lexical similarity (WLS) of the pair would be $\overline{s_{wls}}(T_6, H_6) = \frac{6.089}{8} = 0.761$ when proper nouns are not single tokens.

Longest common subsequence

The *longest common subsequence* (LCS) feature can be viewed as an extension of the simple lexical overlap, but the only version of it that has been used in an RTE system is the plain token LCS similarity. It can be defined as an absolute measure or a relative measure. Let $lcs(T, H)$ be the longest common subsequence between T and H, then the absolute LCS is [179]:

$$s_{lcs}(T, H) = |lcs(T, H)| \tag{3.6}$$

where $|lcs(T, H)|$ is the number of tokens in the sequence, and the relative LCS is:

$$\overline{s_{lcs}}(T, H) = \frac{|lcs(T, H)|}{|H|} \tag{3.7}$$

For example, we can compute both absolute and relative LCS for the pair $\langle T_6, H_6 \rangle$. Given that $lcs(T_6, H_6) = $ "*seven refineries located in Lake Charles*", the LCS will be $s_{lcs}(T_6, H_6) = 6$ and $\overline{s_{lcs}}(T_6, H_6) = \frac{6}{10} = 0.6$. It is worth noticing that the longest common subsequence can be augmented with weights and expanded with similarity measures over tokens as in the methods described above.

3.4.2   STRUCTURED SIMILARITY FEATURES

Structured similarity features extend the token-level similarity measures discussed above, capturing the similarity between a structure $\mathcal{I}(T)$ representing the text T and a structure $\mathcal{I}(H)$ representing the hypothesis H. Structures could represent the syntax of the text or its semantics but, in many cases, the similarity features defined over structures can in theory be oblivious to *what* is represented and depend only on the structure used—trees, planar graphs, and directed acyclic graphs cover many linguistic representation structures. As with the token level, we can define absolute structured similarity features that measure similarities between the two graphs—these could be parse trees, semantic parsing representation, and graphs that represent multiple levels of preprocessing—and relative structured similarity features that normalize the absolute values, dividing them by the size of the graph representing H. Then, given the graph representation of the text $\mathcal{I}(T)$ and the hypothesis $\mathcal{I}(H)$, and a structured similarity type t, we can divide the problem of determining similarity features into two parts:

- $s_t(\mathcal{I}(T), \mathcal{I}(H))$: the similarity between the two graphs $\mathcal{I}(T)$ and $\mathcal{I}(H)$

- $\|\mathcal{I}(H)\|_t = s_t(\mathcal{I}(H), \mathcal{I}(H))$: the norm of the graph $\mathcal{I}(H)$

The absolute value of any of these similarity features f is $f = s_t(\mathcal{I}(T), \mathcal{I}(H))$ and the relative value of these features f is $f = \frac{s_t(\mathcal{I}(T), \mathcal{I}(H))}{\|\mathcal{I}(H)\|_t}$.

The similarity of $s_t(\mathcal{I}(T), \mathcal{I}(S))$ is computed in many ways within the RTE research community, but all can be thought of in terms of "noisy" graph isomorphism. Generally, structured RTE approaches seek the best embedding of $\mathcal{I}(H)$ in $\mathcal{I}(T)$, somehow penalizing imperfect substructure matches (at the level of nodes and edges). Three popular methods are: designing a piecewise scoring function for local structure; counting how many subgraphs are common to two structures; and determining the largest shared subgraph. The latter two problems can be defined more formally, and we address these below. A broader class of approaches that covers piecewise scoring functions is described in Section 3.5.

Common subgraph counting and maximal common subgraph detection are strictly related with the graph isomorphism problem [99] which is NP-complete. However, for some types of graphs, e.g., trees, the problem is tractable and we will present an approach studied by Collins and Duffy [64]. For general graphs, the similarity function has instead been approximated and we will review these models.

The graph similarities used in RTE heavily exploit node and edge labels. Yet, as described in the previous section, we can also consider equivalent nodes having different labels, e.g., preterminal nodes like *nouns* anchored to *verbs* (see the example in Figure 3.1 where the verb *acquired* should be linked to the noun *purchase*). This equivalence must be given by an external resource, as discussed in the previous section. The similarity is then computed in two steps:

- Node alignment: the best node alignment between relevant nodes in $\mathcal{I}(T)$ and $\mathcal{I}(H)$ is determined.

- Graph similarity computation: given the node alignment, the two graphs $\mathcal{I}(T)$ and $\mathcal{I}(H)$ are compared.

Node alignment is a specific case of the candidate alignment generation and alignment process described in Section 3.2 and it may represent the first step of the "noisy" graph isomorphism, i.e., finding the function f that maps nodes of two graphs.

We next describe common approaches that address these two problems, either separately or together.

Basic graph similarity measure: common edges
The first and easiest model for computing the graph similarity $sim(\mathcal{I}(T), \mathcal{I}(H))$ is to compute the number of edges in common between $\mathcal{I}(T)$ and $\mathcal{I}(H)$. We will call this function $\overline{s_e}(\mathcal{I}(T), \mathcal{I}(H))$. The first step is to determine a mapping function m between the nodes N_T and N_H. This can be obtained with the alignment process. Assuming that E'_T are the edges of E_T where the mapping m has been applied, the second step is to compute the $\overline{s_e}(\mathcal{I}(T), \mathcal{I}(H))$ as follows:

$$\overline{s_e}(\mathcal{I}(T), \mathcal{I}(H)) = \frac{|E'_T \cap E_H|}{|E_H|} \tag{3.8}$$

This similarity feature is often used with syntactic/semantic dependency models. In these cases, it captures the pairs of words in common between the text T and the hypothesis H, where words in each pair are connected with a comparable dependency or syntactic parse edge. In this case, the norm of the relative feature is simply $||\mathcal{I}(H)||_e = |E_H|$. This simple approximated similarity measure can be extended to paths up to a specified length as in [99].

For example, Figure 3.3 shows a possible dependency-based syntactic analysis of the pair $\langle T_6, H_6 \rangle$. The type of the syntactic dependencies is omitted for simplicity. In this case the computation of $\overline{s_e}(\mathcal{I}(T), \mathcal{I}(H))$ does not require the computation of the E'_T set as equivalent nodes have trivially the same name (i.e., represent the same word). In this case, $s_e(\mathcal{I}(T), \mathcal{I}(H)) =$

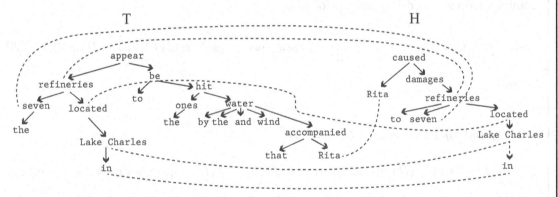

Figure 3.3: A syntactic dependency analysis of an entailment pair with anchors.

4 for the absolute similarity and $\overline{s_e}(\mathcal{I}(T), \mathcal{I}(H)) = 4/8 = 0.5$ for the relative similarity.

Largest common subtree
If we focus our attention on trees, there are other ways to define the similarity function between T and H. Trees are basic representation structures for many syntactic and semantic linguistic

theories: for example, constituency-based syntactic trees [56], and projective and non-projective dependency trees [239]. There is a basic and efficient algorithm for computing whether two trees are equal, i.e., isomorphic. Two trees, α and β, are isomorphic if:

1. α and β are two single-node trees labeled in the same way, i.e., $L(\alpha)=L(\beta)$.

2. α has a root α_r with direct children $\alpha_1,...,\alpha_n$ and β has a root β_r with direct children $\beta_1,...,\beta_n$ such that

   - $L(\alpha_r)=L(\beta_r)$,
   - for $i = 1..n$, $L(\alpha_i)=L(\beta_i)$,
   - for $i = 1..n$, the tree rooted in α_i is isomorphic to the tree rooted in β_i

The two steps above recursively build the bijective function f: step 1 imposes the constraint that $f(\alpha) = \beta$; step 2 enforces the condition that $f(\alpha_r) = \beta_r$ and for each $i = 1..n$ $f(\alpha_i) = \beta_i$. If the two properties are recursively satisfied for the two trees, the function f is defined by construction. This kind of algorithm is implicitly used in the kernel function proposed in [64].

This algorithm offers some interesting possibilities for defining the similarity between T and H and it efficiently solves the alignment problem.

The first tree-based similarity measure, $\overline{s_{lcs}}(\mathcal{I}(T), \mathcal{I}(H))$, computes the size of the largest common subtree. The definition is as follows:

$$s_{lcs}(\mathcal{I}(T), \mathcal{I}(H)) = \max_{n_T \in \mathcal{I}(T), n_H \in \mathcal{I}(H)} |largest\_common\_subtree(\mathcal{I}(T)(n_T), \mathcal{I}(H)(n_H))| \quad (3.9)$$

where:

- n_T and n_H are nodes of $\mathcal{I}(T)$ and $\mathcal{I}(H)$;

- $\mathcal{I}(T)(n_T)$ and $\mathcal{I}(H)(n_H)$ are subtrees of $\mathcal{I}(T)$ and $\mathcal{I}(H)$ respectively rooted in n_T and n_H;

- $largest\_common\_subtree(\mathcal{I}(T)(n_T), \mathcal{I}(H)(n_H))$ computes the largest common subtree of the two subtrees.

The last function can be easily obtained using the general algorithm for determining isomorphism between two trees. As with the similarity measures, we can compute the relative tree similarity by dividing the absolute score by the $norm(\mathcal{I}(H))$.

Figure 3.4 shows a possible syntactic constituency analysis of the pair $\langle T_6, H_6 \rangle$. The largest common subtree is the following:

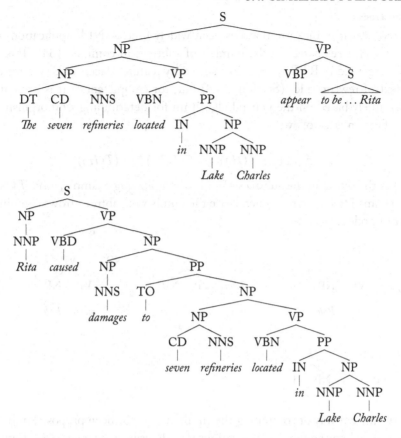

Figure 3.4: A constituency syntactic analysis of a sentence pair.

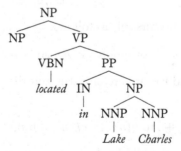

In this case, if we compute the size of the trees according to the number of non-terminal nodes, the absolute similarity is $s_{lcst}(\mathcal{I}(T), \mathcal{I}(H)) = 9$ and the relative similarity is $\overline{s_{lcst}}(\mathcal{I}(T), \mathcal{I}(H)) = 9/21 = 0.43$.

Common subtrees

A second tree similarity measure that has been widely used in NLP applications computes the similarity between trees based on the number of subtrees in common [64]. This similarity has not been directly used in RTE systems in a similarity feature space. RTE systems used it mostly in the context of rewrite rules (Section 3.4.4) but, for completeness, it is presented here. This similarity is largely based on the general algorithm for determining isomorphism between two trees. The definition is as follows:

$$s_{ct}(\mathcal{I}(T), \mathcal{I}(H)) = |\mathcal{T}(\mathcal{I}(T)) \cap \mathcal{T}(\mathcal{I}(H))| \tag{3.10}$$

where $\mathcal{T}(\tau)$ is the set of all the subtrees of τ. In the following example, a set $\mathcal{T}(\tau)$ is presented. We use a very small tree as in the general case the number of subtrees grows combinatorially with the number of nodes .

A very efficient way of computing the similarity $\overline{s_{ct}}$ has been proposed in [64] and refined in [172]. It is based on the following equations that describe a recursive algorithm:

$$s_{ct}(\mathcal{I}(T), \mathcal{I}(H)) = \sum_{n_T \in \mathcal{I}(T), n_H \in \mathcal{I}(H)} \Delta(n_T, n_H) \tag{3.11}$$

where the Δ function is defined recursively as follows:

1. $\Delta(n_T, n_H) = 0$ if the productions rooted in n_T and n_H are not equal;

2. $\Delta(n_T, n_H) = 1$ if n_T and n_H are preterminals and the productions rooted at n_T and n_H are the same;

3. $\Delta(n_T, n_H) = \prod_{i=1}^{nc(n_T)}(1 + \Delta(ch(n_T, i), ch(n_H, i))$ otherwise;

where $ch(n, i)$ represents the i-th child of the node n and $nc(n)$ is the number of children of node n (notice that, if the productions in n_T and n_H are the same, then it must be the case that $nc(n_T) = nc(n_H)$). The use of dynamic programming techniques in the computation of the Δ function allows us to evaluate the similarity function $\overline{s_{ct}}(\mathcal{I}(T), \mathcal{I}(H))$ in time $O(|\mathcal{I}(T)||\mathcal{I}(H)|)$.

To summarize the perspective of similarity features and similarity feature spaces presented so far it is useful to consider the question: how are these being used in the context of a machine learning approach to RTE? The key observation is that, depending on the quality of the generated feature space (and the level of preprocessing used to generate it) most of the information is already in the representation. Consequently, classifiers based on these features often only learn a decision threshold, although it is also possible to learn how to weight different similarity features, e.g., using a linear decision function. It is also possible to learn multiple thresholds, defining intervals of similarity scores that distinguish entailment cases from non-entailment cases.

The rather straightforward use of the similarity feature spaces discussed so far serves also to illustrate the limitations of this approach. Many (T, H) pairs are "similar" even when the corresponding entailment values vary. For example, at the lexical level, two similar texts are not in an entailment relation if they differ only by a negation. Similarly, at the syntactic level, the entailment relation can hold between two very dissimilar text spans when a syntactic alternation (e.g. active/passive, paraphrases) or *downward* and *upward monotonicity* is involved. In the following example, T_7 entails H_7 but it does not entail H_8:

$T_7 \Rightarrow H_7$	
T_7	*"At the end of the year, all solid companies pay dividends"*
H_7	*"At the end of the year, all solid insurance companies pay dividends."*

$T_8 \nRightarrow H_8$	
T_8	*"At the end of the year, all solid companies pay dividends"*
H_8	*"At the end of the year, all solid companies pay cash dividends."*

In the similarity feature spaces introduced above, the two examples could be represented as follows:

$$
\begin{array}{c|c||c}
 & \langle T_7, H_7 \rangle & \langle T_8, H_8 \rangle \\
\hline
f_l & 1 & 1 \\
f_{lcs} & \frac{8}{12} = 0.667 & \frac{10}{12} = 0.833 \\
f_{lcst} & \frac{17}{21} = 0.809 & \frac{18}{21} = 0.857
\end{array}
$$

By this measure, these two examples are almost indistinguishable.

This example serves to illustrate that, while the use of similarity features offers an important way to address the RTE task, there is a need to develop feature spaces that capture additional information.

3.4.3 ENTAILMENT TRIGGER FEATURE SPACES

In this section we discuss a class of feature spaces that extends the similarity feature spaces and is called, following [264], *entailment trigger feature spaces*. The general idea of these feature spaces is to directly use a given set R of pre-existing and known textual entailment recognition rules (for positive and for negative cases) as features. Given a set of entailment rules, we could either use each rule as a feature (direct mode) or use the right-hand side and the left-hand side as separate features (disjoint mode).

In the *direct* mode, for each rule ρ_i in R, we have a corresponding Boolean feature f_i. The space $\mathcal{R}$ then contains n Boolean features f_i modeling each rule $\rho_i = LHS_i \rightarrow RHS_i$. Given a pair $\langle T, H \rangle$, the feature vector $(f_1, ..., f_n) \in \mathcal{R}$ is determined as follows:

$$f_i = \begin{cases} 1 & \text{if } LHS_i \text{ subsumes } T \text{ and } RHS_i \text{ subsumes } H \\ 0 & \text{otherwise} \end{cases}$$

In the *disjoint* mode, for each rule ρ_i in R, we have two corresponding Boolean features f_i^{LHS} and f_i^{RHS}. The space $\mathcal{R}$ then contains $2n$ Boolean features f_i^{LHS} and f_i^{RHS} modeling each rule $\rho_i = LHS_i \rightarrow RHS_i$ in R. Given a pair $\langle T, H \rangle$, the feature vector $(f_1^{LHS}, ..., f_n^{LHS}, f_1^{RHS}, ..., f_n^{RHS}) \in \mathcal{R}$ is determined as follows:

$$f_i^{LHS} = \begin{cases} 1 & \text{if } LHS_i \text{ subsumes } T \\ 0 & \text{otherwise} \end{cases}$$

and

$$f_i^{RHS} = \begin{cases} 1 & \text{if } RHS_i \text{ subsumes } H \\ 0 & \text{otherwise} \end{cases}$$

where, in the above definitions, "subsumes" simply indicates that the rule "fires" in T or H.

Some realized feature spaces

The *entailment trigger feature space* $\mathcal{R}$ overcomes some of the limitations of the similarity feature spaces, as it can model complex relations between T and H. However, this class of feature spaces requires a given set of rules R, and a decision on the type of modeling we want to adopt: direct or disjoint. These rules are, in general, first-order rules written with respect to the level of preprocessing supplied, i.e., the interpretation model.

This approach has been explored in works such as [79], where the use of the following features was shown to be successful:

- *Polarity feature*: presence/absence of negative polarity contexts (*not, no, few, without*).

- *Antonym feature*: presence/absence of antonymous words in T and H. These features capture cases such as: "*Oil price is surging*" $\nrightarrow$ "*Oil prices are falling*";

- *Adjunct feature*: dropping/adding of syntactic adjunct when moving from T to H, as in: "*all solid companies pay dividends*" $\nrightarrow$ "*all solid companies pay cash dividends*";

- *Passive feature*: presence/absence of a transformation from active to passive moving from T to H or vice versa.

Note that any rule can be represented as a feature and then evaluated. For example, the *passive rule* can be represented by the following syntactic rule: ρ_{pass}="$\boxed{X}$ *are (VBN* $\boxed{Y}$*) by* $\boxed{Z}$"→"$\boxed{Z}$ *(VBZ* $\boxed{Y}$*)* $\boxed{X}$". Conversely, we can model a Boolean feature f_{pass} that is *true* if the left-hand side of ρ_{pass} is active in T and the right-hand side is active in H.

Notice that rules modeling entailment triggers can be both *ground rewrite rules*, i.e., without variables (like the antonyms rule ρ_{ant}="*good*"→"*bad*") and *first-order rewrite rules*, i.e., with variables (as in the example above).

Learning algorithms used over these feature spaces will assign learned weights to these features and, as before, learn a threshold of acceptability.

This approach has two clear limitations. First, a set of rules needs to be given in advance. Second, the rules, and thus the features, depend on the level of preprocessing, and are thus sensitive to noisy interpretations. Specifically, given that rules are written under the assumption of a correct interpretation they may not fire given the noisy preprocessed text, and we may need other approaches that can address this limitation.

3.4.4 REWRITE RULE FEATURE SPACES

We describe below a class of rewrite rule feature spaces that is, in principle, just an extension of the previous class, i.e., the entailment trigger feature space. The key difference is that this space allows for the exploration of all possible rules whereas in the previous class of spaces, only a small fraction of possible rules is—the set of rewrite rules known in advance. This opens the possibility of overcoming the two limitations discussed earlier: we can both learn weights of rules and, in some sense, adapt or better learn rules despite incorrect interpretations generated by the preprocessing stage.

The Kernel tool is used to describe these potentially huge feature spaces. We will use it to describe two classes of spaces: the class of ground rewrite rule feature spaces and the class of first order rewrite rule feature spaces.

Background: Classification with Kernels and Kernel Machines

To introduce the next classes of features we need the notion of kernels. In this section, we first introduce an important perspective on classification algorithms that are attractive from the RTE perspective since they allow a concise definition of expressive feature spaces.

We typically think of linear classifiers $y = C(x)$ as functions of the *feature representation* of instances in X; that is, the learning process determines a weight for each feature, and the prediction with respect to an instance x is computed by summing up the weights of the features in the representation of x. This is called the *primal* representation of the classifier. Equivalently, it is possible to represent the same linear classifier as a function of the examples used to learn it; in this *dual* representation, we maintain a list of examples rather than a list of weights, and the prediction with respect to an example x is computed as a linear combination of the *similarity* between x and the examples observed earlier. Below we briefly discuss the equivalence between these representations to facilitate some of the RTE classification presentation. More details can be found in [71, 130].

The key insight relevant to our discussion of machine learning in RTE is that kernels give us a direct means of thinking about *similarity measures* in terms of *features*, and so helps us to present a unifying view of decision functions in RTE systems. The important (and often nonintuitive) difference is that, while earlier we discussed similarity functions between T and H, when dealing with kernels we discuss similarities between two pairs (T, H) and (T', H').

We illustrate the equivalence between the primal (more standard) and dual views using the Perceptron [208]. Perceptron is a well known online learning algorithm that makes use of the aforementioned feature-based representation of examples. The Perceptron is a binary classification function:

$$y = C(x) = sgn(\bar{w} \cdot \bar{x})$$

where $\bar{w} \in \mathbb{R}^n$ is a weight vector and $sgn(\cdot)$ is a sign function. The decision is then $y = -1$ or $y = 1$ representing two classes.

The Perceptron learning algorithm aims to estimate $\bar{w}$ using the set *Train* of training examples. The algorithm initializes $\bar{w} = (0, \cdots, 0)$. Upon receiving an example $(\bar{x}, y) \in$ *Train* the algorithm predicts according to the linear threshold function $\bar{w} \cdot \bar{x} \geq 0$. If the prediction $C(x)$ is 1 and the label y is -1 then the vector $\bar{w}$ is set to $\bar{w} - \bar{x}$, while if the prediction $C(x)$ is -1 and the label y is 1 then $\bar{w}$ is set to $\bar{w} + \bar{x}$. No change is made if the prediction is correct.

It is therefore easy to see that the hypothesis w of the Perceptron is a $\pm$ sum of the previous examples on which prediction mistakes were made. Let $L(x) \in \{-1, 1\}$ denote the label of example x; then $w = (\sum_{\bar{v} \in M} L(v)\bar{v})$ where M is the subset of examples on which the algorithm made a mistake. Thus the decision function $f(x)$ for Perceptron can be represented as:

$$f(x) = \bar{w} \cdot \bar{x} = \left(\sum_{\bar{v} \in M} L(v)\bar{v} \right) \cdot \bar{x} = \sum_{\bar{v} \in M} L(v)(\bar{v} \cdot \bar{x})$$

The final prediction function is $C(x) = sgn(f(x))$.

We see that the prediction made by Perceptron on instance x is a function of the dot product of $\bar{x}$ with all previous mistakes $\bar{v}$ on which the perceptron made mistakes during the learning process. This dot product operation can be viewed as a "similarity" between $\bar{x}$ and $\bar{v}$, measured in the feature space. When the feature space is very expressive, this computation may become too expensive, but it is sometimes possible to compute this dot product without writing down all the features explicitly. For example: if $\bar{x}$ and $\bar{v}$ represent subtrees of a tree representation of the sentences x and v, computing the dot product between these two representations of x and v can be done without explicitly enumerating all the subtrees, but rather directly from the two trees. A function that computes the dot product in this way is called a Kernel. In the terms presented above, the dot product $\bar{v} \cdot \bar{x}$ is replaced with $K(v, x)$ to give:

$$f(x) = \sum_{v \in M} L(v)K(v, x)$$

Many learning algorithms that depend on the dot product of two examples (e.g., Percep-tron [130, 208], SVM [67, 245], and others) can gain from the use of kernels. Many kernels can be designed to measure the similarity between examples x and v; notice that computing the kernel is equivalent to first blowing up the feature space (e.g., enumerating subtrees of some type) and then computing the dot product. The trade-off between computing the dot product between x and v via the kernel (dual representation) or first blowing up an explicit feature representation (primal method) is well understood (see for example [71]). Fundamentally, it boils down to the ratio between the number of training examples and the size of the feature space (the larger the ratio, the larger the advantage of primal methods is). Nevertheless, it is sometimes convenient to articulate the type of features the classifier depends on by describing the kernel, even when the implementation explicitly computes the features.

In the rest of this section we will provide examples of the use of kernels to articulate feature spaces that were found useful for RTE.

Ground Rewrite Rule Feature Spaces

Following the discussion in Section 3.4.3 we begin with a set R of all the possible rewrite rules and derive the sets R_{LHS} and R_{RHS} of all the left-hand sides and right-hand sides. As before, for the two modes, the possible features are: $F_{dir} = R_{LHS} \times R_{RHS}$ (direct) and $F_{dis} = l(R_{LHS}) \cup r(R_{RHS})$ where $l(X) = \{l(x)|x \in X\}$ and $r(X) = \{r(x)|x \in X\}$ (disjoint). In contrast to the previous rewrite rules treatment, here we will assume that R_{LHS} and R_{RHS} cover all rules that the algo-rithms can induce from training examples.

As these spaces are generally not used in an explicit form, their definition is usually speci-fied using a function $\mathcal{F}$ that determines the active features of each instance: namely, the space is defined by a function $\mathcal{F}(\langle T, H \rangle)$ that determines a value for each pair $\langle T, H \rangle$. Given this func-tion, we can now define the corresponding kernel function $K(\langle T', H' \rangle, \langle T'', H'' \rangle)$. Without loss of generality, we consider results of $\mathcal{F}(\langle T, H \rangle)$ as sets. The kernel function $K(\langle T', H' \rangle, \langle T'', H'' \rangle)$ is then defined as follows:

$$K(\langle T', H' \rangle, \langle T'', H'' \rangle) = |\mathcal{F}(\langle T', H' \rangle) \cap \mathcal{F}(\langle T'', H'' \rangle)| \tag{3.12}$$

In order to instantiate this general idea we assume a function $\mathcal{T}(.)$ that acts on both the text T and the hypothesis H and outputs fragments of the two elements, e.g., words, subtrees, subgraphs. For example, in:

$T_9 \Rightarrow H_9$	
T_9	*"Yahoo bought Overture"*
H_9	*"Yahoo owns Overture"*

assuming, for simplicity, a function that only returns tokens, we have the two sets: $\mathcal{T}(T_9) =$ *{Yahoo, bought, Overture}* and $\mathcal{T}(H_9) =$ *{Yahoo, owns, Overture}*. A ground rewrite rule is always an element $\langle t, h \rangle$ in the set $\mathcal{T}(T) \times \mathcal{T}(H)$, and it represents the rule $t \; \to \; h$.   For the above example, the active ground rules are:

$$\mathcal{T}(T_9) \times \mathcal{T}(H_9) = \{\langle Yahoo, Yahoo \rangle, \langle Yahoo, owns \rangle, \langle Yahoo, Overture \rangle,$$
$$\langle bought, Yahoo \rangle, \langle bought, owns \rangle, \langle bought, Overture \rangle,$$
$$\langle Overture, Yahoo \rangle, \langle Overture, owns \rangle, \langle Overture, Overture \rangle\}$$

The pair $\langle bought, owns \rangle$, for example, represents the lexical rule $bought \rightarrow owns$. The key point, as described earlier, is that we will not need to explicitly generate these sets in order to compute the value of the kernels, and therefore in order to learn a decision function over this representation. Next, we define the kernel functions for the *direct* and the *disjoint* modes.

In the direct mode, the set $\mathcal{F}_{dir}(\langle T, H \rangle)$ is simply the set of rules activated by the example $\langle T, H \rangle$, i.e.:

$$\mathcal{F}_{dir}(\langle T, H \rangle) = \mathcal{T}(T) \times \mathcal{T}(H) \tag{3.13}$$

The kernel functions for this class of spaces are defined as:

$$
\begin{aligned}
K_t(\langle T', H' \rangle, \langle T'', H'' \rangle) &= |\mathcal{F}_{dir}(\langle T', H' \rangle) \cap \mathcal{F}_{dir}(\langle T'', H'' \rangle)| \\
&= |\mathcal{F}(T') \cap \mathcal{F}(T'')||\mathcal{F}(\langle H') \cap \mathcal{F}(\langle H'')| \\
&= K_t(T', T'')K_t(H', H''),
\end{aligned}
$$

where t is the type of kernel chosen.

To illustrate, we compare it with this pair:

$T_{10} \Rightarrow H_{10}$	
T_{10}	"*Wanadoo bought KStones*"
H_{10}	"*Wanadoo owns KStones*"

The result is $K_t(\langle T_9, H_9 \rangle, \langle T_{10}, H_{10} \rangle) = |\{\langle bought, owns \rangle\}| = |\{bought\}||\{owns\}|$.

Similarly, in the disjoint mode, the set $\mathcal{F}_{dis}(\langle T, H \rangle)$ is the set of right-hand sides and left-hand sides of the rules activated by the example $\langle T, H \rangle$, i.e.:

$$\mathcal{F}_{dis}(\langle T, H \rangle) = l(\mathcal{F}(T)) \cup r(\mathcal{F}(H)) \tag{3.14}$$

The kernel for this class of spaces is thus:

$$
\begin{aligned}
\widehat{K}_t(\langle T', H' \rangle, \langle T'', H'' \rangle) &= |\mathcal{F}_{dis}(\langle T', H' \rangle) \cap \mathcal{F}_{dis}(\langle T'', H'' \rangle)| \\
&= |l(\mathcal{F}(T')) \cap l(\mathcal{F}(T''))| + |r(\mathcal{F}(H')) \cap r(\mathcal{F}(H''))| \\
&= K_t(T', T'') + K_t(H', H''),
\end{aligned}
$$

where t is the type of kernel chosen.

In the above example, the result is $\widehat{K}_t(\langle T_9, H_9 \rangle, \langle T_{10}, H_{10} \rangle) = |\{l(bought), r(owns)\}| = |\{l(bought)\}| + |\{r(owns)\}|$.

With the similarity measures defined in Section 3.4 for different data structures and the definition for kernels we can now produce a large variety of different kernels as we now illustrate.

At the token level, we can use many of the metrics defined in Section 3.4.1. For example, we can model the space of all the lexical rules, i.e., rules changing a word with another, such as $buy \rightarrow own$. We can also model the space of all weighted lexical rules where the weighting function of the lexical rules depends on an external weighting scheme such as tf*idf. To do that, we can simply use the s_{wl} function (defined in Section 6) in the kernels.

Notice that while we do not explicitly generate all the rule-driven features here, we assume a function that can return similarity values, and this function will potentially have to touch a lot of the rules. Following the ideas presented in Section 3.4.2, we can use the idea of kernels to derive larger structural feature spaces. For example, using the basic graph similarity measure over a syntactic or a semantic graph (eq. 3.8), we can model the two kernels:

$$K_e(\langle T', H' \rangle, \langle T'', H'' \rangle) = s_e(T', T'') s_e(H', H'') \tag{3.15}$$
$$\widehat{K}_e(\langle T', H' \rangle, \langle T'', H'' \rangle) = s_e(T', T'') + s_e(H', H'') \tag{3.16}$$

In this case, we are modeling the space of the ground rewrite rules transforming an edge of the Text to an edge of the Hypothesis. Likewise, using a tree-based similarity measure (Eq. 3.10) that counts the number of common subtrees, we can model an interesting ground rewrite rule space. The two kernel functions are the following:

$$K_{ct}(\langle T', H' \rangle, \langle T'', H'' \rangle) = s_{ct}(T', T'') s_{ct}(H', H'') \tag{3.17}$$
$$\widehat{K}_{ct}(\langle T', H' \rangle, \langle T'', H'' \rangle) = s_{ct}(T', T'') + s_{ct}(H', H'') \tag{3.18}$$

Such spaces are expressive enough to potentially solve complex cases such as the examples $\langle T_7, H_7 \rangle$ and $\langle T_8, H_8 \rangle$. Let us assume that T and H are represented as syntactic trees, as follows:

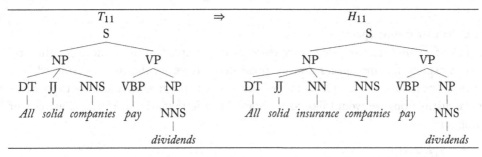

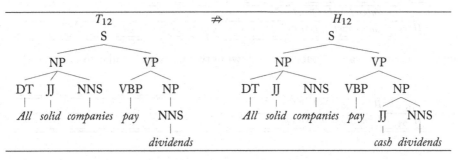

While in the distance feature space $\langle T_{11}, H_{11} \rangle$ and $\langle T_{12}, H_{12} \rangle$ are identical, here they are represented by two different points, since H_{11} and H_{12} have different syntactic structures ("*all solid insurance companies*" is different from "*all solid companies*" and "*dividends*" is different from "*cash dividends*"). Thus, these examples activate different features in this syntactic space. If we then want to classify the following example:

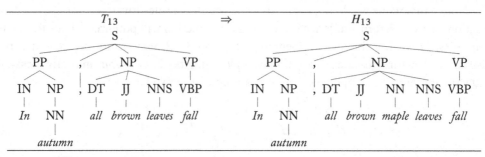

in this feature space would find that its structure is more similar (i.e., there is a higher number of common tree fragments) to $\langle T_{11}, H_{11} \rangle$ than to $\langle T_{12}, H_{12} \rangle$. In other words, we implicitly apply to $\langle T_{13}, H_{13} \rangle$ the following *ground rewrite rule*, learned from the feature space of $\langle T_{11}, H_{11} \rangle$:

$$
\rho_{14} =
\begin{array}{c}
\text{S} \\
\diagup\diagdown \\
\text{NP} \quad \text{VP} \\
\diagup\uparrow\diagdown \quad | \\
\text{DT JJ NNS VBP} \\
| \\
\textit{all}
\end{array}
\rightarrow
\begin{array}{c}
\text{S} \\
\diagup\diagdown \\
\text{NP} \quad \text{VP} \\
\diagup\uparrow\diagdown \quad | \\
\text{DT JJ NN NNS VBP} \\
| \\
\textit{all}
\end{array}
$$

First-order rule feature spaces

The class of *ground rewrite rule feature spaces* is very important as it addresses the limitations of earlier, explicit features spaces that we presented. However, the rules considered here are all grounded. The following example illustrates a case in which a ground rule is not expressive enough to make distinctions we would like to support. Assume that we have the following pair in the training set:

$T_{15} \Rightarrow H_{15}$	
T_{15}	"*Yahoo bought Overture*"
H_{15}	"*Yahoo owns Overture*"

In a syntactic content feature space, the following two pairs are similar to $\langle T_{15}, H_{15} \rangle$:

$T_{16} \Rightarrow H_{16}$	
T_{16}	"*Wanadoo bought KStones*"
H_{16}	"*Wanadoo owns KStones*"

$T_{17} \not\Rightarrow H_{17}$	
T_{17}	*"Wanadoo bought KStones"*
H_{17}	*"KStones owns Wanadoo"*

but T_{16} entails H_{16}, while T_{17} does not entail H_{17}. In both cases we would apply the following rule derived from $\langle T_{15}, H_{15} \rangle$:

$$\rho_{18} = \qquad\qquad\qquad\qquad \rightarrow$$

However, in order to distinguish $\langle T_{16}, H_{16} \rangle$ from $\langle T_{17}, H_{17} \rangle$ we would need to use the following *first-order rewrite rules*:

$$\rho_{19} = \qquad\qquad\qquad\qquad \rightarrow$$

This rule can be applied to the first example but not to the second. Therefore, a feature space learning *first-order rewrite rule* is needed to leverage a text representation in which the use of variables is allowed. We now briefly describe such expressive feature spaces; more details can be found in [262].

Once again, we use kernels, this time making use of defining similarity functions over graphs. However, these similarity functions must be more general than the ones proposed in the previous sections, so that it is possible to model *variables*. [262] describes a method for doing this using the representation language of tripartite graphs (TGs); this representation provides a way to model the matching of a first order rule to a sentence pair as a graph matching problem, and thus a way to model first-order rule feature spaces using the kernels introduced earlier for ground rewrite rules.

More details on this approach, together with concrete RTE examples, are described in [260, 261]) and we will not provide them here.

3.4.5   DISCUSSION

We have presented a study of feature spaces used for RTE. In many respects the selection of feature spaces is the crucial step in allowing a learning algorithm the opportunity to learn from observed examples a model that supports the appropriate RTE decision. It is important to realize that computing the features over a pair (T, H), requires that we align the representations of T and H (or consider all possible alignments). In the next section we describe work focusing on alignment; the quality of this process, along with that of the preprocessing step, are significant in determining the quality of the eventual feature-based representation of an entailment pair.

3.5 LEARNING ALIGNMENT FUNCTIONS

In previous sections, we have defined alignments over words and syntactic structures that allow us to derive a feature-based representation for an entailment pair such as $\langle T, H \rangle$. The methods described so far either use a hand-crafted, deterministic approach to determine such alignments, or use similarity approaches that implicitly consider all alignments, albeit over a constrained set of representations. But alignment can potentially use multiple levels of representation—words, phrase chunks, syntactic parse trees, semantic role labeled verb-argument structures, and so on; as an alternative to designing a kernel function, we can try to learn an alignment function directly that will provide the best support for the eventual classification process $C(\langle T, H \rangle) \rightarrow$ *Entailed/Not–Entailed*.

3.5.1 LEARNING ALIGNMENT FROM GOLD-STANDARD DATA

The most direct method to learn an alignment function is to use a hand-annotated set of alignments for entailment examples. Attention has so far focused on aligning entailment pairs at the *lexical* level: each word in the Hypothesis may be mapped to one or more contiguous words in the Text. A sample lexical mapping is presented in Figure 3.5. The appeal of this lexical-level mapping is that it does not commit to a specific interpretation $\mathcal{I}(\cdot)$, but given the lexical mapping for an entailment pair and an interpretation of the pair, the interpretation can be mapped based on the lexical level mapping (for example, dependency parse subtrees can be mapped based on the lexical alignments of their yields).

Given such a lexical level gold alignment and its mapping to the desired representation $\mathcal{I}(\cdot)$, features can be defined in terms of lexical items (for example: Are the words identical? Do they share a lemma? What is their distributional similarity based on some reference corpus? Are they related by synonymy? By meronymy? By hypernymy?) and the representation over them (e.g., given a pair of tokens in H aligned to a pair of tokens in T, what are the paths through the dependency trees that link each pair? How long are these paths? Are they identical?). These features can then be assigned weights based on the gold-standard alignment data: when a pair of components (H_i, T_j) are aligned in a gold standard example, the corresponding feature weights are promoted; when they are present but *not* aligned, they may be demoted. If a global alignment quality term is defined in terms of features, these too can have their weights updated using the gold standard annotations.

Note that this view of alignment is not directly related to *entailment* labels: it simply accounts for which pairs of words or interpretation components should be aligned in a given entailment pair. Note also that features can be based on fixed metrics such as similarity scores computed

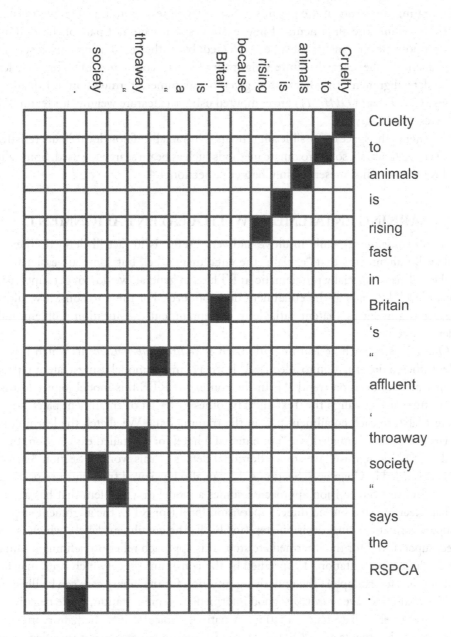

Figure 3.5: A sample hand-annotated lexical alignment for an entailment pair.

from some reference corpus or external resource; in this case, the learned weight can be viewed as incorporating a measure of the metric's reliability with respect to the alignment task.

To determine the alignments of new examples that were not part of the training data, a search over possible alignments must be conducted; but rather than using a fixed set of specified scoring functions, the learned feature weights are used to compute scores for each active edge in a candidate alignment. In other words, given the alignment formulation in Equation 3.1, the functions $s(H_i, T_j)$ and $Q(H_i, T_j)$ are computed using the feature weights for features related to active edges.

In general, the space of possible alignments is intractable if non-local characteristics are part of the objective function, so approximate methods such as beam search are used. Some alignment-focused RTE research is presented in Chapter 4, Section 4.4.

3.5.2   LEARNING ENTAILMENT WITH A LATENT ALIGNMENT

The notion of *alignment*, while intuitive and very useful, is in fact ill-defined. There could be multiple valid alignments that "explain" the entailment label, but some are easier to deal with than others. This is especially problematic in RTE as in general, we do not get supervision at the alignment level, but only at the entailment decision level. For these reasons, it would be useful to consider alignment as a latent variable in the entailment classification problem, rather than consider it directly.

One relevant machine learning approach is *indirect supervision*, in which a weak signal provides sufficient information to adequately learn a complex model using a latent representation of an intermediate decision step [51]. In the context of RTE this model jointly learns weights for the features used to align the Text and Hypothesis of a set of entailment pairs, and to assign the correct label to each entailment pair in the training data. We sketch the learning model for the binary RTE task ("entailed" vs. "not entailed") here; for a detailed explanation, the reader is referred to [51], though we give some additional details of this work in Section 3.5.2; the work by [201] described in Chapter 4, Section 4.2.2 can also be viewed from this perspective.

The Indirect Supervision approach assumes a model of a problem that has a complex intermediate decision step but no direct supervision for it (for RTE, the alignment step), together with supervision at the final decision step (for RTE, the entailment label), which is considered "indirect supervision" for the intermediate step. This approach relies on defining a suitable space of intermediate representations $\mathcal{V}$, specified by the constraint set $\mathcal{C}$ (which itself may be defined by a set of rules, for example). The underlying intuition for the binary case can be illustrated thus: all positive examples have *at least one* good intermediate representation, while negative examples have *no* good intermediate representation. A natural choice of intermediate representation for RTE is that of alignments of $\mathcal{I}(T)$ with $\mathcal{I}(H)$. The alignment step is not specified as a separate, stand-alone task; rather, the gold standard training labels of the target application are used together with the space of valid alignments in an optimization approach to determine the *optimal intermediate representation* for the *target* task, i.e., the representation that maximizes performance on the target task. This obviates the need for expensive annotation efforts on the intermediate structure.

The learning process takes place over a number of iterations. At the beginning of each iteration, the learner has a current model for the alignment (i.e., a set of weights $\bar{w}$ associated with the set of pre-defined alignment features $\mathcal{F}$) and for the entailment decision function (which could be weights $\bar{v}$ for a different set of features derived from a single alignment, or simply a threshold on the alignment score for a binary learning task). For each entailment example, the best-scoring alignment $h \in \mathcal{H}$ is found using $\bar{w} \cdot \mathcal{F}(h)$. This best-scoring alignment h_{best} is then used as input to the decision function. If h_{best} results in the correct entailment label, the weights w are not changed. However, an incorrect prediction causes w to be demoted (if the label was "entailed" and the prediction was "not entailed") or promoted (if the label was "not entailed" and the prediction was "entailed").

This model has the advantage of learning the alignment function that leads to the best performance on the entailment recognition task for a given specification of features. If multiple different representation levels are present in $\mathcal{I}(\cdot)$, and specific subsets of features $\mathcal{F}$ relate to these different representation levels, this model effectively learns similarity functions for the different representations. However, it is important to recognize that the primary goal of this approach is to learn a good entailment classification function.

CHAPTER 4

Case Studies

The previous chapters have identified the following key tasks that must be performed by end-to-end textual inference systems:

1. **Conversion of natural language to a meaning representation.** The meaning representation must be defined (i.e., What is the set of predicates? Of functions? Of variables?) and the variability of natural language must be handled in identifying the underlying meaning in the specified terms.

2. **Control of error propagation.** Either the process for inducing meaning representation must be (almost) error-free, or the inference process must allow for errors introduced at this stage.

3. **Acquisition and application of supporting knowledge.** Setting aside the linguistic knowledge required to induce the meaning representation from raw text, many entailment pairs require application of background knowledge about causes, locations, times, types, numbers, and more.

In this chapter we present summaries of specific RTE systems, mapping each system to the framework outlined in Section 2.4. While we compare system performance to statistics for the relevant RTE evaluation(s), we did not use this as our primary criterion for selecting work to present: rather, we have sought to identify promising concepts that we feel could underlie successful future RTE work. We have tried to group related research directions, but the works described in such a group are generally not strictly comparable even when evaluated on the same RTE task, as different resources are used or different research goals are targeted.

Each system so described is also summarized in a summary table that identifies the basic mapping to the conceptual architecture outlined in Chapter 2, section 2.4. Statistics for the relevant RTE tasks are given in the summary tables; these give the mean and maximum scores for systems that participated in the named evaluation (so some later works occasionally outperform the highest-scoring system reported during the given task).

4.1 EDIT DISTANCE-BASED RTE

Edit distance is a widely used heuristic for string similarity, and is an intuitive approach to apply to RTE. Since syntactic dependency structure can be extracted for well-formed text with respectable accuracy (at least within the domain for which the parser being used was developed), it seems natural to refine a simplistic, purely word-level approach and manipulate entailment pairs using the syntactic dependency representation.

Tree Edit Distance (typically based on dependency parse structure) was first used for textual inference by Punyakanok et al. [198] to select answers in the task of Question Answering. Several teams later applied Tree Edit Distance to the task of Recognizing Textual Entailment (for example, Kouylekov and Magnini [136] in RTE 1). The following examples represent successful and/or innovative implementations of tree edit distance approaches.

4.1.1   OPEN SOURCE TREE EDIT-BASED RTE SYSTEM

Mehdad et al. [158] propose an open-source framework for textual entailment called the Edit Distance Textual Entailment Suite (EDITS), which provides a basic, customizable framework for systematic development and evaluation of edit distance-based approaches to RTE. The framework allows the computation of edit distance to transform the Text into the Hypothesis using edit operations at the string-, token-, and tree-level. In addition, it allows costs to be associated with entailment and contradiction rules. The EDITS framework also defines a common text-annotation format to represent the input text-hypothesis pair and the entailment and contradiction rules. Training data must be used to learn a distance model. The EDITS workflow is shown in Fig. 4.1.

In the system submitted to TAC RTE 5, the preprocessing step uses dependency parsing, part-of-speech tagging, lemmatization, and morphological analysis. The graph generation and alignment selection steps are integrated. The lowest cost edit distance is determined using a set of operations (insertion, deletion, and substitution), each of which has an associated cost. These costs are learned using an optimization algorithm together with a threshold score that maximizes performance on the development set. Word-level substitution resources were derived from VerbOcean [54], WordNet [90], and Latent Semantic Analysis of Wikipedia. The inference step compares the computed edit distance with the learned threshold score: if the pair's edit distance is greater than the threshold, the system assigns the label "Not Entailed;" otherwise, it assigns the label "Entailed."

The EDITS-based RTE system achieved a score of 60.2% in RTE 5 (see Table 4.1), but could probably be improved by investigating new substitution resources, and possibly by enriching the input structures with Named Entity information (and using a specialized named entity similarity measure in the inference step).

4.1.2   TREE EDIT DISTANCE WITH EXPANDED EDIT TYPES

Heilman and Smith [116] use an enhanced tree edit distance model with operations that move subtrees, reorder child nodes, and replace a tree's root node with a different node from that tree. Intuitively, this addresses a gap in the standard edit distance model for textual inference, because it captures in single edits certain kinds of syntactic variation (such as passivization) that would, in a standard edit model, require multiple sequential edits, and which therefore cannot be directly learned.

Because these new operations introduce non-local changes to the tree, the authors do not try to find a dynamic programming solution, but instead use a greedy search process that uses a heuristic to estimate the cost to reach the target tree from the current state; thus at each step the process seeks to minimize the difference between the current and target trees. The search space is constrained to avoid insertion operations that introduce terms not in the target tree, and to constrain move operations to affect only nodes whose lemmas are in the target tree. In addition, insertion operations introduce edges labeled with the most frequent edge label for the POS of the inserted node. A hard limit is imposed on the search depth.

The heuristic function used is a tree kernel that measures the similarity between all pairs of nodes in the trees being compared, normalized using the geometric mean of the self-similarity of the two trees. The kernel computes the similarities using contiguous ordered subsequences of children, summing over all pairs of subtrees. The kernel contains decay factors relating to child subsequence length and subtree height, with the goal of favoring smaller edits (i.e., edits involving fewer nodes).

The tree representation is derived using a part-of-speech tagger and a dependency parser. WordNet is used to lemmatize the words of the underlying text; no additional information from WordNet is used. Features are specified that identify the kinds of changes made by edit operations (such as whether they change a part of speech, lemma, proper name, pronoun, or numerical expression, or whether they remove a verb or noun) in addition to general features such as the number of each basic edit type and total number of edits.

The system uses a statistical classifier trained using the edit sequences derived for the RTE 3 development set plus all the RTE 1 and RTE 2 data, and achieves an accuracy of 62.8% on the RTE 3 test set (see Table 4.1).

4.2   LOGICAL REPRESENTATION AND INFERENCE

First Order Logic and related representations/inference methods are well studied in the context of expressiveness and tractability, and a number of off-the-shelf systems exist that can potentially be used by RTE systems. However, standard approaches are not error-tolerant, and precise specification of requisite background knowledge is difficult and time-consuming, and may be complicated by the constrained expressiveness of the chosen formalism. The approaches we survey here explore ways to overcome these difficulties. All induce a logical representation of the Text and Hypothesis, and then seek to determine whether or not the Hypothesis is entailed by the Text combined with a knowledge base representing background knowledge.

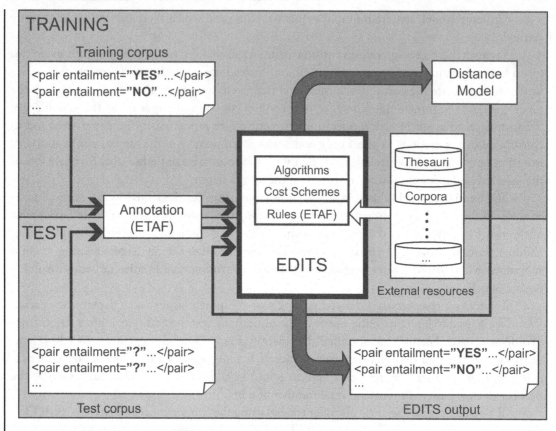

Figure 4.1: EDITS workflow, as described in [158].

4.2.1   REPRESENTATION

RTE systems as a rule do not define a standard canonical logical representation: given the open domain nature of the RTE task, such a definition alone would be a formidable research challenge. Instead, approaches use predicates to directly encode the linguistic structure (or a simplified version thereof) as induced by NLP tools in the preprocessing stage, such as syntactic structure; localized semantic information (such as whether a term refers to a Named Entity); and binary relations from closed classes such as "Lives In" based on relation identifiers trained on specialized corpora, including certain relations expressed by noun compounds. As such, the induced representation can be thought of as a quasi-formal interpretation, with an associated quasi-formal semantics.

The COGEX system of Fowler et al. [94] formulates a predicate for every noun, verb, adjective, adverb, preposition, and conjunction in the Text and Hypothesis. Predicate names are

Table 4.1: Characteristics of selected edit distance based-RTE systems. Accuracy statistics in the left-most column indicate the evaluation task, together with the mean score/maximum score for that task (based on the original scores reported for that task)

System ID	Mehdad et al. '09	Heilman and Smith '10
System Type	Approach 1	Approach 1
Preprocessing	POS, Dependency, Lemma, Morphological analysis	POS, Dependency, Lemma
Enrichment	-	-
Candidate Alignment Generation	VerbOcean, WordNet, Wikipedia	-
Alignment Selection	exhaustive search	heuristic search
Classification	minimum edit distance cost plus threshold	statistical classifier
Accuracy: RTE 3 (61.4/80.0)	-	62.8
Accuracy: RTE 5 (61.5/73.5)	60.2	-
Main Innovation	Open source edit distance system	Extended set of tree edit operations

formed by concatenating the lexeme and the associated part-of-speech of the relevant word. Adjectival and adverbial predicates take a single argument (the term modified). Nominal predicates take a single argument. Noun compounds and conjunctions are treated as grouping predicates with two or more arguments, while prepositional predicates relate two arguments, one of which is itself a predicate modified by the other argument (the prepositional object). Named Entity predicates are also constructed by concatenating the associated semantic class of the entity and the suffix "NE." An example of this representation is shown in Figure 4.2. Raina et al. [201]'s logical representation uses a syntactic-dependency-based logical form similar to that of the CO-GEX system, but add annotations for Named Entities and basic semantic roles (agent/patient): these additional annotations are not rendered in the logical representation, but are used as features when determining the cost of rule applications.

Bos and Markert [32] use a CCG parser to generate a semantic representation based on Kamp and Reyle [128]'s Discourse Representation Structures, and includes the use of certain triggers to infer presuppositional use (such as the modifier "new" implying the existence of a pre-existing entity of the type of its modified object). This representation fully specifies scope. A schematic of their representation is shown in Figure 4.3.

The Boeing Language Understanding Engine (BLUE) system by Clark and Harrison [59] is also based on a formal logical approach to RTE. In its preprocessing stage it transforms the text into a logical form induced from a syntactic parse, which is then modified using syntactic rewrite rules to derive ground logical assertions (see Figure 4.4).

Example:

Heavy selling of Standard & Poor's 500-stock index futures in Chicago relentlessly beat stocks downward.
Logical form:
heavy_JJ(x1) & selling_NN(x1) & of_IN(x1,x6) & Standard_NN(x2) & &_CC(x13,x2,x3) & Poor_NN(x3) &s_POS(x6,x13) & 500-stock_JJ(x6) & index_NN(x4) & future_NN(x5) & nn_NNC(x6,x4,x5) & in_IN(x1,x8) & Chicago_NN(x8) & relentlessly_RB(e12) & beat_VB(e12,x1,x9) & stocks_NN(x9) & downward_RB(e12)

Figure 4.2: COGEX syntax-based logical form; Raina et al. uses a similar representation.

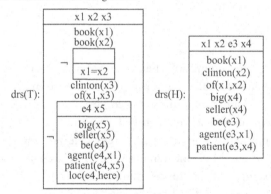

Example: 78 (FALSE)
T: Clinton's new book is not big seller here.
H: Clinton's book is a big seller.

Figure 4.3: A schematic view of Bos and Markert's Discourse Representation Structure representation for Textual Entailment pairs.

4.2.2 LOGICAL INFERENCE WITH ABDUCTION

Raina et al. [201]'s underlying theorem-proving technique—unit resolution—runs in polynomial time, but is very limited in terms of performance: their published results do not include the per-

Example:

A soldier was killed in a gun battle.

Logical Form:

(DECL
((VAR _X1 "a" "soldier")
(VAR _X2 "a" "battle" (NN "gun" "battle")))
(S (PAST) NIL "kill" _X1 (PP "in" _X2)))

Derived Ground Clauses:

object(kill01, soldier01),
in(kill01, battle01),
modifier(battle01,gun01)

Figure 4.4: BLUE's logical form.

formance of the non-abductive theorem prover, but it can be assumed to be close to their TFIDF baseline results of 51.8%. This is consistent with the performance of another logic-based system reported by Bayer et al. [16].

There are two intuitive ways to relax the strict theorem proving approach: 1) introduce rules that model abduction by allowing predicates and arguments in the representation of the Text or Hypothesis to be ignored (effectively, temporarily treating them as background knowledge or as entailed from the existing KB); and 2) allow rules to have associated *costs* and to use these costs to determine the confidence one has in a proof of entailment, and allow potentially unreliable rules to be included in the system KB.

The COGEX system [94] extends the basic axiom/theorem-proving mechanism of standard logical inference processes by allowing arguments to be "relaxed" and propositions in the entailment pair to be "dropped;" these operations are treated, in effect, as abductive rules. Proofs are scored based on the number and types of operations required to derive the Hypothesis from the Text. The costs associated with each type of proof step (resolution, application of a standard rule, and application of an abductive rule) are set by hand. The resulting system achieved an accuracy of 55.1% on the RTE 1 data set (see Table 4.2).

Raina et al. use a similar approach, but use machine learning techniques to induce weights for the different inference operations. They specify three abduction operations corresponding to term matching, verb argument dropping, and non-identical constant mapping (introduced to allow for coreference). Rather than assign costs to these abduction operations heuristically, they formulate a learning problem to find the best costs for the operators using the binary-labeled RTE data. They define a set of features based on: similarity resources such as WordNet; commonality of POS or Named Entity tags; syntactic role; and coreference cues. Each operation is associated with its own set of weights for these features, allowing different costs to be assigned for two different operations on the same predicate in the same example, and two different costs to be assigned for the same operation on two different predicates. For a given entailment example, a minimum cost proof can then be found that includes abduction operations by summing the costs of operations used to derive the Hypothesis from the Text.

To learn the weights of these features for each type of abduction operation, a logistic prediction model is assumed, and a discriminative likelihood function over the entire data set is formulated. Because this function is not convex, an iterative process is followed in which the minimum cost proofs for all examples in the corpus are found using the current feature weight vectors, and then new feature weights are learned by gradient descent over the likelihood function. The authors note that the approach relies on a good initialization of feature weights. The resulting system scored competitively with the best systems that participated in RTE-1, achieving an accuracy of 57.0% (see Table 4.2).

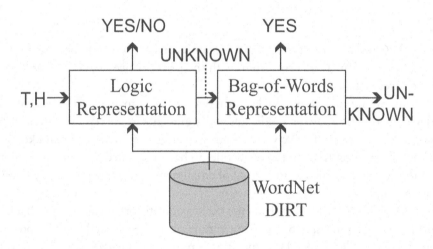

Figure 4.5: BLUE system architecture [59].

4.2.3   LOGICAL INFERENCE WITH SHALLOW BACKOFF SYSTEM

Bos and Markert [32, 33]'s DRS-based representation is used as input to a theorem prover and to a model builder. Predictably, neither approach yields sufficiently informative answers to do well

Table 4.2: Characteristics of selected logic-based RTE systems with abduction. Accuracy statistics in the left-most column indicate the evaluation task, together with the mean score/maximum score for that task (based on the scores reported in the *original task evaluation*)

System ID	Raina et al. '05	Fowler et al. '05
System Type	Approach 1	Approach 1
Preprocessing	POS, Dependency, Named Entity	POS, Dependency, Named Entity
Enrichment	Hand-coded rules	Hand-coded rules; Rules derived from WordNet
Candidate Alignment Generation	Rule-level feature vector, machine-learned weights	-
Alignment Selection	Implicit	Implicit
Classification	Proof score + threshold	Proof score + threshold
Accuracy: RTE-1 (54.8/58.6)	57.0	55.1
Main Innovation	Feature-based, machine learned rule costs; abductive rules	Abductive rules

on the RTE task. To address this problem, they define eight coarse entailment features derived from the outputs of the theorem prover and model builder, including domain and model sizes: the former counts the number of entities in the Text and Hypothesis, and the latter accounts for the complexity of the derived model in terms of relations with arity greater than one. The entailment features express the differences in domain size and complexity between models for the Text alone versus the Text and Hypothesis combined. These features are used as inputs to a decision tree learner, together with the Task label from the corpus, for a final performance of 61.2% on the RTE-1 dataset (see Table 4.3). Note that this evaluation was performed after the RTE-1 shared task was conducted, and as a result, exceeds the highest score reported in that evaluation (and hence in Table 4.3).

The BLUE system of Clarke and Harrison consists of a two-stage pipeline, as shown in Fig. 4.5. Initially, the Text and Hypothesis are parsed into a logical representation, using a bottom-up GPSG chart parser [113]. The logical form encodes a simplified tree structure with logic-type elements. Its pre-processing steps include dependency parsing, POS tagging, and pronoun and reference resolution. Some attributes, such as plurality, tense, and negation, are represented by special predicates in the logical form. This logical representation is used by a proof-theoretic process based on subsumption and equivalence using WordNet and DIRT Inference rules. If the logical inference step fails to determine either entailment or contradiction, a bag-of-words alignment model is used (in conjunction with WordNet and DIRT inference rules) as a back-off inference module. The logic-based part of the approach maps directly to the model described in Chapter 2, Section 2.1, while the backoff model is analogous to weighted similarity as described in Chapter 3, Section 6.

BLUE's proof-theoretic component tries to find an explanation for the entailment decision by finding a chain of reasoning from Text to Hypothesis. It is, however, limited by errors in the knowledge sources and the pre-processing stages such as parsing and semantic analysis. According to the analysis presented in Clark and Harrison [59], the presence of implicit relations in text, combined with lack of knowledge to bridge the semantic gap between the Text and Hypothesis, further limits the performance of the system (61.5% accuracy on the RTE-5 data set; see Table 4.3).

One strong positive characteristic of this system is that for those examples for which it can derive a proof chain, it produces an explanation of its label, which potentially allows the user to identify sources of errors, and to assess the reliability of the system: if the explanation is plausible for a given set of entailment examples, we may be more confident that this system will perform well on unseen examples from a similar domain.

4.3 TRANSFORMATION-BASED APPROACHES

Transformation-based approaches closely follow the intuitive model presented in Chapter 2, Section 2.1, using a set of rules to perturb the entailment pair with the goal of making the Text and Hypothesis identical. After the rule set has been exhausted (when either no more changes can be effected by applying rules, or some heuristic limit is reached), if the Text and Hypothesis match, the entailment pair is labeled as "entails," and if they don't, it is labeled as "not entails." (In theory, this can be extended to include a method for assigning the label "contradicts.") They are distinct from edit-distance-based approaches in that they entertain a set of transformations that are at once more complex than standard edit-distance operations, and more restricted in that the goal is to entertain only transformations that yield valid natural language sentences as their result.

4.3.1 TRANSFORMATION-BASED APPROACH WITH INTEGER LINEAR PROGRAMMING

Braz et al. [34] propose and implement a transformation-based RTE system that uses a hierarchical graph-based representation of syntactic and shallow semantic structure, shown in Figure 4.6, together with a set of hand-coded rules designed to capture alternative expressions of information at the lexical, phrasal, syntactic, and shallow semantic levels. They provide a model-theoretic justification of this approach, wherein each rule application makes some underlying meaning of the

Table 4.3: Characteristics of selected hybrid systems with logic-based components. Accuracy statistics in the left-most column indicate the evaluation task, together with the mean score/maximum score for that task (based on the scores reported in the *original task evaluation*)

System ID	**Bos and Markert '05**	**Clarke et al. '09**
System Type	Approach 1	Approach 1
Preprocessing	CCG parser	POS, Coreference, GPSG Parser
Enrichment	Hand-coded rules; WordNet	Hand-coded rules; WordNet; DIRT rules
Candidate Alignment Generation	WordNet-based; GoogleAPI (back-off system)	-
Alignment Selection	Greedy (back-off system)	Greedy (back-off system)
Classification	statistical classifier	First stage: Proof; second stage: word overlap + threshold
Accuracy: RTE-1 (54.8/58.6)	62.1	-
Accuracy: RTE-5 (61.5/73.5)	-	61.5
Main Innovation	Uses model builder as component; CCG-derived logical forms	Two-stage architecture, clean separation of theorem prover and shallow back-off

Text explicit. Given precise rules and a correct induced representation of the text, the result is a sound inferential process, whose completeness is contingent on the coverage of the rules available to the system.

The system's algorithm attempts to apply each available rule in turn; if a rule head matches the Text, the rule is applied and an alternative version of the Text is generated. After each perturbation resulting from application of a rule, the system checks whether the Text subsumes the Hypothesis. The system repeats the process to allow chaining of rules, but uses a fixed limit to avoid trivial rule chaining (such as alternating between possessive structures "A's B" and "B of A"). In order to reduce the number of rules used by the system, lexical mappings based on Word-Net were encoded as a metric applied during the check for subsumption (termed "functional subsumption").

The subsumption is formulated as an Integer Linear Programming (ILP) problem, which is used to find the optimal minimum-cost subsumption of the Hypothesis by the Text. Rules have associated costs, and these costs are further weighted depending on the level of the representation at which the rule is expressed (the intuition being that it is more important to match relations—and therefore verbs—than individual terms like determiners). The objective function weights different levels of structure to emphasize the level that gives the most reliable information for entailment, using hand-set weights.

There is no explicit alignment selection step; the inference step formulates the ILP problem and determines the minimum cost of subsumption of the Hypothesis by the Text. If the cost exceeds a threshold (tuned on a development set), the entailment pair is labeled "Not Entailed;" otherwise, it is labeled "Entailed." This system was shown to outperform a smart lexical baseline on a subset of the RTE-1 development set, and achieved an accuracy of 56.1% on the RTE-1 test set (see Table 4.4).

4.3.2   SYNTACTIC TRANSFORMATION WITH LINGUISTICALLY MOTIVATED RULES

Bar-Haim et al. [10] apply their syntactic transformation-based approach (described in [9], which maps cleanly to the approach described in Chapter 2, section 2.3.3) to the RTE task. Figure 4.7 shows an example of a syntactic transformation in terms of the representation they use, together with the corresponding transformation rule. To mitigate the problems with rule coverage and, indirectly, with noisy inputs, the classification step of their system uses a cost function that compares both lexical and syntactic similarity, the parameters of which are tuned using a held-out development set. This version of their system scored 61.1% on the RTE-3 data set (see Table 4.4).

Later work (Bar-Haim et al. [7]) extends their system by using a compact forest representation, which is used to more efficiently encode the various augmentations of a given entailment pair. In addition, a machine learning component is introduced. A heuristic distance metric is used to identify the most closely matching pair of Text-Hypothesis representations from among all those possible in the augmented entailment pair, and then features are extracted from this pair. These features, which include lexical matching features (coverage of terms in the Hypothesis by terms in the Text; presence of polarity terms) and lexical-syntactic matching features (degrees of predicate-argument matches between the Hypothesis and Text), are used by a classifier to predict the entailment label. To train the classifier, the same steps are run, the features extracted, and the feature representation of each entailment pair together with the pair's label are used in the standard supervised Machine Learning paradigm. This system improved the accuracy on RTE-3 to 66.4%, and achieved an accuracy of 60.6% on RTE-4. Mirkin et al. [163] extend this system by adding rules based on Extended WordNet and a location gazetteer indicating "is-in" relations, and achieved 63.8% accuracy in the RTE-5 main task (see Table 4.4).

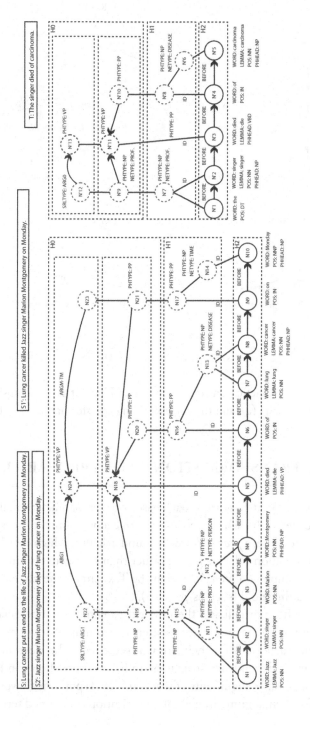

Figure 4.6: Representation of text used by Braz et al. [34].

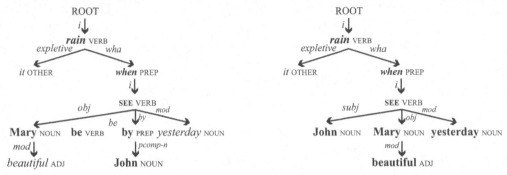

Source: it rained when beautiful Mary was seen by John yesterday

Derived: it rained when John saw beautiful Mary yesterday

(a) Application of passive to active transformation

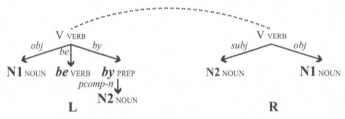

(b) Passive to active transformation (substitute rule). The dotted arc represents alignment.

Figure 4.7: An example of a syntactic transformation in Bar-Haim et al.'s system showing the system representation of entailment pairs (a), and the corresponding transformation rule (b).

4.3.3 SYNTACTIC TRANSFORMATION WITH A PROBABILISTIC CALCULUS

Harmeling [111] proposes an edit-based approach based on a probabilistic entailment calculus—a simple model that associates with each transformation rule a probability of preserving the entailment label. The goal is, therefore, a *probabilistically* sound calculus, which may be a more realistic goal than a sound transformation calculus per se: rather than simply determine an entailment label, the resulting system computes a *probability* that the Text entails the Hypothesis; a prediction can then be made using a threshold (such as $p > 0.5$).

As its initial step, after normalizing the raw text to eliminate superficial differences, the system rewrites the raw text to create separate sentences from appositives and relative clauses, and removing these constructions from their original sentences. The Text and Hypothesis are then represented as syntactic dependency structures similar to those shown in Figure 4.7.

A fixed number of possible alignments of words in the Hypothesis to words in the Text are heuristically selected. For each alignment, possible substitutions of aligned terms are entertained

Table 4.4: Characteristics of selected transformation-based systems. Accuracy statistics in the left-most column indicate the evaluation task, together with the mean score/maximum score for that task (based on the scores reported in the *original task evaluation*)

System ID	Braz et al. '05	Bar-Haim et al. '07, '09; Mirkin et al. '09
System Type	Approach 1	Approach 1
Preprocessing	Part-of-Speech; Named Entity; Syntactic parse; Semantic Role Labeling	Dependency parse
Enrichment	Hand-coded rules; WordNet	Hand-coded rules; WordNet
Candidate Alignment Generation	WordNet similarity	-
Alignment Selection	implicit (ILP)	hand-crafted scoring function
Classification	ILP + threshold	statistical classifier
Accuracy: RTE-1 (54.8/58.6)	56.1	-
Accuracy: RTE-3 (61.4/80.0)	-	66.4
Accuracy: RTE-4 (61.4/80.0)	-	60.6
Accuracy: RTE-5 (61.5/73.5)	-	63.8
Main Innovation	Noisy subsumption; Integer Linear Programming formulation	Linguistically motivated syntactic transformation; packed forest representation

together with grammatical perturbations that make the Text and Hypothesis more similar. Remaining differences are resolved by rotation/deletion operations on nodes of the Text dependency structure.

Operations are typed, and Harmeling uses labeled RTE data to learn weights for each operation; a simple feature vector representation of proofs is used where each feature corresponds to a transformation type, and is assigned a value equal to the number of times that transformation operation was applied in the proof. Intuitively, this method must give high probabilities only to operations that appear in proofs for "entails" examples that do not also appear in proofs for "does not entail" examples, and low probabilities to operations that appear in proofs for "does not entail" examples but not in proofs for "entails" examples. The system achieves an accuracy of 55.6% on RTE-2 and 57.5% on RTE-3 (see Table 4.5).

4.3.4 SYNTACTIC TRANSFORMATION WITH LEARNED OPERATION COSTS

Work by Stern and Dagan [227] (with later implementation improvements by [229]) augments the syntactic transformation approach of [7] with an algorithm to estimate transformation costs, which allows entailment labels to be assigned based on proof cost (the sum of the transformation costs). The idea is similar to that of [201], but uses a simpler hill-climbing parameter estimation approach. Like [201], this system defines a set of features that are associated with each transformation operation/rule; a weight vector for each operation is learned based on the training data. Features include a rule-specific confidence measure; the part-of-speech and phrase label of inserted elements; and distance of move operation.

They also augment the transformations used by [7] with additional rule sets derived from DIRT and other sources, and with a custom set of abductive operations (including deletion and insertion operators for different types of constituents, operators for simplifying multi-word expressions, and "type-raising"-like behavior) to allow finer-grained abductive behavior. The resulting system performed consistently well on four different RTE data sets, with scores significantly above the median performance of systems participating in those tasks, achieving an accuracy of 63.5% on RTE-5 (see Table 4.5). Moreover, the system can provide a complete proof for each entailment decision.

4.3.5 NATURAL LOGIC

MacCartney and Manning [151] propose a framework, "NatLog," based on a natural logic-based representation of meaning that combines an edit-distance approach with a logical calculus based on monotonicity relations between concepts. Like approaches described in Section 4.2, NatLog encodes structural relations between components as predicates, and names events in the text with their lexical surface form, avoiding full semantic interpretation. NatLog specifies a set of relations that represent different kinds of entailment between elements of text (such as noun phrases) in terms of monotonicity. For example, *semantic containment* identifies when one concept generalizes another, while *semantic exclusion* indicates when one concept, if true, precludes the other being true. These relations are listed in Figure 4.8.[1] In addition, NatLog specifies a set of semantic functions encoding polarity (modality and negation) and general quantifiers (which correspond to the examples of entailment triggers described in Chapter 3, Section 3.4.3). These functions and their behavior when inserted or deleted closely follow work by [176]; an example is given in Figure 4.9.

---

[1] This figure and others relating to Natural Logic are from Bill MacCartney's PhD thesis [148].

Table 4.5: Characteristics of selected transformation-based systems. Accuracy statistics in the left-most column indicate the evaluation task, together with the mean score/maximum score for that task (based on the scores reported in the *original task evaluation*)

System ID	Harmeling '09	Stern and Dagan
System Type	Approach 1	Approach 1
Preprocessing	Dependency parse	Dependency parse, Coreference
Enrichment	Hand-coded rules; WordNet	Hand-coded rules; Word-Net; DIRT; Wikipedia; Directional Similarity; Lin Similarity
Candidate Alignment Generation	-	-
Alignment Selection	heuristic, k-best	exhaustive (subsumption check)
Classification	proof score + threshold	proof score + threshold
Accuracy: RTE-1 (54.8/58.6)	-	57.3
Accuracy: RTE-2 (60.0/75.4)	55.6	61.6
Accuracy: RTE-3 (61.4/80.0)	57.5	67.1
Accuracy: RTE-4 (61.4/80.0)	-	-
Accuracy: RTE-5 (61.5/73.5)	-	63.5
Main Innovation	Probabilistic transformation calculus	Full proofs with weighted transformation rules

The NatLog inference process models a transformation-based approach whereby a series of edits to an entailment pair are made to make the Hypothesis and Text identical. In this model, the Text and Hypothesis are represented by semantic composition trees, where each node corresponds to a constituent of the underlying text (fragments of composition trees are shown in

Venn	symbol	name	example
●	P = Q	equivalence	*couch = sofa*
◐	P ⊏ Q	forward entailment (strict)	*crow ⊏ bird*
◐	P ⊐ Q	reverse entailment (strict)	*European ⊐ French*
▮	P ∧ Q	negation (exhaustive exclusion)	*human ∧ nonhuman*
●●	P | Q	alternation (non-exhaustive exclusion)	*cat | dog*
▮	P ‿ Q	cover (exhaustive non-exclusion)	*animal ‿ nonhuman*
◕	P # Q	independence	*hungry # hippo*

Figure 4.8: The entailment relations of Natural Logic.

	signature	example		β (DEL)	β (INS)
implicatives	+ / -	*he managed to escape* ≡	*he escaped*	≡	≡
	+ / o	*he was forced to sell* ⊏	*he sold*	⊏	⊐
	o / -	*he was permitted to live* ⊐	*he lived*	⊐	⊏
implicatives	- / +	*he forgot to pay* ∧	*he paid*	∧	∧
	- / o	*he refused to fight* |	*he fought*	|	|
	o / +	*he hesitated to ask* ?	*he asked*	?	?
nonfactives	o / o	*he wanted to fly* #	*he flew*	#	#

Figure 4.9: The behavior of semantic functions in Natural Logic.

Figure 4.11). A path from a constituent to the root of a semantic composition tree corresponds to the interaction of nested polarity-marked expressions from the most nested expression to the outermost expression.

When an edit is made to one of the composition trees, the entailment relation between the modified tree and the original tree must be determined. The edit operation has an associated monotonicity relation which must be applied to the modified node, and which will interact with any semantic function affecting the node. An example showing the interactions between negation and the entailment operations is shown in Figure 4.10. If a change in polarity results, the change must be projected up through the composition tree to determine whether it affects the polarity of higher-level constituents, and thereby affects the overall entailment relation between the two composition trees. These interactions are defined by a projectivity calculus that encodes the effects of deleting or inserting a semantic function on a (local) entailment relation. An example of an edit and the resulting projection is given in Figure 4.11.

Finally, *sequences* of edits must be composed to determine the final entailment label, as individual edits may result in incompatible entailment labels. The composition calculus defines interactions between different entailment operations of the form $R_1(a, b) \bowtie R_2(b, c) \Rightarrow R_3(a, c)$. These interactions are listed in Figure 4.12.

The application of this model to textual entailment requires an alignment between elements of the Text and Hypothesis based on a phrase-level chunking of the underlying text. This chunking is derived from a syntactic representation (rather than the desired compositional semantic representation), interpreted sufficiently to canonize the semantic functions and their scopes, in which the chunks can be thought of as premises represented in the original entailment pair Text and Hypothesis. A hand-coded cost function aligns the Hypothesis chunks with the Text chunks based on minimum cost edit distance, using the standard insertion/deletion/substitution operations and a dynamic programming algorithm. The NatLog system then orders the edit sequence, determines the local entailment labels (for each individual edit), and finally determines the global entailment label by composing the individual edit labels.

In the resulting RTE system, a statistical classifier is used to predict which entailment relation holds for a given edit. Features such as WordNet relations, string similarity, part of speech, and numeric equivalence are used as inputs to the classifiers, which are trained using a small set of hand-crafted entailment examples designed to exercise the feature space.

This approach works well on simple sentences, such as those in the FraCaS corpus [65], but it becomes much harder to reliably extract the basic premises from the Texts in entailment pairs from the PASCAL and NIST RTE corpora, as world knowledge is often required to infer relations more closely reflecting the structure of those in the Hypothesis. To apply the Natural Logic inference to the RTE task, MacCartney and Manning combine the alignment system described in Section 4.4.1 with the NatLog system via a straightforward linear function, and achieve a score of 59.4% on the RTE-5 data set (see Table 4.6).

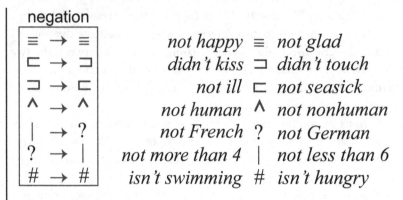

Figure 4.10: Interactions between negation and NatLog's entailment relations.

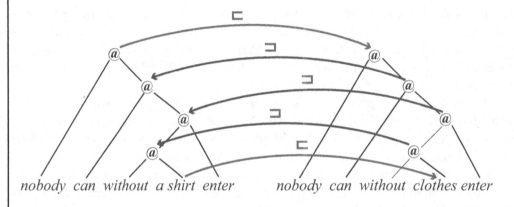

Figure 4.11: An example of projection of polarity resulting from an edit to a semantic composition tree.

4.4   ALIGNMENT-FOCUSED APPROACHES

This section highlights RTE research where the alignment selection task is directly addressed. Such approaches view alignment as a key, explicit part of the inference process, with the design or statistical learning of the alignment selection function as a focus of their research.

4.4.1   LEARNING ALIGNMENT SELECTION INDEPENDENTLY OF ENTAILMENT

MacCartney et al. [150] argue for a two-stage RTE architecture, where an alignment selection stage determines the most relevant portions of the Text to align with the (typically shorter) Hy-

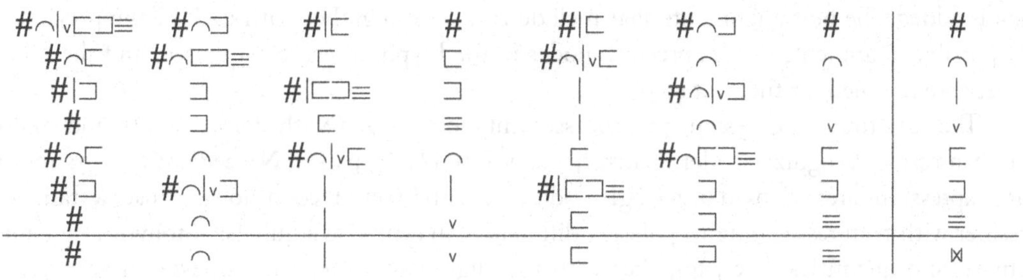

Figure 4.12: Composition calculus for Natural Logic entailment relations.

Table 4.6: Characteristics of the NatLog system. Accuracy statistics in the left-most column indicate the evaluation task, together with the mean score/maximum score for that task (based on the scores reported in the *original task evaluation*)

System ID	MacCartney and Manning '08
System Type	Approach 1
Preprocessing	POS, Syntactic Parser
Enrichment	Polarity; number identification
Candidate Alignment Generation	statistical classifiers with WordNet, string similarity, POS features
Alignment Selection	hand-crafted scoring function
Classification	minimal edit distance and derived entailment label
Accuracy: RTE-3 (61.4/80.0)	59.4
Main Innovation	Calculus for monotonicity and polarity interactions

pothesis, independently of Recognizing Textual Entailment. They propose that alignment selection be thought of as identifying *relevant* portions of the Text, and argue that this separation is necessary. A two-stage architecture finds, in theory, the best embedding of the Hypothesis in the Text with the alignment selection step, and determines polarity and monotonicity effects in a later step that uses *global* features of the aligned graphs.

MacCartney et al. use a hand-crafted scoring metric for the alignment selection step, and find the highest-scoring alignment using beam search. At each search step a new Hypothesis node is added; the best alignments that include this node together with each of the previous k best possible alignments for the previous nodes in the Hypothesis are computed, and the k best of these are retained for the next step.

The resulting RTE system preprocesses entailment pairs with named entity and multi-word expression recognizers; a lemmatizer; and a dependency parser. Named entities and multi-word expressions are collapsed into single nodes. The entailment recognition step uses a statistical classifier with features relating to polarity, differences in syntactic adjuncts, antonymy, modality, factivity, and quantities/dates, together with the alignment score, and achieves an accuracy of 59.1% on the RTE-1 data set (see Table 4.7).

De Marneffe et al. [78] continue this line of work, but focus on the alignment selection step, with the goal of *learning* the alignment selection function. They use a sample of the RTE-1 data set annotated with lexical-level alignments (with named entities collapsed into a single phrasal chunk), where edges indicate semantic equivalence, containment, or antonymy.

In the alignment system, the Text and Hypothesis are preprocessed with named entity and multi-word expression recognizers; a lemmatizer; a quantity expression normalizer; a coreference resolver; and a dependency parser. Named entities and multi-word expressions are collapsed into single nodes. Alignment selection is formalized as an optimization problem that accounts for alignments of individual tokens in the hypothesis and of pairs of hypothesis tokens connected by a dependency edge. Specifically, they seek to maximize the cost of the following function:

$$G(\{(H_i, T_j)\}) = \sum_{(H_i,T_j)} S(H_i, T_j) + \sum_{(i,j)\in e(h)} s_e((h_i, h_j), (a(h_i), a(h_j))) \qquad (4.1)$$

in which the first term corresponds to the component-level alignment score in Equation 3.1, and the second corresponds to its quality term $Q()$, which measures the compatibility of a pair of aligned nodes in the Text, together with the dependency structure connecting them, with the corresponding pair of nodes in the Hypothesis, and their dependency structure. There is no normalization term in the De Marneffe et al. formulation. The edge and node similarity functions are formulated as weighted feature vectors whose weights are learned using structured perceptron [63] with the MIRA update of Crammer and Singer [69].

The optimization problem is solved using stochastic search, which initializes the alignment with the best greedy word-level alignment, then proceeds to explore the space of all possible alignments using Gibbs sampling. The Gibbs sampler is modified with a soft-max function parameterized by a temperature value that decreases according to a cooling schedule. As this work focuses only on alignment selection and not on Recognizing Textual Entailment, the evaluation given relates only to performance in replicating the hand-annotated alignment data.

MacCartney et al. [149] generalize this alignment formulation to the phrase level (where *phrase* simply means *contiguous text span*). As in de Marneffe et al.'s work, they use a stochastic search process to explore the space of possible alignments; however, the alignment score is formulated in terms of phrase edit distance, with operations for equality, substitution, insertion, and deletion of phrases in the Text with respect to the Hypothesis. Their alignment score is simply the sum of the edit scores required to map the Hypothesis to the Text. Edit scores are, like the alignment scores in de Marneffe et al., derived from weighted feature vectors where the weights are learned from gold alignment data.

The model is trained using lexical alignment labelings generated by Brockett [35]. While they report an improvement over two lexical-level alignment baselines, they did not observe significant differences in performance between the phrase-level system and a token-level alignment by the same system (i.e., where the phrase size is fixed at one token) (see Table 4.7). The system scored 60.3 on the RTE-2 data set, using only the alignment score (i.e., without an additional entailment labeling step using features and a statistical classifier).

Table 4.7: Characteristics of selected alignment-focused systems. Accuracy statistics in the left-most column indicate the evaluation task, together with the mean score/maximum score for that task (based on the scores reported in the *original task evaluation*)

System ID	MacCartney et al. '06	MacCartney et al. '08
System Type	Approach 2	Approach 2
Preprocessing	Dependency parser; multi-word expressions; named entities; lemmas	Dependency parser; multi-word expressions; named entities; lemmas; quantities; coreference
Enrichment	-	-
Candidate Alignment Generation	hand-crafted similarity functions	statistical weighted feature model for nodes and dependency edges
Alignment Selection	hand-crafted scoring function	stochastic search
Classification	statistical classifier	alignment score + threshold
Accuracy: RTE-1 (54.8/58.6)	59.1	-
Accuracy: RTE-2 (60.0/75.4)	-	60.3
Main Innovation	Separate alignment step	Stochastic alignment with learned edge functions

4.4.2 HAND-CODED ALIGNMENT FUNCTION

Iftene et al. [123, 124, 125] develop a system based around hand-coded local and global similarity functions. A block diagram of their system is shown in Figure 4.13.

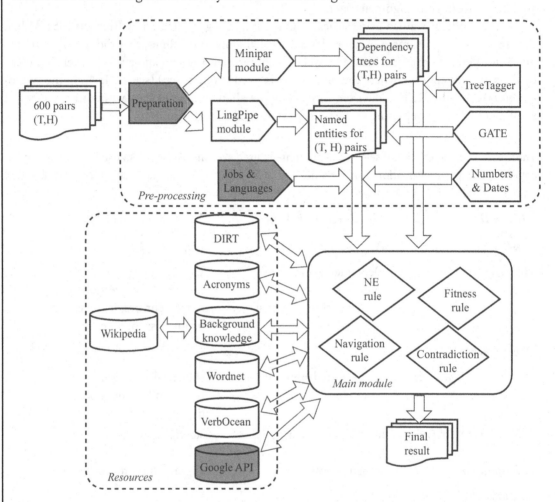

Figure 4.13: Block diagram representation of Iftene and Moruz's textual entailment system.

In the preprocessing step, the text of the entailment pair is first normalized to expand contractions (e.g., "is not" instead of "isn't") and replace some punctuation characters; this improves the performance of the preprocessing components. The induced representation of the entailment pair is based on a dependency parse tree, enriched with Named Entity information. [123] improves the system by adding a POS tagger that replaces the POS tags in the dependency parse output, and supplements the named entity annotation with the output of GATE [72]; in addition, a numerical quantity recognizer/normalizer is added. In [125], the representation is enriched with specific relations (such as "work-for") and terms relating to languages and nationalities.

The alignment selection step comprises local and global scoring functions, where the global function is based on tree-edit distance; all possible alignments are considered. Each Hypothesis constituent is mapped to the best candidate Text constituent. This process includes the application of rules derived from WordNet, DIRT, Wikipedia, and a set of acronyms. [123] supplements these with VerbOcean [54], and [125] add a distance measure based on retrieval results obtained with the Google API. These resources are used to identify possible mappings between dissimilar Text/Hypothesis term pairs; these mappings have associated hand-crafted "local fitness functions" that compare nodes, accounting for their parents and the corresponding dependency edges, and assign similarity scores.

These local alignment scores are then integrated using another hand-crafted similarity function, which makes adjustments based on certain global characteristics of the alignment, such as whether the Named Entities in the Hypothesis are matched by Entities in the Text, and whether an aligned predicate is negated in one of the Text and Hypothesis but not the other. [123] adds a contradiction rule component that detects disagreements in polarity between corresponding verbs due to negation, modal constructions, and antonymy (which is detected using a combination of WordNet synonyms and antonyms and VerbOcean's "opposite" relation).

The inference step applies two thresholds to the resulting score: a higher threshold that distinguishes between "Entailed" and "Not Entailed," and a lower threshold that separates the "Not Entailed" examples into the two categories "Unknown" and "Contradicted." These thresholds are tuned to maximize performance on the three-way task for the Development set; the two-way labeling score is derived directly from the three-way labeling by combining the "Unknown" and "Contradicted" labels to generate "Not Entailed" labels. The role of Machine Learning is minimized in this approach, as only the thresholds are directly driven by the data.

The [124] system scored 69.1% on the RTE-3 task. The [123] system scored 68.5% on the RTE-4 three-way task, and 72.1% in the two-way task. The [125] system achieved accuracies of 68.5% on the RTE-5 three-way task and 73.5% on the two-way task (see Table 4.8).

4.4.3   LEVERAGING MULTIPLE ALIGNMENTS FOR RTE

Sammons et al. [213] attempt to address two difficulties faced by RTE system developers who wish to use deeper NLP analytics in a structured similarity model (see Chapter 3, Section 3.4.2): the integration of NLP analyses operating at different granularities (word, phrase, syntax, and predicate-argument levels), and the application of similarity metrics or other knowledge resources (such as rules) in a consistent way across these different layers of representation. The latter problem is in essence one of *scaling*: most knowledge resources, whether similarity metrics or inference rules, are designed with a confidence score; but even when such scores have the same range (or are normalized), the same score from two different resources may not be interpretable as meaning equal confidence. For example, suppose a Named Entity metric returns a score in the range [0, 1]; a

Table 4.8: Characteristics of selected alignment-focused systems. Accuracy statistics in the left-most column indicate the evaluation task, together with the mean score/maximum score for that task (based on the scores reported in the *original task evaluation*)

System ID	Iftene and Balahur-Dobrescu '07, Iftene '08, Iftene and Moruz '09	Sammons et al.
System Type	Approach 2	Approach 2
Preprocessing	part-of-speech, dependency parse, named entities; quantities ('08)	part-of-speech, shallow parse, named entities, syntactic parse, semantic role labeling, quantities, coreference
Enrichment	relations, languages/nationalities ('09)	-
Candidate Alignment Generation	DIRT, acronyms, Wikipedia, WordNet; VerbOcean ('08); Google API ('09)	WordNet, named entity, predicate-argument similarity functions
Alignment Selection	brute force search	brute force search
Classification	alignment score + threshold	statistical classifier
Accuracy: RTE-3 (61.4/80.0)	69.1	-
Accuracy: RTE-4 2-way (56.6/74.6)	72.1	-
Accuracy: RTE-4 3-way (47.7/68.5)	68.5	-
Accuracy: RTE-5 2-way (61.5/73.5)	73.5	66.6
Accuracy: RTE-5 3-way (57.6/68.3)	68.3	-
Main Innovation	Successful integration of specialized local similarity scores	Compares multiple alignments

score of 0.6 might indicate relatively low similarity. Suppose a WordNet-based metric also returns a score in the range [0, 1]; it is quite possible that for the WordNet metric, a score of 0.6 indicates a relatively high similarity. The outputs of the two metrics are then not *compatible*, because the same returned score does not have an equivalent meaning.

Sammons et al. describe a multi-view approach in which different sources of NLP analysis are represented in separate views of the data, though comparable levels of representation may be combined in the same view. The Text and Hypothesis are annotated with part-of-speech, shallow parse, named entities, syntactic parse, semantic role labeling, coreference, and quantities. Specialized knowledge resources are encoded as metrics operating on these individual views. Their system uses multiple alignments of the Text and Hypothesis in each entailment pair, separating views with incompatible metrics into separate alignments. Each alignment is scored using a global function of the form of Equation 3.1:

$$G(\{(H_i, T_j)\}) = \frac{\alpha \sum_i \Delta(e(H_i, T_j), e(H_{i+1}, T_k)) + \sum_{(H_i, T_j)} S(H_i, T_j)}{m} \tag{4.2}$$

subject to the constraint $\sum_j I[e(H_i, T_j)] \leq 1$, where m is the number of tokens in the hypothesis; $S(H_i, T_j)$ is the magnitude of the score of a metric comparing Hypothesis token i with Text token j; α is a parameter weighting the distance penalty; and $\Delta(e(H_i, T_j), e(H_{i+1}, T_k))$ measures the distance, in tokens, between the Text constituent aligned to Hypothesis token i and the Text constituent aligned to Hypothesis token j. $I[e(H_i, T_j)]$ is the indicator function indicating that token i of the Hypothesis is aligned to token j of the Text.

Features are defined over individual alignments and also between alignments, based on the observations that different information sources may be more or less reliable, and that disagreements between reliable information sources may be crucial for entailment detection. For example, if lexical-level alignments or Semantic Role-based predicate-argument structure alignments indicate entailment, but alignments using Numerical Quantity metrics do not, this is a good indication that the Text does not entail the Hypothesis.

The multi-view, multi-alignment model allows a modular approach to integrating new NLP analytics and knowledge resources, and the machine-learning based inference component allows the system to determine the reliability of cues from different sources of analysis. The system scored 66.6% on the RTE-5 two-way task (see Table 4.8).

4.4.4   ALIGNING DISCOURSE COMMITMENTS

Hickl et al. [118] propose a framework for recognizing textual entailment based on extraction of discourse commitments. The assumption is that the text consists of many simpler constructs that are true even if the particular Text-Hypothesis pair does not entail. Figure 4.14 shows a sample entailment pair with all discourse commitments; the block diagram of the system is shown in Fig. 4.15.

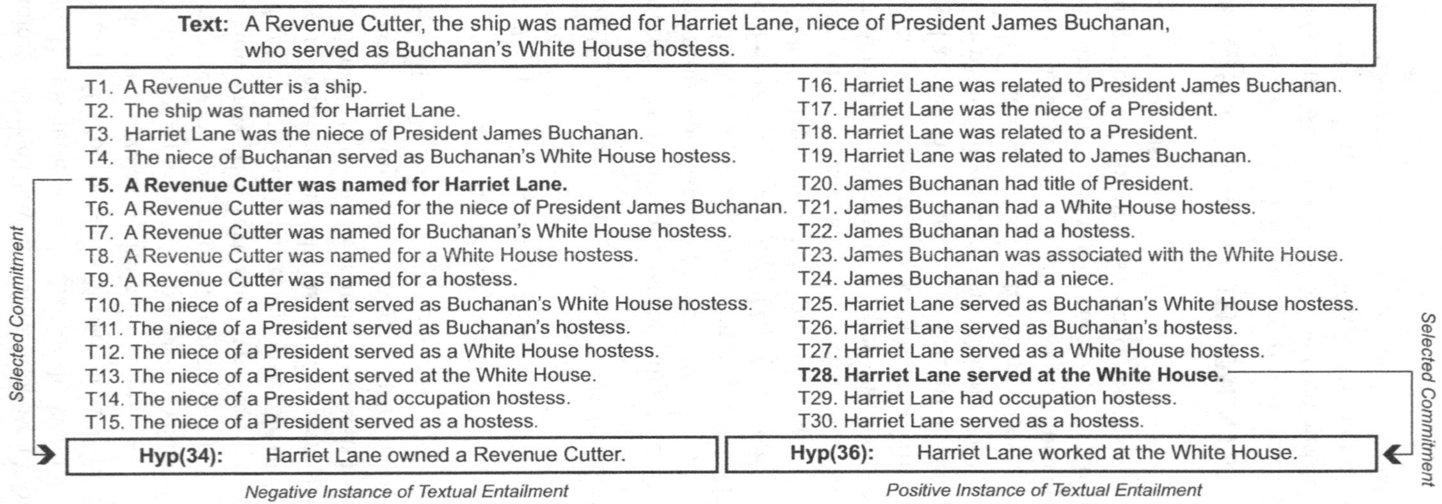

Text: A Revenue Cutter, the ship was named for Harriet Lane, niece of President James Buchanan, who served as Buchanan's White House hostess.

Selected Commitment

T1. A Revenue Cutter is a ship.
T2. The ship was named for Harriet Lane.
T3. Harriet Lane was the niece of President James Buchanan.
T4. The niece of Buchanan served as Buchanan's White House hostess.
T5. A Revenue Cutter was named for Harriet Lane.
T6. A Revenue Cutter was named for the niece of President James Buchanan.
T7. A Revenue Cutter was named for Buchanan's White House hostess.
T8. A Revenue Cutter was named for a White House hostess.
T9. A Revenue Cutter was named for a hostess.
T10. The niece of a President served as Buchanan's White House hostess.
T11. The niece of a President served as Buchanan's hostess.
T12. The niece of a President served as a White House hostess.
T13. The niece of a President served at the White House.
T14. The niece of a President had occupation hostess.
T15. The niece of a President served as a hostess.

T16. Harriet Lane was related to President James Buchanan.
T17. Harriet Lane was the niece of a President.
T18. Harriet Lane was related to a President.
T19. Harriet Lane was related to James Buchanan.
T20. James Buchanan had title of President.
T21. James Buchanan had a White House hostess.
T22. James Buchanan had a hostess.
T23. James Buchanan was associated with the White House.
T24. James Buchanan had a niece.
T25. Harriet Lane served as Buchanan's White House hostess.
T26. Harriet Lane served as Buchanan's hostess.
T27. Harriet Lane served as a White House hostess.
T28. Harriet Lane served at the White House.
T29. Harriet Lane had occupation hostess.
T30. Harriet Lane served as a hostess.

Hyp(34):   Harriet Lane owned a Revenue Cutter.

Negative Instance of Textual Entailment

Hyp(36):   Harriet Lane worked at the White House.

Selected Commitment

Positive Instance of Textual Entailment

Figure 4.14: Example of discourse commitments from text [118].

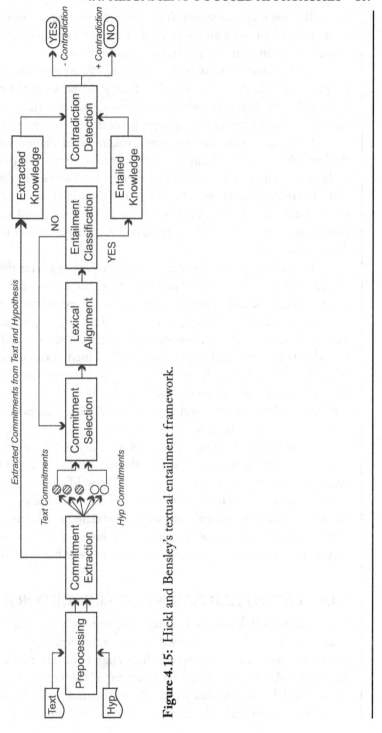

Figure 4.15: Hickl and Bensley's textual entailment framework.

The preprocessing step includes syntactic parsing and semantic-dependency parsing, named entity recognition, coreference resolution, and numeric quantity recognition. The outputs of these systems are unified in a single graph representation.

In the enrichment step, the Text and Hypothesis sentences are decomposed into sets of simpler sentences that are themselves true, irrespective of the truth value of the pair. A relation extractor is used to recognize known relations, such as owner-of, location-near, employee-of, etc.; and supplemental expressions, such as parenthesis, as-clauses, and appositives.

In the alignment selection step, a token-based aligner is applied to the commitments from the Hypothesis to identify the most relevant commitment from the Text for each. The aligner uses multiple similarity metrics including metrics for Levenstein distance, WordNet similarity[188], named entity similarity, and the Dice coefficient [82] (for word association). The alignment selection inference is performed by solving a maximal weighted matching problem, using the metric outputs as features; the model is trained using a hand-annotated set of alignments of the RTE-3 development set.

In the classification/inference step, the system selects the best-aligned commitment from the Text for each commitment extracted from the Hypothesis, based on the weighted matching score found in the alignment selection step and a reciprocal best hit approach (following Mushegian and Koonin [175]). Using these commitments, it extracts features based on entity and argument matches, and a decision-tree classifier is used to decide if a commitment pair represents a valid entailment instance. The classifier is trained in the standard way, using features extracted for each example in the development corpus. Features were based on alignment characteristics (longest common subsequence; number of unaligned elements); entity, argument, and predicate match; modality; factivity; and other polarity-related elements. The system scored 80.4% on the RTE-4 task (see Table 4.9).

A later experiment used a large proprietary corpus of entailment pairs to improve the performance of the entailment classifier; the use of 25,000 additional pairs resulted in a maximum accuracy of 82.3% on the RTE-3 Test set. A modified version of the system scored 74.6% on the RTE-4 data set (see Hickl [117]); this differed from the previous system in using a paraphrase resource to generate multiple versions of extracted commitments. In addition, the system used a relaxed, k-best version of reciprocal best hit to determine the best match between Text and Hypothesis commitments, where the value of k was tuned on the development data.

4.4.5   LATENT ALIGNMENT INFERENCE FOR RTE

Chang, et al. [49] develop a joint learning approach that learns to make entailment decisions in tandem with learning an intermediate representation that aligns Texts and Hypotheses. No supervision is assumed at the intermediate alignment selection level: the assumption is that while alignment selection is an important element of entailment decisions, the "correct" alignment selection model is simply that which allows the most reliable entailment decisions, and does not necessarily correspond to human intuitions of "best alignment."

Chang et al. apply the general learning framework described in Section 3.5.2 to RTE, and extend it to use a semi-supervised approach. They use alignment as the intermediate representation in an iterative process: at each iteration the optimal alignment is computed for every entailment pair under its current model, using the approach described in Chapter 3, Section 3.2. The alignment edges have costs derived from a weighted feature vector, where features indicate for each pair of aligned words their similarity according to a WordNet-based metric [86]; a named entity metric; the relationship between aligned words' POS tags; and whether or not each is negated. Features for aligned edges are based on the features of their corresponding word mappings. The alignment objective function is:

$$G(\{(H_i, T_j)\}) = \sum_i W^T \phi(S(H_i, T_j)) + \sum_i W^T \phi(e(r(H_j, H_k), r(T_l, T_m))) \qquad (4.3)$$

where W is a weight vector and ϕ is a feature mapping defined over the chosen constituent alignments. The first sum computes the contribution of token and entity alignments, and the second computes the contribution of aligned edges. Consistency between the two terms is enforced with the constraint: $\forall(j, k, l, m) e(r(H_j, H_k), r(T_l, T_m)) \Leftrightarrow e[H_j, T_l] \wedge e[H_k, T_m]$. This requires all aligned edges to have aligned end nodes.

The framework uses a declarative Integer Linear Programming (ILP) inference formulation (see Chang et al. [50]), where the intermediate representation can be easily defined in terms of binary variables and knowledge can be injected as constraints in the model. During training, if the model generates a "good" (valid) alignment—in the sense that the resulting entailment decision based on the features activated by this alignment is correct—the learning stage uses this as a positive example for the entailment classifier and also to provide feedback to the alignment selection model. Unlabeled data can be added to the labeled data pool, following the standard semi-supervised approach.

The Text and Hypothesis are represented as graphs, where the words and phrases are nodes and dependency relations between words form the edges. In addition, directed edges link verbs to the head words of their semantic-role-labeled arguments. The mappings between the nodes and edges in the Text graph and the Hypothesis graph define the alignment. These alignment variables are constrained using relations between word mappings and edge mappings: for instance, an edge mapping is active only if the corresponding word mappings are active.

Chang et al. apply their framework to transliteration discovery, paraphrase identification, and recognizing textual entailment. For the RTE task, the preprocessing step uses part-of-speech, named entity, dependency parse, semantic role labeling, and coreference resolution and collapses them into a single, canonical graph structure. The graph generation step uses similarity metrics for words and Named Entities (see Do et al. [86]) but also computes alignment edges between edges in the Text and the Hypothesis, where the edges' sources and sinks are also aligned. Chang et al.'s system achieved an accuracy of 66.8% in the two-way task for the RTE-5 corpus (see Table 4.9).

Table 4.9: Characteristics of selected alignment-focused systems. Accuracy statistics in the left-most column indicate the evaluation task, together with the mean score/maximum score for that task (based on the scores reported in the *original task evaluation*)

System ID	Hickl and Bensley	Chang et al. '10
System Type	Approach 2	Approach 3
Preprocessing	syntactic parse, dependency parse, named entities, coreference, quantities	part-of-speech, named entities, syntactic parse, semantic role labeling, coreference
Enrichment	decomposition rules	-
Candidate Alignment Generation	string similarity, hand-crafted similarity functions	statistical weighted feature model
Alignment Selection	maximal weighted matching	iterative, integer linear programming formulation minimizing objective function
Classification	statistical classifier	alignment score + threshold
Accuracy: RTE-3 (61.4/80.0)		-
Accuracy: RTE-4 2-way (56.6/74.6)	74.6	-
Accuracy: RTE-5 2-way (61.5/73.5)	-	66.8
Main Innovation	Decomposition of text into simpler "commitments"	Learn alignment as latent structure

4.5   PAIRED SIMILARITY APPROACHES

The system of Zanzotto, et al. [262], in addition to modeling similarities between the Text and Hypothesis of entailment pairs, also compares aligned Text-Hypothesis pairs with each other using a tree kernel measure. The goal is to learn (implicitly) patterns that abstract common valid syntactic translations (i.e., first order transformation rules) over many entailment pairs. As such, it is a batch learning algorithm that tunes both parameters encoding similarity between the Text and Hypothesis of individual entailment pairs, and parameters encoding pairwise similarity between the entailment pairs themselves. Their system uses a dependency tree based representation, with abstraction of nodes via lexical/semantic match (which can be thought of in terms of enrichment via simple rules).

The system has a preliminary heuristic lexical alignment selection stage, which establishes potential subtree matching locations, called "anchors." These focus the application of the subtree matching component, which determines the final alignment between Text and Hypothesis for each entailment pair.

To train the inference model, these anchors are then abstracted into generic placeholders in a syntactic dependency representation. An intra-pair tree-kernel-based similarity function identifies (implicitly) the features of the intra-pair entailment graph, and a second tree-kernel-based similarity function is applied to compare patterns of alignments between entailment pairs. The goal is to learn more general structural correspondences that apply over multiple entailment pairs, by replacing the lexical anchors with variables. A Support Vector Model is trained using this inter-pair distance metric and the entailment example labels; this model is applied at the inference step of their RTE system. The system scored 63.0 on the RTE-1 data set, and 63.9 on the RTE-2 data set (see Table 4.10).

Later work by Moschitti and Zanzotto [173] improves the efficiency of the kernel-based matching, and Pennachiotti and Zanzotto [193] increase the expressiveness of the model by allowing anchors and placeholders to be typed by meronymy, hypernymy/synonymy, and antonymy, and related by surface similarity or semantic similarity. The types derive from the resource used to connect the different anchors in the inter-pair similarity function. This updated version of the system scored 66.8% on the RTE-3 data set (see Table 4.10).

Mehdad et al. [160] add more semantic information to increase the expressiveness of the intra-pair matching component with a similarity measure based on proximity of terms in Wikipedia. This system attained a score of 66.2% on the two-way labeling task of RTE-5 (see Table 4.11).

Wang and Neumann [247] use a similar approach to learn an entailment classification function over a subset of entailment pairs. Their subsequence kernel uses a linearized representation of the differences between the syntactic parse of the Text and Hypothesis to represent each entailment pair amenable to such a representation, then uses a subsequence kernel to compute the similarity between each entailment pair.

The verbs and nouns of the dependency parse trees of the Text and Hypothesis in each entailment pair are first aligned; if the aligned nodes fall along a dependency path in both the Text and Hypothesis, these paths ("Tree Skeletons") are extracted (see Figure 4.16). Next, the paths are compared, and a representation of the difference between the two paths (an "Entailment Pattern") is formulated that abstracts the differences into a closed set of categories. The differences for a given pair are represented by a four-tuple that consists of a Boolean value indicating whether the root nodes of the pair match; a Boolean value indicating whether or not the subject and object

Table 4.10: Characteristics of selected pairwise similarity systems. Accuracy statistics in the left-most column indicate the evaluation task, together with the mean score/maximum score for that task (based on the scores reported in the *original task evaluation*)

System ID	Zanzotto et al. '06	Pennachiotti and Zanzotto '07
System Type	Approach 1	Approach 1
Preprocessing	syntactic dependency	syntactic dependency
Enrichment	-	-
Candidate Alignment Generation	WordNet relations, Levenstein string edit distance	WordNet relations, Levenstein string edit distance
Alignment Selection	greedy	greedy
Classification	statistical classifier	statistical classifier
Accuracy: RTE-1 (54.8/58.6)	63.0	-
Accuracy: RTE-2 (60.0/75.4)	63.9	-
Accuracy: RTE-3 (61.4/80.0)	-	66.8
Main Innovation	Learned inter-pair entailment distance function; implicit First Order rule learning from RTE data	Generalize anchors using typed placeholders

relations are consistent; and sequences of closed category substitutions for the left and right part of the entailment pattern that represent the differences in dependency paths for the Text and Hypothesis. (Note that the first two components correspond to some of the entailment triggers described in Section 3.4.3.) Wang and Neumann found that 37% of pairs in the RTE-3 corpus could be represented in this way.

The subsequence kernel is used to compute the similarity between the left category substitution sequences and the right category substitution sequences, and these are integrated via weighted sum with trivial kernels for the other Entailment Pattern components. The weights in this sum are learned using the training data. Shallow backoff methods based on dependency edge overlap and on lexical overlap are used for the entailment pairs for which Tree Skeletons cannot

T: *For their discovery of ulcer-causing bacteria, Australian doctors* **Robin Warren** *and* *Barry Marshall have* **received** *the 2005* **Nobel Prize** *in Physiology or Medicine.*

H: Robin Warren was awarded a Nobel Prize

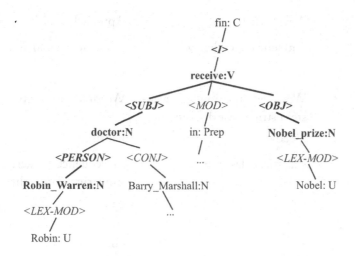

Figure 4.16: Tree Skeleton representation of an entailment pair.

be induced. This system scored 63.6% on the RTE-2 dataset and 66.9% on the RTE-3 dataset (see Table 4.11).

4.6   ENSEMBLE SYSTEMS

This section describes RTE systems that combine other entailment systems; they are specifically distinct from other approaches in that they offer a very straightforward mechanism for composing specialized systems.

4.6.1   WEIGHTED EXPERT APPROACH

Tatu et al. [238] develop a system that combines two different versions of the COGEX logic prover with a lexical overlap measure, using a weighted expert approach.

The COGEX components use two representations of the text, one based on a constituency parse and another based on a dependency parse: the first supports better shallow semantic analysis, while the second captures syntactic dependencies more reliably. The logical forms of both are augmented with negation information (terms for adverbs "not" and "never" are dropped, and the

Table 4.11: Characteristics of selected pairwise similarity systems. Accuracy statistics in the left-most column indicate the evaluation task, together with the mean score/maximum score for that task (based on the scores reported in the *original task evaluation*)

System ID	Mehdad et al. '09	Wang and Neumann '07
System Type	Approach 1	Approach 1
Preprocessing	syntactic dependency	syntactic dependency
Enrichment	-	-
Candidate Alignment Generation	WordNet relations, Levenstein string edit distance	WordNet similarity
Alignment Selection	greedy	heuristic
Classification	statistical classifier	subsequence kernel/global similarity score + threshold
Accuracy: RTE-2 (60.0/75.4)	-	63.6
Accuracy: RTE-3 (61.4/80.0)	-	66.9
Accuracy: RTE-5 (2-way: 61.5/73.5)	66.2	-
Main Innovation	Enhance tree kernel with lexical similarity	"Tree Spine" representation, subsequence kernel

corresponding verb terms are negated), with quantification, and with Named Entity annotations (all terms in a proper noun are treated as a single term). The dependency-based logical form reflects that shown in Figure 4.2. The constituency-based form is similar, but represents phrase-level constituents as predicates taking the child constituents as arguments. The constituency-based logical form (which reflects that shown in Figure 4.17) is augmented with shallow semantic information such as semantic roles like "theme" and "temporal modifier;" and select background knowledge relations such as Kinship, Cause, and Belief. Temporal expressions, and temporal relations between events, are detected by an additional preprocessing component that generates a canonical temporal representation.

The representations are further augmented using WordNet-derived rules and hand-coded axioms to identify coordination relations and relations implicit in compound nominals, together with about 450 hand-coded world knowledge rules. Finally, a set of rules to identify relations from combinations of semantic relations are added—for example, relating different Kinship relations, part-whole relations, and IsA relations. Abduction operators are also used when the knowledge

---

Example:

Gilda Flores was kidnapped on the 13th of January 1990.
Augmented, syntactic constituency parser-based logical form:

Gilda_NN(x1) & Flores_NN(x2) & nn_NC(x3,x1,x2) & _human_NE(x3)
& kidnap_VB(e1,x9,x3) & on_IN(e1,x8) & 13th_NN(x4) & of_NN(x5) &
January_NN(x6) & 1990_NN(x7) & nn_NNC(x8,x4,x5,x6,x7) &
_date_NE(x8) & THEME_SR(x3,e1) & TEMPORAL_SR(x8,e1) &
time_TMP(BeginFn(e2),1990,1,13,0,0,0) &
time_TMP(EndFn(e2),1990,1,13,23,59,59) & during_TMP(e1,e2)

Figure 4.17: COGEX syntax-based logical form augmented with semantic role and temporal predicates, as used in RTE-2 and RTE-3.

base has been exhausted. Proof costs are derived in the same way as the earlier version of the COGEX system (described in Section 4.2.2), and the scores are normalized so that they fall in the range [0, 1].

The lexical overlap component computes an edit distance, where the cost of an edit varies depending on the part of speech of the associated word, and allowing use of synonyms as zero-cost replacements (presumably, using WordNet as the source). The edit cost is normalized to yield a score in the interval [0, 1].

To integrate the three components, the output score for each component system is modified by a weight, and the sum is computed. The component weights are tuned on the development set; a different weight is computed for each component for each RTE subtask to maximize performance. Positive labels are assigned for a combined score greater than a threshold of 0.5. Weights were found by grid search. This system scored 73.8% on the RTE-2 data set (see Table 4.12).

4.6.2   SELECTIVE EXPERT APPROACH

Wang and Neumann [248] expand their Tree-Structure system (described in Section 4.5) by combining it with additional entailment components for times and for named entities.

The Time-Anchoring component, based on [249], extracts and normalizes temporal expressions, and identifies the events to which they are attached (where events are expressed by verbs or nouns). Wang and Neumann define a simple entailment calculus for comparing temporal expressions. The resulting representation is a set of 2-tuples for the Text and Hypothesis, each of which contains an event and a normalized temporal expression. Each tuple from the Hypothesis is compared to every tuple from the Text, using lexical resources WordNet and VerbOcean to improve event match coverage. The induced representation for events and times gives only partial coverage of the entailment pair; as a result, if all Hypothesis tuples are unmatched by Text tuples, the module predicts "not entailed," otherwise it predicts "unknown."

The Named Entity component works in a similar way to the Time-Anchoring component: named entities are identified and linked to events expressed as nouns or verbs, and sets of tuples for the Text and Hypothesis are extracted that represent events, their time and location, and the set of participants (person names or organization names). If any event tuple in the Hypothesis is unmatched by any event tuple from the Text, this module predicts "not entailed."

Two shallow back-off measures based on lexical overlap and dependency-edge overlap are used as two additional modules.

The overall system, shown in Figure 4.18, selects among the three main modules based first on whether one of the primary modules makes a prediction. If neither makes a prediction, the backoff modules are consulted. When more than one primary module makes a prediction, the one known to have a higher accuracy is selected—in effect, the modules form a decision list ordered by accuracy, where the prediction of the first module on the list to return a non-null decision is taken. The system achieved a performance of 70.6% on the two-way RTE-4 task, and of 61.4% on the three-way RTE-4 task (see Table 4.12).

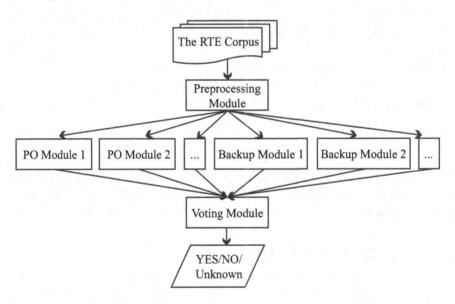

Figure 4.18: Wang and Neumann's divide-and-conquer system architecture.

Table 4.12: Characteristics of selected ensemble systems. Accuracy statistics in the left-most column indicate the evaluation task, together with the mean score/maximum score for that task (based on the scores reported in the *original task evaluation*)

System ID	Tatu et al. '06	Wang and Neumann '08
System Type	Approach 1	Approach 1
Preprocessing	syntactic constituency and dependency parse; named entities; temporal expressions and relations; polarity; quantifiers	syntactic dependency parse; temporal expressions; named entities
Enrichment	WordNet-derived rules; hand coded linguistic and world knowledge rules	-
Candidate Alignment Generation	-	WordNet, VerbOcean
Alignment Selection	heuristic	heuristic
Classification	weighted sum + threshold	decision list
Accuracy: RTE-2 (54.8/58.6)	73.8	-
Accuracy: RTE-4 (61.5/73.5)	-	70.6 (2-way), 61.4 (3-way)
Main Innovation	Weighted expert ensemble	Decision-list ensemble

4.7 DISCUSSION

At the time of writing, there are no clear "winners" among the numerous approaches to Recognizing Textual Entailment. There are, however, some comparisons to be made to highlight strengths and disadvantages of the different models described in the previous sections.

Simple similarity approaches such as the tree edit distance models (Section 4.1) are conceptually straightforward. They have some potential for extension by using local distance metrics based on richer similarity resources (e.g., WordNet-based similarity metrics). Heilman et al. [116]'s framework is sufficiently expressive that it can encode a limited set of syntactic transformations, which is an improvement over standard approaches; nevertheless, its overall expressiveness is still quite limited. Simpler approaches are easier to implement and reproduce, but as they strongly constrain the types of resources (knowledge, inference approaches) that can be brought to bear, they appear to have limited potential to significantly improve beyond current performance levels. Nevertheless, given their potential to perform robustly and at scale, they may have a role in textual inference components of larger NLP systems that can use components with only weak predictive capacity.

Paired similarity approaches appear to be quite robust (probably due to the learned inter-pair similarity measure over alignments). However, they still rely on heuristic initial alignments, and it is not straightforward to incorporate knowledge of e.g., syntactic alternations into the tree kernels directly. To automatically learn the space of possible syntactic alternations and comparable anchor terms would appear to require a very large data set. It would be interesting to train them with the (noisy) data sets used by Hickl [117].

Alignment-focused approaches generally view alignment selection as a filtering mechanism, constraining the space of solutions explored by an RTE system. This has clear value when the solution space is large. However, the meaning associated with alignments produced by these models is not clear: for example, it is not immediately clear how to account for implicit (elided) phrases in either the Text or Hypothesis, or to represent alignment for non-trivial contradiction examples. The joint approach of Chang et al. seems intuitively appealing, as alignment properties are not defined ahead of time, but emerge from the constraints chosen and the training corpus. However, alignment selection and local similarity alone do not appear sufficient to determine entailment when the inference process requires consideration of significant linguistic alternations and/or world knowledge.

Logic-based approaches using standard proof-theoretic approaches are brittle, because the representations used (based on e.g., syntactic dependency) and rules in the knowledge base (based on e.g., WordNet) are not sufficiently precise or broad in their coverage, violating necessary conditions for the success of the standard algorithms. Modifications have improved robustness, but more sophisticated models require more complex learning algorithms which need good initialization, and this requires strong intuitions on the part of the system designer (e.g., [201]). So far, these approaches appear to work best in tandem with a back-off model when a logic model has good precision and modest recall.

Transformation-based approaches have come to subsume edit distance approaches by allowing node deletion and insertion, and also search for valid *sequences* of local edit operations [229]. The problems faced are similar to those of standard logic-based approaches; but by opting for a more visually interpretable representation, transformation-based approaches invite alternative strategies for handling errors arising from the induction of representation and from inaccurate or incomplete knowledge. In addition, the representations used in these approaches naturally lend themselves to separating alternative representations of the same underlying text, with the result that they may allow straightforward assessment of individual steps in a proof (transformation sequence) as to the validity of the derived version of the entailment pair. This is an advantage over a logic-based representation that encodes *syntactic* relations as a proxy for *semantic predicates*, where special provision must be made to allow extraction of a particular set of predicates that, combined, represent a given step in the proof in human-readable form. One limitation of these approaches, as with logic-based approaches, is the need for many high-precision rules to capture a large range of possible linguistic alternations; the high cost of producing such rules by hand makes such an effort problematic. However, the straightforward mechanism for incorporating world knowledge is appealing, as the problem of incorporating background knowledge must be overcome to make significant progress in RTE regardless of the representation and inference process used.

NatLog has an appealing underlying model for entailment, though it is limited to simpler phenomena in natural language. Its more complex taxonomy of entailment labels allows a more precise characterization of interactions between scoped semantic phenomena in text spans with comparisons between different surface representations of concepts. One significant limitation is that composition of multiple edit operations (comparisons) often leads to undefined outcomes, as it may result in multiple possible entailment labels for the same abstract semantic structure populated with different concepts. The implementation requires heuristics to replace the conceptual semantic composition representation and inference process using a syntactic parse and a hand coded alignment function to map corresponding elements of the Hypothesis and Text. A significant potential benefit is that the entailment taxonomy may support a divide-and-conquer approach, as it separates out certain linguistic phenomena (modal and presuppositional structures, for example) to be handled separately from quantification and simple monotonicity of concepts.

The decomposition of entailment texts into sets of assertions ("discourse commitments," [118]) is appealing, and similar intuitions underly numerous other approaches (including Wang et al. [251] and Roth and Sammons [209]). Recently, attention has been devoted to systematically identifying distinct inference phenomena in RTE corpora (Bentivogli et al. [18], Sammons et al. [212], LoBue and Yates [147], and Winter et al. [240]); this corresponds to a perceived need to develop specialized inference capabilities that can be integrated and reused. However, broad questions remain about the best way to integrate such capabilities, assuming they can be developed.

To summarize: Simpler RTE approaches such as those based on tree edit distance are easier to work with but have limited potential due to their relative inexpressiveness, but may be practically useful as self-contained components in larger NLP systems that can use weak signals.

In terms of reproducing human performance on entailment recognition, more complex approaches have the potential to deliver more competitive results. Transformation-based and formal logic-based approaches have been extended to provide some degree of robustness against input errors, and offer intuitive strategies for representing and applying linguistic and world knowledge; moreover, they hold the potential to provide explanations (via proofs) of their answers. NatLog's monotonicity calculus suggests an interesting specialization of entailment labels that could form the basis of a more refined model for textual inference, though it may require revisions to address limitations due to the ambiguities arising from composing individual inference operations, and must be extended to more complex sentence constituents. Transformation-based approaches have improved in efficiency and performance, though knowledge acquisition remains a significant obstacle, and models that assign a reliability to rules regardless of context appear to put an upper limit on potential performance. Latent alignment selection models offer a principled way to use the concept of alignment which can potentially improve the efficiency of other approaches by restricting the space of solutions considered.

No single approach tried so far has all the answers; it seems logical to explore ways of combining complementary approaches like alignment and transformations.

CHAPTER 5

Knowledge Acquisition for Textual Entailment

As described throughout this book, textual entailment recognition requires background knowledge, which captures inference relations both within the language as well as in the external "real world" discussed in texts. Accordingly, practically all entailment systems employ some form of external knowledge in their architecture. Such knowledge has been obtained from various types of resources and knowledge acquisition algorithms, which were often developed in other semantic processing contexts rather than specifically for textual entailment.

Since the availability of vast amounts of knowledge is perceived as crucial for effective textual inference, this chapter provides a high-level overview of knowledge resources and acquisition methods that were either employed for textual entailment recognition or are clearly relevant to the task. The chapter may thus be useful for two types of readers: those interested in building inference systems, and who need to understand the potential knowledge resources they can use; and those interested in conducting future research to improve inference knowledge acquisition. Both types of readers are encouraged to follow the cited literature for further detail.

5.1 SCOPE OF TARGET KNOWLEDGE

Loosely speaking, knowledge is usually used to identify that a certain language expression in the text implies the meaning of a different language expression in the hypothesis. In a simple case, such knowledge may correspond to a lexical-semantic relation between two words (or lexical terms), which indicates meaning implication. For example, knowing that *stock* is synonymous to *inventory* in certain contexts enables recognition that the sentences "*I enlarged my stock*" and "*I enlarged my inventory*" entail each other. While synonymy is a symmetric relation, hyponymy illustrates a directional semantic relation useful for directional inference, such as recognizing that "*I have a cat*" entails "*I have a pet*" (but not vice versa). In the context of entailment recognition it is common to refer to these relations as *entailment rules*, or *inference rules*, as they support inferring the Hypothesis from the Text. The above lexical relations may thus be represented by the two rules *stock* → *inventory* and *inventory* → *stock* for these synonymous words (or *stock*↔*inventory* for short), and by *cat* → *pet* for the hyponym relation.

The above examples correspond to classical lexical-semantic relations that have been traditionally used for inference. However, useful meaning implications also hold in more subtle cases. For example, the sentence "*I went to a concert to see Madonna*" entails "*I went to a pop concert,*" suggesting the usefulness of the rule *Madonna→pop*. Similarly, "*I bought diapers for my son*" textually entails "*My son is a baby*," suggesting the rule *diaper → baby*. Obviously, the underlying semantic relationships which license inference in these cases are more complex. In the latter example, proper inference would involve an explicit reasoning step that if someone uses diapers then most likely that someone is a baby. However, such complex knowledge is currently beyond the scope of typical textual inference systems and applications, making a lexical rule such as *diaper → baby* an acceptable substitute. In a typical entailment system, such shallow inference allows us to increase the overall entailment likelihood for the hypothesis, thanks to lexical coverage, even though it does not fully assess the entailment relation between the two texts.

As exemplified earlier in this book, entailment rules may capture meaning implication between more complex structures than just lexical terms. A prominent example is where each side of the rule consists of a template that includes some variables, typically denoting entailment between predicates where the variables specify corresponding argument positions—for example, the rule *X causes Y→Y is a symptom of X*, which is valid in medical contexts. The rule templates may be specified at different levels of linguistic representation, ranging from linear token sequences, possibly including wild cards, to part-of-speech-tagged sequences, up to syntactic parse tree fragments. In the latter case, the left-hand-side of the above rule may be represented as '$X \xleftarrow{subj} cause \xrightarrow{obj} Y$', in this case corresponding to a path in a dependency parse. Finally, entailment rules may capture inferences between purely syntactic structures (not containing any content words), such as a rule denoting that a passive-form sentence can be inferred from the equivalent active form, or that a predicate applied to a conjoined noun phrase typically applies to each of the conjuncts (e.g., "*John and Mary left*" entails "*Mary left*").

The remainder of this chapter reviews various knowledge resources and acquisition methods that have been used for RTE or have a clear potential for it. Section 5.2 describes the use of manually constructed knowledge resources; which were originally constructed either for computational purposes (like WordNet) or for human consumption (like Wikipedia). Next, Section 5.3 reviews the main bulk of work on corpus-based knowledge acquisition, focusing on the use of standard monolingual corpora. It first presents the two main approaches for corpus-based acquisition, namely distributional and co-occurrence based methods, and then provides a short overview of the use of special types of corpora, including parallel and comparable monolingual corpora and bilingual corpora. We then proceed in Section 5.4 to describe approaches for integrating multiple pieces of evidence, including the integration of multiple information sources regarding the same entailment rule as well as information from multiple rules. Section 5.5 discusses the context sensitivity of entailment rules and approaches proposed to address this aspect. The concluding section of this chapter (5.6) provides some perspectives on the current state of research and points at directions for further research. It also refers to the automatic acquisition of entailment-related corpora, which may be used for training entailment recognition methods as well as for further knowledge acquisition of entailment-related knowledge.

As a final note, this chapter focuses on relevant knowledge resources and acquisition methods, rather than on how they have been used within RTE systems. The latter aspect has been included in the descriptions of specific RTE approaches in Chapter 4. Beyond these system-oriented descriptions, several papers in the literature paid special attention to the utility of knowledge and knowledge resources for RTE (e.g., [12, 84, 167]). An additional illuminating perspective on knowledge resources utility is provided by the ongoing endeavor of organized ablation tests as part of the recent RTE challenges. As part of these challenges, participants were asked to submit additional runs of their system, where in each run a major knowledge resource or system module had been ablated. The results of these ablations were included in the organizers' paper of each campaign, measuring the (positive or negative) impact found for various resources in the different systems. Tables consolidating the ablation results from the campaigns are published at the RTE Knowledge Resources page,[1] under the ACL-Wiki Textual Entailment Portal.[2]

5.2   ACQUISITION FROM MANUALLY CONSTRUCTED KNOWLEDGE RESOURCES

A promising source for mining semantic inference knowledge is in knowledge resources that were constructed by humans, and hence are likely to include quite accurate information. Such knowledge resources may be partitioned to two types: those constructed for computational purposes and those constructed for human consumption.

5.2.1   MINING COMPUTATION-ORIENTED KNOWLEDGE RESOURCES

WordNet [90] is by far the most widely used computational lexical resource in Natural Language Processing. It specifies lexical-semantic relations between lexical items such as *hyponymy*, *synonymy*, and *derivation*, where many of its relations capture various cases of meaning implication and correspond directly to lexical entailment rules. For example, the WordNet relation specifying that *'chair'* is a hyponym of *'furniture'* corresponds to the entailment rule *chair → furniture*. Indeed, WordNet has been the most widely used resource in RTE systems, as well as in specific semantic inference applications such as question answering and information extraction.

An immediate issue that has to be considered when using WordNet relations for textual inference is word sense ambiguity. WordNet relations are specified for synonym sets (synsets), where each synset corresponds to a particular sense of the words it contains. Thus, before properly applying the above mentioned rule to an occurrence of the word *chair*, the inference system has to verify that this occurrence corresponds to the furniture sense of the word. One way to address this issue is to apply a Word Sense Disambiguation (WSD) algorithm or tool to determine the appropriate WordNet sense of the targeted word in context. However, since robust and accurate

---

[1]See http://aclweb.org/aclwiki/index.php?title=RTE_Knowledge_Resources for the ablation tests. The page also includes a table of many knowledge resources, often publicly available, which were used by RTE systems including many described in this chapter, along with summary information about their usage in various systems.

[2]http://aclweb.org/aclwiki/index.php?title=Textual_Entailment_Portal

WSD technology is not that commonly used for inference, RTE systems have typically either ignored sense ambiguity or applied simple heuristics, such as considering WordNet relations only if they correspond to the most frequent sense of the involved words. With recent advances in WSD technology, including publicly available state-of-the-art WSD tools, it seems appealing to further investigate their potential utility for textual inference. However, when following such a line of investigation, one should consider the inherent subjectivity in the definition of WordNet senses, and the typical low inter-annotator agreement when manually assigning WordNet senses to words in context. While better WSD success has been obtained with course-grained senses, it is not straightforward to determine how WordNet relations should be mapped to the coarse-grained level, raising additional questions for further research. Section 5.5 discusses more broadly the need to identify the right contexts in which inference rules can be validly applied, and reviews some initial approaches proposed to address this need.

Even though WordNet has been used so extensively, there is no clear consensus about exactly which of its various relations should be exploited for semantic inference, and how. For example, *synonymy* is quite trivially used for symmetric inference, as in the *stock* ↔ *inventory* example given above. *Hyponymy* is typically used for directional inference, such as in the "*I have a cat*" entailing "*I have a pet*" example. However, it should be considered that hyponymy can be used to recognize entailment in this direction only in upward monotone contexts [151], as in this example. In a downward monotone context the inference direction should be reversed, as "*I do not have a pet*" entails "*I do not have a cat*" but not vice versa. However, while models for handling non-monotonicity were proposed in [151] and related work, robust recognition of the monotonicity direction still seems beyond state of the art in most applied systems. Thus, in practice, systems generally assume the upward monotonicity case, which is by far more frequent. Another subtle case involves the *meronym* (part-of) relation, which may trigger entailment in some cases but not in others (see the discussion in [269]).

For verbs, the *troponymy* relation is analogous to hyponymy for nouns, e.g., *sleep* → *rest*. The verb *entailment* relation specifies that the action denoted by one verb implies that denoted by the other, corresponding to entailment rules such as *win* → *compete*. The *antonym* relation, e.g., *sleep* vs. *wake*, is also potentially useful for inference in negated contexts or for detecting contradictions, e.g., *sleeping* entails *not waking*, though inference in this case may be more subtle and has to consider temporal aspects. The *derivationally related* relation links words where one is a morphological derivation of the other, which typically imply each other's meaning as in *acquire* ↔ *acquisition*.

WordNet has notable limitations as a source for entailment rules when predicates are involved. While it indicates the meaning implication between lexical items denoting the predicates, it does not specify the corresponding mapping of arguments for which entailment would hold. For example, WordNet specifies that there is an entailment relation between the predicates '*pay*' and '*buy*', but does not describe the way in which arguments are mapped: *X pay Y for Z* → *X buy Z from Y*. Thus, using WordNet directly to derive predicative entailment rules with predicate-argument templates is possible only for semantic relations such as hyponymy and synonymy, where arguments typically preserve their syntactic positions on both sides of the rule (e.g., *X sleep → X rest*). This limitation of WordNet was partly addressed in the Argument-mapped WordNet method (AmWN) [234], described below. Furthermore, WordNet usually does not cover complex predicate expressions, such as *"cause a reduction in,"* which have been captured by various corpus-based methods as described further below.

A critical aspect to consider when using WordNet relations as entailment rules is *transitivity*. By its logical nature, entailment is a transitive relation. For example, having the two rules *nap → sleep* and *sleep → rest*, both corresponding to troponyms in WordNet, we expect *nap → rest* to be a valid rule as well. However, if we transitively traverse too many WordNet links the textual entailment relation might not be preserved along the whole chain of links, due to sense drift or reaching very abstract terms, such as *object*. Hence, researchers often limit entailment inference to follow WordNet links chains of limited length, such as those consisting of two or three transitivity steps. For example, Shnarch et al. [222] experimented with rule chaining of up to length 4, and presented results where using chains of length two performs better than no chaining, while in [220] they report results for chains of up to length 3. Extended WordNet[3] [170, 171] is a publicly available knowledge resource derived from WordNet which allows transitive chaining of original WordNet links, combined with links that were automatically derived from WordNet's textual glosses (dictionary-style definitions), and has been used in some early RTE systems. It should also be noted that some types of entailment recognition systems, such as transformational approaches (described earlier in Section 2.3.3), transitively chain inferences stemming from multiple entailment rules as part of the inference process. Overall, however, finding an optimal strategy for transitively chaining entailment rules remains an open problem, when using WordNet links and similarly when using other sources of entailment knowledge.

Finally, another limitation of WordNet is that it provides symbolic information, which is not explicitly accompanied by quantitative measures that would help in assessing its likelihood of being effective for practical textual inference. For example, the last sense of the noun *sleep* in WordNet is the euphemism of death, as in *"they had to put their family pet to sleep."* However, employing the rule *sleep → death* in a practical textual entailment system is likely to cause more harm than benefit. The damage in using such unlikely inferences is further amplified when entailment rules are chained, yielding rules such as *nap → death*. One approach to avoid such cases is the first-sense heuristic (or k-first), where entailment rules are derived only from the first sense of each word (or first *k* senses, for some parameter *k*). Another possible approach is to use measures for quantifying semantic similarity or relatedness based on WordNet links [36, 188], hoping that it will correlate with the likelihood of entailment when applying the corresponding rules. Estimating the likelihood of validity of applying a certain entailment rule is also related to the problem of ambiguity, or context matching in general. In particular, a rule derived for a certain sense of a word in WordNet should be applied, in principle, only for occurrences of this word

---

[3]http://xwn.hlt.utdallas.edu/index.html

having the same sense. However, since Word Sense Disambiguation (WSD) is rarely applied within RTE systems or related applications, such sense matching is not performed. The general issue of matching entailment rules in context is further discussed in the concluding section of this chapter.

Some other computational lexical resources provide complementary information to that found in WordNet, which addresses some of WordNet's shortcomings. The Categorial-Variation Database[4] (Catvar) [107] is a database specifying sets of derivationally related lexical items with their part-of-speech in English (e.g., *'trick::noun', 'trick::verb', 'trickery::noun', 'trickery::adjective'*). It thus overlaps with the derivationally related links in WordNet, but provides broader coverage of derivations. In [222] it improved the performance of a lexical entailment system over using WordNet alone. Nomlex [152] is a lexical database that goes a step further with regard to nominalizations, and provides the mapping of arguments between nominal and verbal forms of predicates. Based on this information, it has been used to derive predicative entailment rules, such as *X's treatment of Y ↔ Y's treatment by X ↔ X treat Y* [161, 234].

FrameNet [5] is a lexicographic resource that is arranged around "frames:" each frame corresponds to an event type and includes information on the predicates and argument roles relevant for that specific event, supplemented with annotated examples that specify argument positions. For instance, FrameNet contains an *'attack'* frame, and specifies that *'attack'* events include an *'assailant'*, a *'victim'*, a *'weapon'*, etc. In addition, Framenet provides a list of lexical items that belong to the *'attack'* frame, such as *'attack', 'bomb', 'charge', 'invade'*, and more. Ben Aharon et al. [17] consolidated various types of information in FrameNet to generate predicative entailment rules, which specify both an entailment relation between predicates, and the corresponding argument mapping: for example, *cure X → X recover*. Their method induces entailment relations between certain predicates within the same frame and across related frames that are linked by certain relations indicative of entailment. Argument mapping is based on the semantic role indications available in FrameNet. Finally, the resulting set of rules is augmented through transitive closure. Manual evaluation of a random sample of the resulting rule resource, named FRED,[5] indicated an accuracy of 69%. Results of an experiment using the ACE 2005 event extraction dataset[6] showed improved performance relative to the earlier LexPar rule resource extracted from FrameNet by Conyne and Rambow [68]. LexPar contains mostly entailment relations that can be identified in WordNet, and hence its rules can be viewed as an intersection of WordNet and FrameNet lexical relations, accompanied with argument mappings based on FrameNet argument roles. Following these exploitations of FrameNet, future work may investigate the potential utility of PropBank [131], which bears similarities to FrameNet and contains a corpus of sentences annotated with predicates and their role-labeled arguments.

---

[4]Available at http://clipdemos.umiacs.umd.edu/catvar/
[5]Available at http://www.cs.biu.ac.il/nlp/downloads
[6]http://projects.ldc.upenn.edu/ace/

5.2.2 MINING HUMAN-ORIENTED KNOWLEDGE RESOURCES

The resources reviewed so far were created for computational purposes and were consequently exploited for mining entailment-related knowledge, even though they were not necessarily designed primarily for this purpose. Beyond the exploitation of such resources, it also makes sense to mine entailment knowledge from resources that were created primarily for human consumption, through automatic analysis of the information they contain. The first and most natural candidate for providing such knowledge is dictionary definitions. These definitions have long been identified as a valuable source for semantic relations between words, as they describe words in terms of other words [122]. Definitions typically describe the defined concept by giving a genus term, which is usually a hypernym of that concept. For example, the definition of *car* would refer to its genus *vehicle*, along with additional differentiating properties such as moving on wheels. Many works on extracting information from machine readable dictionaries (MRD) have tried to extract such textually expressed information and make it explicitly available for computational use. Chodorow et al. [55] observed that the genus term is typically the head of the defining phrase and suggested simple heuristics to extract it. Other methods use a specialized parser or a set of regular expressions tuned to a particular dictionary (e.g., [180]; [255] describes the extensive early lines of work on MRDs, including an overview of automatic techniques for analyzing them). With respect to the Extended WordNet resource mentioned above, Moldovan and Rus [171] parse the definitions ("glosses") in WordNet and transform them into logical form, enabling explicit representation of the relations they express. Similarly to information mined from WordNet, once the knowledge expressed in dictionary definitions is made explicit, much of it may be turned into entailment rules (e.g., *car* → *vehicle*, per the example above).

More recently, the vast encyclopedic and lexical knowledge available in Wikipedia has become an attractive target for extracting semantic information. Shnarch et al. [219] focused particularly on extracting entailment rules from Wikipedia and provide a knowledge base of about 8 million rules.[7] Similar to knowledge extraction from dictionary definitions, they start by analyzing the syntactic structure of the first sentence of a Wikipedia article and identifying the main copula (*is a*) construction it contains, resulting in high-precision rules like *Jim Carrey* → *actor* and *Jim Carrey* → *comedian*. A similar approach was applied by Kazama and Torisawa for first sentences in Wikipedia articles [129]. Shnarch et al. also heuristically created rules for which the left-hand side is the concept name defined by the article and right-hand side is any head noun or base noun phrase appearing in the first sentence of the article (termed *All-Nouns*). This results in lower precision rules, but provides additional cases of lexical entailment other than hyponymy, which is the type of relation typically extracted from copula structures. In addition to the textual information in the definition sentence of the article, they exploit three types of more structured information appearing in Wikipedia: (1) *Redirect* links, which typically capture synonyms, alternative names, and spelling variations for the same concept or named entity, generating bi-directional rules between the alternative terms (*CPU* ↔ *Central processing unit*, *Hypertension* ↔ *Elevated*

---

[7]Available at `http://u.cs.biu.ac.il/~nlp/downloads/index.htm`

blood-pressure, U.S. ↔ USA); (2) disambiguation terms, which appear in parenthesis following a searched Wikipedia concept in a disambiguation page (*graph → mathematics, graph → data structure*); (3) hyperlinks in an article text pointing to another Wikipedia article. For each link a rule is generated where the left-hand side is the linking text and the right-hand side is the title of the linked article (*pet → Domesticated Animal, Gestaltist → Gestalt psychology*). Shnarch et al. evaluated manually the accuracy of each of the above extraction types over a random sample, which yielded accuracies ranging from 0.87 (for *redirect* rules) to 0.7 (hyperlink rules), with the exception of the 3 million (out of 8 million) *All-Nouns* rules whose accuracy is about 0.5. This rule base was later used within the BIUTEE system at the RTE-7 challenge [228] and contributed 1.56% to its F1 score (being a substantial contribution relative to typical single-resource impacts).

Other works mined Wikipedia and generated hierarchical concept taxonomies, which may serve as an additional source for entailment rules similar to the use of WordNet for this purpose. Ponzetto and Strube [195] identify the subsumption (IS-A) relation between Wikipedia category tags using basic syntactic, connectivity-based, and pattern-based methods. Suchanek et al. [230] use category tags to extract entities and facts from Wikipedia, which are then unified with Word-Net using rule-based and heuristic methods, creating the YAGO semantic knowledge base which integrates the two resources. In a somewhat similar vein, Yamada et al. [256] extend WordNet with hypernyms and siblings appearing in Wikipedia, determining their position in WordNet (their *synset*) by integrating evidence derived from the structure of an article in Wikipedia and distributional similarity of terms. Their experiments show that the method can identify synsets for over 2 million terms appearing in Wikipedia with a precision of 0.84.

Finally, the TAREC (TAxonomic RElation Classifier) algorithm of Do and Roth [85] is related to the works above in that it tries to determine taxonomic relations (*ancestor* and *sibling*) based on information in Wikipedia. However, rather than extracting all possible term relationships and building a stationary hierarchical structure for them, TAREC is a classifier that recognizes on the fly the taxonomic relation between any two terms given as input. TAREC simulates a reference ontology by searching and selecting the top relevant articles in Wikipedia for each input term; taxonomic relations are then recognized based on the features extracted from these articles and relations in the Wikipedia category structure. The authors suggest this approach as an appealing alternative to using stationary resources, and present an experimental evaluation showing that their approach significantly outperforms other systems built upon existing well-known knowledge sources.

5.3   CORPUS-BASED KNOWLEDGE ACQUISITION

While manually constructed knowledge resources provide relatively accurate information, their coverage of semantic information is inevitably incomplete. Hence, a prominent line of ongoing research is dedicated to automatic learning of semantic knowledge from corpora. This section provides an overview of corpus-based methods for semantic knowledge acquisition that have either been used for RTE or have a clear potential for it. These include acquisition from regular "off-line" corpora, as well as the use of the web as a corpus, which has an impact on the computational processing techniques that can be used.

Generally speaking, two major types of corpus information have been exploited to learn semantic relationships between language expressions (terms and templates): (1) distributional similarity information, which considers occurrences of the target expressions throughout the corpus and comparing the contexts in which they occur; (2) co-occurrence information, which considers adjacent occurrences of the target expressions, usually in the same sentence, and exploits their co-occurrence patterns. The following two subsections review these two approaches, followed by a subsection dedicated to the use of special types of corpora (parallel and comparable monolingual corpora and bilingual parallel corpora). Broader approaches which consider the integration of these and other sources of information are described in the next section. The interested reader is directed to the survey articles of Madnani and Dorr [154] and Androutsopoulos and Malakasiotis (Section 4) [4], which include overviews of relevant acquisition methods for paraphrasing and textual entailment.

5.3.1   DISTRIBUTIONAL SIMILARITY METHODS

Distributional similarity methods follow the classical *distributional hypothesis* [112], which suggests that words that tend to occur in similar contexts have similar meanings. Accordingly, these methods gather information about the contexts in which two words (or other language expressions) occur and assess the degree of similarity between their context representations, in order to determine the degree of semantic "similarity" between the two words. While the notion of semantic similarity that can be identified by this approach is somewhat loose, distributional similarity often coincides with semantic equivalence or entailment relations, and was therefore incorporated in several entailment systems and studies (see [167] for a comparative study including distributional similarity and other entailment knowledge sources). The basic distributional similarity technique has been investigated and described extensively in language technology textbooks and papers; we first illustrate it briefly, and then describe extensions which were geared more concretely to acquire inference-related knowledge.

Distributional similarity for terms and predicative templates
Distributional similarity algorithms typically represent the target language elements whose similarity we want to assess as vectors of context features. In the simplest configuration, the target elements are words or lexical terms, and the context features are other words with which the target words occur throughout the corpus. For example, for the target words *book* and *novel*, the context vector for each word would consist of other words with which the target word occurred, such as *author*, *write*, *read*, and *interesting*. Next, in order to assess the semantic similarity between the two words their context vectors are compared using some vector similarity measure. In our example, we expect the similarity between the two context vectors to be high, since the sets of context words with which *book* and *novel* occur are likely to have a substantial overlap.

The language processing literature includes numerous variants of this scheme. For example, rather than considering context features to be words in a surrounding window, many works defined them to be words that are syntactically related to the target word via a dependency relation in a parsed corpus, in which case the feature consists of the combination of the word and the connecting dependency relation (e.g. [141]). Various vector similarity measures have been employed for comparing feature vectors, such as cosine similarity (following the Information Retrieval tradition), Weighted Jaccard, information theoretic measures ([140]), and others. As an illustration, we present here the widely used similarity measure of Dekang Lin [141].

Denoting two target words to be compared by u and v, and their corresponding sets (vectors) of features by F^u and F^v, Lin first defines the *weight* of each feature f in a word's vector by the pointwise mutual information between the feature and the corresponding word: $w^u(f) = \log \frac{Pr(f|u)}{Pr(f)}$, where the probabilities are computed using maximum likelihood over the corpus, and a zero weight is assigned if f never occurs with u. The *Lin* similarity measure for the two words u and v is then defined by:

$$Lin(u, v) = \frac{\sum_{f \in F^u \cap F^v} [w^u(f) + w^v(f)]}{\sum_{f \in F^u} w^u(f) + \sum_{f \in F^v} w^v(f)} \tag{5.1}$$

As can be seen from the equation, the similarity measure indeed captures the relative overlap in the two words' contexts: it is proportional to the cumulative weight of their overlapping features, normalized by the sum of feature weights in both vectors. As can be expected, this measure often captures synonymy and hyponymy relations, which may or may not be available from manually constructed resources. However, distributional similarity also captures other types of entailment-related lexical relations. For example, in the study mentioned above, Mirkin et al. [167] illustrate other types of valid entailment rules that were produced by the Lin similarity method, such as *government → official, mortgage → bank* and *childbirth → motherhood*. The first two examples were learned with features corresponding to words appearing in the proximity of the target word, while the latter was learned when features corresponded to words related to the target word through a dependency relation. Additional examples for variants of the distributional similarity scheme include the work of Pasca and Dienes [187], who extract word and phrase paraphrases from an unparsed web snapshot in an unsupervised manner, where context features are n-grams. Bhagat and Ravichandran [29] present an unsupervised method for extracting paraphrases from a large 150GB pos-tagged corpus, where elements are POS-tagged phrases and features are nouns or noun-noun compounds.

When learning entailment rules for predicative templates, the elements correspond to these templates, often containing some syntactic information, while the features are the arguments that instantiate the template's variable slots throughout the corpus. Using this representation, one would expect to discover high distributional similarity between entailing templates, which tend to take the same sets of arguments. For example, we expect that *buy X* and *own X* would have similar sets of arguments throughout the corpus, since any object that can be bought can also be owned.

Lin and Pantel [143] introduced the highly cited *DIRT* algorithm for learning inference rules between binary templates, each including a pair of variables, such as *X buy Y* and *X own Y*. This algorithm applies the above *Lin* similarity measure over the template-based representation. The predicates are represented by *binary propositional templates*, which are dependency paths in a parsed sentence between two arguments of a predicate, where the arguments are replaced by variables. Note that in a dependency tree, a path between two arguments must pass through their common predicate. Also note that if a predicate has more than two arguments, then it is represented by more than one binary template, where each template corresponds to a different pair of arguments. For example, the propositional template *'X buy Y for Z'* contains a predicate and three argument positions. It would therefore be represented in the DIRT algorithm by the following three templates, each including another pair of dependency edges: '$X \xleftarrow{subj} buy \xrightarrow{obj} Y$', '$Y \xleftarrow{obj} buy \xrightarrow{prep} for \xrightarrow{pcomp-n} Z$' and '$X \xleftarrow{subj} buy \xrightarrow{prep} for \xrightarrow{pcomp-n} Z$'.

For each template DIRT computes two feature vectors F_X and F_Y, containing the nouns that instantiate the argument slots X and Y, respectively, from a large corpus. Then, to determine the similarity between two templates u and v, the algorithm computes the Lin similarity score separately for the X vectors of the two templates and for their Y vectors, yielding two corresponding similarity values, $Lin_X(u, v)$ and $Lin_Y(u, v)$. The overall similarity between the two templates, termed *DIRT*, is the geometric average of the scores for the two variable slots:

$$DIRT(u, v) = \sqrt{Lin_x(u, v) \cdot Lin_y(u, v)} \tag{5.2}$$

If $DIRT(u, v)$ is high, this means that the templates u and v share many "informative" arguments and so the predicates are semantically similar. While this does not guarantee an entailment relation between the predicates, Lin and Pantel proposed DIRT as an algorithm for learning inference rules in the context of Question Answering. Their evaluation showed that many of the learned rules yielded valid inferences, although accuracy was mediocre since many other learned rules were invalid. Some examples given in their paper for rules that yielded valid inferences include *X manufactures Y ↔ X produces Y* and *X manufactures Y ↔ X is supplier of Y*.[8]

A notable limitation of the distributional measures discussed so far, including the DIRT algorithm, with respect to entailment inference is that they are *symmetric*. That is, the similarity value between u and v is identical to that between v and u. This is why we considered the above two DIRT rules to be bidirectional, as DIRT does not provide any information regarding the entailment direction. However, while the first rule above is indeed bidirectional, since *manufacture* and *produce* are largely synonymous, the second rule is not, and holds only in the left-to-right direction: a manufacturer of a product typically supplies it, but a supplier is often not the original

---

[8]As of the time of writing, the set of rules produced by the original DIRT implementation may be obtained upon request from the DIRT authors. The output of a re-implementation of the algorithm by the Bar-Ilan University NLP lab, run over the Reuters corpus, is available at `http://u.cs.biu.ac.il/~nlp/downloads/index.htm`.

manufacturer. Hence, since entailment is a directional relation, it is desirable to devise *directional* similarity measures to predict the entailment direction, as described next.

Directional distributional similarity

Most directional distributional similarity approaches were based on the intuition that semantically broader expressions occur in more contexts than semantically narrower ones. Thus, if the contexts of a term or predicate u are (almost) properly *included* in the contexts of v, then this might imply that $u \rightarrow v$, even though entailment might not hold in the opposite direction. For example, we can observe that *biscuit* co-occurs with words such as *tasty, homemade, prepare,* and *ingredient,* and expect that its hypernym *food* will co-occur with all of them as well. However, the broader term *food* will co-occur with many other words that are unlikely to occur with *biscuit,* such as *fast* and *juicy.*

Geffet and Dagan [100] suggested this idea as a *distributional inclusion hypothesis,* and presented a concrete implementation of it using web queries to obtain comprehensive information about word-context co-occurrences when testing for inclusion. Bhagat et al. designed the LEDIR algorithm [28] for learning predicative inference rules, which first uses a symmetric similarity measure, but then attempts to recognize the true directionality of each predicative entailment rule based on the number of contexts with which the left-hand side and right-hand side of the rule occur, assuming that more general predicates occur in more contexts. They use the same template representation for predicates as in the DIRT algorithm, but their features were based on the *semantic classes* of the arguments rather than on individual argument terms. A similar rationale of context inclusion was used to learn concept hierarchies in the formal context analysis of Cimiano et al. [58].

As part of investigating a broader similarity scheme, Weeds and Weir [252] defined a directional distributional similarity measure that incorporates the inclusion principle directly into the similarity formula, introducing the *Cover* measure:

$$Cover(u, v) = \frac{\sum_{f \in F^u \cap F^v} w^u(f)}{\sum_{f \in F^u} w^u(f)} \tag{5.3}$$

This measure quantifies the relative degree by which the contexts of u are included in those of v. It can be noted at this point that in cases where most contexts of u do appear with v, but many contexts of v do not occur with u, a symmetric measure like *Lin* would yield a relatively low score. This is because symmetric measures quantify the degree of feature overlap relative to the accumulated weight of *both* vectors (the normalization factor in the denominator). On the other hand, the directional *Cover* measure would yield a high similarity score because it normalizes only by the accumulated weight of u's features.

Szpektor and Dagan [233] examined the *Cover* measure for learning entailment rules for predicate templates and discovered that it tends to produce noisy entailment rules due to the very strict inclusion test. For example, if a predicate u is infrequent and occurred in the corpus with rather few context features then we might obtain for it, by chance, high inclusion proportions within vectors of some frequent predicates that occasionally occurred with many different context features. To reduce such noisy effects, they counter-balanced the strict inclusion test by averaging it with the symmetric *Lin* measure. Their proposed *Balanced Inclusion (BInc)* measure is the geometric mean of the *Cover* and *Lin* measures:

$$BInc(u, v) = \sqrt{Lin(u, v) \cdot Cover(u, v)} \qquad (5.4)$$

In their evaluations, Szpektor and Dagan show that *Balanced Inclusion* outperformed DIRT and LEDIR when tested over the same predicate representation (using unary templates, described below).

More recently, Kotlerman et al. [135] conducted data analysis of various aspects of directional lexical similarity. Consequently, they developed a novel type of distributional inclusion measure, called *APinc*, which is derived from the *Average Precision* (AP) ranking evaluation measure. Following the general scheme of the AP measure, *APinc* considers feature ranks in the vectors of both the narrower and broader terms, as well as overall vector length. Like *Balanced Inclusion*, they also found that it is better to balance the inclusion measure with a symmetric one, yielding their final *balAPinc* measure which is the geometric mean of *APinc* and *Lin*. Their evaluation showed that *balAPinc* typically outperforms prior measures in detecting entailment direction and in an event detection setting that is based on directional lexical inference. Their lexical entailment rule knowledge base was made publicly available,[9] and was used within the BIUTEE system at the RTE-7 challenge [228], contributing almost 1% to its F1 score.

Choices in feature, template, and rule representation
When applying distributional similarity methods, different representations may be chosen both for the features and for the elements between which similarity is measured, particularly when measuring similarity for predicate templates whose structure is more complex.

As already noted, when the elements are lexical items, like *novel* or *book*, features may be either individual words appearing in their context, like *read*, or words that are syntactically related to the target element through a dependency relation together with that relation, for example *<read, subj-head>* or *<interesting, adj-modifier>*. Another choice, as used in the LEDIR algorithm, is to consider as features the semantic class of an argument word rather than the word itself, obtaining generalized features and reducing data sparsity.

When the elements are predicate templates, the features are derived in some way from the arguments appearing in their variable slots throughout the corpus. As described above, DIRT employs two separate feature vectors, one for each argument position, in which the features are the corresponding argument words. Schoenmackers et al. [215, 216] made several different choices in their representations. Regarding features, a feature in their work is a *pair* of arguments (e.g., *(Microsoft,Redmond)*), as opposed to computing a separate similarity score for each argument,

[9]http://www.cs.biu.ac.il/nlp/downloads

which effectively decouples the arguments from one another. Although this decoupling alleviates sparsity problems, it disregards an important piece of information, namely the joint appearance of arguments. For example, consider the following propositions: *"coffee increases blood pressure," "coffee decreases fatigue," "wine decreases blood pressure," "wine increases fatigue."* A method like DIRT would identify that the predicates occur with similar subject arguments and object arguments, considered separately, and might mistakenly infer that *"decrease ↔ increase."* However, looking at pairs of arguments reveals that the predicates do not share a single pair of arguments. Schoenmackers et al. prefer to use the more informative pairs of arguments as features since their data is a large web-based corpus, providing substantial information also at the sparser pair level. This type of feature representation is also shared by Szpektor et al.'s web-based method TEASE [237] (described below), which uses argument pairs, as well as the LEDIR algorithm, which uses pairs of argument semantic classes.

Other different choices made by Schoenmackers et al. regard template representation. Their syntactic representation of propositions is much shallower—no parsing is performed, and binary propositions are represented simply as tuples of strings $argument_1$,predicate,$argument_2$, or equivalently $pred(arg_1, arg_2)$. Further, arguments are typed, that is, variables slots may be restricted to be, for example, some type of *country*, *disease*, *profession*, etc. Hence, a propositional template is a *typed predicate* described as $pred(X_{Type_1}, Y_{Type_2})$.

In the above mentioned work of Szpektor and Dagan [233], where the directional *balanced inclusion* measure was introduced, they also proposed a modified predicate representation. Instead of using binary propositional templates as elements, Szpektor and Dagan represented predicates with *unary propositional templates*, which contain a predicate and a single argument, such as: '$X \xleftarrow{subj} buy$'. Szpektor and Dagan explained that unary templates are more expressive than binary templates, because they can account for arbitrary arity by applying several unary rules for the same predicate during inference. In particular, inference for intransitive verb occurrences can only be encoded using unary templates.

Finally, Schoenmackers et al. allowed a richer structure of the learned inference rules. Their rule representation is inspired by ideas from Inductive Logic Programming [174, 199]. In this framework, the left-hand side of the rule may be composed of a conjunction of propositional templates (also known as *Horn clauses*). A rule might state, for example, that if a company is headquartered in a city, and the city is located in some state, then this implies that the company is based in that state. Such a rule can be denoted by '$IsHeadquarteredIn(X_{Company}, Y_{City}) \land IsLocatedIn(Y_{City}, Z_{State}) \Rightarrow IsBasedIn(X_{Company}, Z_{State})$'. A similar representation has also been recently proposed in the NELL project [43].

Learning predicative entailment rules from the Web

Obviously, we expect that the performance of distributional methods would improve when using larger corpora, which provide richer statistics on element-feature co-occurrence and alleviate data sparseness. This motivation has driven a line of research that exploits the web as a corpus, particularly for learning inference rules for predicates. The main computational difference when using the web is that it cannot be processed exhaustively to collect all predicate-argument co-occurrences. Instead, web search engine queries are used to retrieve texts in which a certain predicate appears and then co-occurring arguments are identified in these texts; or vice versa—retrieving texts in which certain arguments appear and identifying in them co-occurring predicates. A prominent example for applying this approach to learn predicative entailment rules is the TEASE algorithm of Szpektor et al. [237], which applies both types of searches to obtain an unsupervised web-based acquisition method.

TEASE receives as input a list of target predicative templates for which entailment rules are sought, termed *pivots*. Szpektor et al. suggest that such pivots may be obtained automatically from verb lexicons, though other methods may be envisioned to obtain them for a target domain or application. In the first step of the algorithm, given an input template, a sample corpus is generated for this pivot via queries to a search engine by retrieving sentences containing the pivot term.. Each sentence is analyzed to fetch an *anchor set* of noun phrases, which includes the arguments of the template in the sentence and optionally an additional context anchor. The anchor sets are collected from all sentences retrieved for the pivot, and various statistical filters are used to exclude overly specific and overly general anchor sets. For example, for the pivot template *X prevent Y* the identified anchor sets included {*X = sunscreen, Y = sunburn*}, {*X = safety valve, Y = leakage*} and {*X = vitamin D, Y = fractures, context-anchor = elderly people*}.

In the second step of the TEASE algorithm a search query is issued for the words in each anchor set, obtaining a second sample corpus in which each sentence contains one of the anchor sets. The corpus sentences are aggregated into an efficient compact representation, from which maximally specific recurring templates are extracted and ranked by statistical criteria. By construction, these templates occur with several of the anchor sets that originally co-occurred with the pivot template: that is, they share multiple argument tuples with the pivot. Therefore, according to the distributional hypothesis criterion, the extracted templates are suggested as candidates to hold an entailment relation with the original pivot. For the above example of the *X prevent Y* pivot, the candidate templates extracted included *X protect against Y, X lower risk of Y, Y vaccine is X*, and even *X a day keep Y away*. The entailment direction for the corresponding entailment rules, between the pivot and each of the extracted templates, is not predicted by TEASE. Finally, given the new set of extracted templates, the anchor set extraction phase can be repeated for these new templates, yielding an iterative bootstrapping scheme. While in the original TEASE paper [237] only one iteration was performed, an iterative application of TEASE was used by Romano et al. [207] in a relation extraction task to generate a set of entailing templates for the protein interaction relation. In this work, they used TEASE to learn rules for the pivot template *X interacts with Y*.

With respect to the distributional similarity scheme, several properties of TEASE may be noted. First, the anchor sets correspond to the distributional features characterizing each template. As mentioned above, this choice corresponds to the use of argument *pairs* as features by

Schoenmackers et al. Referring to the example given above to illustrate the Schoenmackers et al. method, TEASE would regard each of {*coffee, blood pressure*}, {*coffee, fatigue*}, {*wine, blood pressure*}, and {*wine, fatigue*}, as a separate anchor set. Second, a notable characteristic of TEASE's template extraction phase is that any recurring template structure may be identified, without limiting template structure to a dependency path, as DIRT and other algorithms do. Third, while the statistical criteria of TEASE are symmetric, and hence do not predict the entailment direction, it seems possible to adopt within this framework later principles of the distributional inclusion hypothesis in order to model the directionality aspect.

Evaluations in the original TEASE paper [237], and later in [236] using an improved evaluation methodology, showed that TEASE and DIRT have quite comparable performance in terms of precision and coverage. However, they are largely complementary, with only 15% overlap in their output [236]. It was hypothesized by the authors that this may be because the DIRT rule base was generated from a corpus in the news domain, whereas TEASE learns from the web, extracting rules from multiple domains. Since their precision is comparable, they suggest that it may be best to use both algorithms in tandem.

Ravichandran and Hovy [203] propose an algorithm for learning from the web predicative templates that entail a target predicate in a Question Answering setting. Their algorithm applies a similar scheme to TEASE, in an iterative manner, but use surface patterns to represent templates rather than parse fragments. However, the algorithm they propose requires some seed anchor sets to be identified manually and given to the algorithm as initial input for each target predicate. Only then can some entailing templates be identified based on the seed anchors and the iterations proceed. Obviously, such an approach has limited scalability, as it requires careful manual construction of inputs for each target. Finally, it should be pointed out that iterative bootstrapping schemes of the above kinds were often explored in the Relation Extraction literature, such as in the Espresso system of Pantel and Pennacchiotti [186], where the eventual goal is extracting mentions of a target relation in corpora. To that end, iterative bootstrapping methods are used to learn templates that entail the target relation, which is quite analogous to learning left-hand sides of entailment rules whose right-hand side expresses the target relation.

While web-based methods are attractive in that they make it possible to obtain statistics for relatively rare events, a major drawback is their dependence on issuing web search engine queries. Applying such methods at large scales requires access to very large quotas of web search queries, which are not available to most researchers. Run time is also relatively slow compared to local processing. With the gradual increase in the capacity of computing resources and available corpora size, it has become common to process very large corpora, often based on large web dumps (such as the work of Schoenmackers et al. described above). Still, web-based methods may be suitable whenever the above limitations do not hold, or when aiming to learn entailment rules for a limited number of predicates in a target domain. On the other hand, search-based bootstrapping methods may be useful also for locally indexed large corpora, in cases where it is desireable to avoid exhaustive processing of the full corpus.

5.3.2 CO-OCCURRENCE-BASED METHODS

Co-occurrence-based methods are complementary to distributional similarity methods in that they tap into a different source of information. As described above, when learning an entailment rule, distributional methods examine distinct occurrences of its left-hand side and its right-hand side and determine whether the two tend to occur in similar contexts. Co-occurrence-based methods, on the other hand, examine *joint* occurrences of the two rule sides in the same text. They then examine the patterns which connect these expressions throughout the corpus, looking for patterns that characterize an entailment relation between them. As illustrated below, some of these patterns may be quite reliable in predicting the semantic relation holding between the two elements. However, the downside of this approach is that such indicative joint occurrences of the rule sides may be quite rare, making the co-occurrence based approach more sensitive to data sparseness than distributional methods, typically requiring larger corpora.

Acquiring noun relations through targeted patterns

Learning semantic relations using co-occurrence patterns was first articulated in Hearst's seminal paper [115] on automatic acquisition from large corpora of the *hyponymy* (*is-a*) relation between nouns. The key insight was that the hyponymy relation is quite reliably implied by certain template patterns which connect noun occurrences. For example, the patterns "NP_y *such as* NP_x," as in *fruits such as oranges*, or "NP_x *and/or other* NP_y," as in *oranges and other fruits*, often imply that NP_x is a kind of NP_y. Note that the information conveyed in such patterns is clearly *directional*, indicating which noun is the hyponym (*oranges*) and which is the hypernym (*fruit*). The basic pattern-based approach searches a large corpus for such indicative patterns and proposes noun pairs that occur within them, possibly satisfying some statistical filtering criteria, as candidates for the hyponym-hypernym relation.

Many researchers have expanded on Hearst's work in various ways to automatically acquire the hyponymy relation [41, 57, 138, 254], as well as other generic relations such as *meronymy* (*part-of*)[27, 103] and even certain bio-medical relations between genes and proteins [95]. For example, the patterns "NP_y *is composed of* NP_x" and "NP_y *is constituted of* NP_x" designates that NP_x is a meronym of NP_y.

While Hearst's patterns provide an effective acquisition method, they have been found to extract a substantial proportion of incorrect instances of the hyponymy relation, due to pattern-matching errors and to context-specific expressions of patterns which do not imply a generic hyponymy relation. To increase hyponymy extraction accuracy, Kozareva et al. [137] suggested using more specific *doubly anchored* patterns which are based on those of Hearst. Their setting assumes that a class name is given (the hypernym, like *fruit*), along with a single known seed class member (a single example of a hyponym, like *orange*). The goal is then to find additional members of the given class (additional hyponyms, like *apple* and *banana*).

Given the two input nouns, the method then searches for indicative patterns in which the class name occurs together with the known class member in conjunction with another noun, which is then identified as a candidate for being an additional class member. For example, given the input pair *fruit* and *orange*, the method would search for occurrences of patterns like '*fruits such as oranges and NP$_x$*' and '*oranges and NP$_x$ or other fruits*'. Nouns instantiating NP$_x$ in the pattern occurrences in the corpus are then extracted as additional hyponyms of *fruit*. Such doubly anchored patterns are much less frequent in a corpus, but when found the extracted words have a higher likelihood of belonging to the hypernym class. These patterns also provide disambiguation for different senses of the class name. For example, for the class *president* it is not clear whether country presidents or corporate presidents are sought as class members, but the target sense is disambiguated by the seed class member (e.g., *Obama*). To cope with data sparseness Kozareva et al. used a large Web corpus.

In a followup work, Kozareva et al. [137] applied the doubly anchored patterns in a typical bootstrapping scheme in order to extract a richer taxonomy of nouns falling under a root concept. The algorithm receives as input the root concept name and one seed example for a hyponym. It then works in alternating rounds: extracting additional hyponyms, by instantiating the doubly anchored patterns with a known class name and a class member (as described above), and extracting new hypernym terms that are subordinate to the root concept, by instantiating the patterns with previously acquired pairs of class members and looking for new instantiations of the class name.

Co-occurrence-based acquisition without pre-specified patterns

The approaches mentioned above rely on a limited set of patterns that have been identified as reliable indicators for a target semantic relation. Snow et al. [224] propose an important extension to the pattern-based approach for learning hyponyms. Instead of using a limited set of designated patterns, they consider *all* syntactic dependency patterns that are found to connect pairs of nouns in a large corpus. In this way, they exploit tens of thousands of patterns while learning each pattern's importance with respect to the target hyponymy relation using a supervised linear classifier. For every pair of nouns, they extract all sentences in which the nouns co-occur, and then use the syntactic patterns linking the nouns as features, represented as dependency paths. Hence, a pair of nouns is represented by a feature vector where each entry counts the number of times in which a certain syntactic pattern links the pair of nouns in the corpus.

To generate a training set for the classifier Snow et al. employ "distant supervision," that is, positive and negative examples are generated automatically using a lexicographic resource (in this case, WordNet). A pair of WordNet nouns is considered a positive example if they are hyponyms in WordNet, and a negative example if both nouns exist in WordNet and neither one is the ancestor of the other in the hyponymy hierarchy. A classifier is then trained on the training set and is used to classify new unseen pairs of nouns. Snow et al. show that this method significantly outperforms the use of the pre-specified Hearst patterns in hyponymy extraction.

Table 5.1: The five pattern groups suggested by Chklovsky and Pantel and an example pattern for each group

Semantic relation	Example pattern
similarity	V_1 i.e., V_2
strength	V_2 and even V_1
enablement	to V_2 by V_1ing the
antonymy	either V_1 or V_2
happens-before	to V_1 and subsequently V_2

Co-occurrence-based acquisition of verb relationships

Co-occurrence based methods are typically more suitable for nouns than for verbs, since nouns tend to co-occur in sentences more often than verbs do. Nevertheless, some works developed co-occurrence-based approaches for learning semantic relationships between verbs. Notably, Chklovsky and Pantel [54] used pre-specified lexical patterns to discover semantic relations between verbs in their *VerbOcean* system. In a method similar to that of Hearst, they manually constructed 33 patterns divided into five pattern groups, with each group indicating a different target semantic relation: *similarity, strength, antonymy, enablement,* and *happens-before.* Table 5.1 specifies the five pattern groups and provides an example pattern for each group. For example, from the sentence *"He scared and even startled me."* one may infer that *"startle"* is semantically stronger than *"scare."* Pairs of verbs were then classified to semantic relations according to their frequency of occurrence in each of the 33 patterns. Since verbs rarely instantiate lexical patterns in a sentence, Chklovsky and Pantel used the web as their corpus via search engine queries, and constructed the substantial VerbOcean knowledge resource of verb relationships.[10]

With respect to entailment, the VerbOcean *similarity* relation often corresponds to mutual entailment between the two verbs (e.g., *produce* ↔ *create*), the *strength* relation often corresponds to directional entailment (e.g., *startle* → *scare*), while *antonymy* indicates contradiction (e.g., *close* vs. *open*). The relations of *enablement* (e.g., *win* → *fight*) and *happens-before* (e.g., *buy* → *own*) may also serve as looser indicators of entailment, though the entailment direction for them is less predictable (e.g., in *divorce* → *marry* the temporal order is reversed to that in *buy* → *own*). Thanks to its large scale, the VerbOcean resource has been employed in about a dozen RTE systems.[11]

An alternative to looking for specific highly indicative co-occurrence patterns is to adopt a more "relaxed" notion of co-occurrence, in order to improve coverage. In particular, instead of looking for cases where a pair of verbs instantiates a lexical pattern, one can consider any verb co-occurrence in the same sentence and encode information about the relation between the two verbs with more general features. Tremper [241] presented such an approach, suggesting a supervised method for learning the *presupposition* relation (a subtype of entailment) with features such as the

---

[10]http://demo.patrickpantel.com/demos/verbocean/
[11]http://aclweb.org/aclwiki/index.php?title=RTE_Knowledge_Resources

distance between verbs in a sentence, the part-of-speech tags preceding and following the verbs, the tense and aspect of the verb, etc.

Another, somewhat hybrid, approach considers the co-occurrence of a pair of verbs in larger text segments, such as paragraphs or documents. Since such distant co-occurrence does not indicate the semantic relation between the two verbs, similarity is computed by checking whether the pair of verbs share the same arguments throughout the discourse. Thus, this approach can be viewed as a blend of both distributional similarity and co-occurrence since we check whether a pair of verbs co-occurs in a document *and* appears with similar arguments. Pekar [189] suggested an unsupervised approach along these lines for detecting entailment, focusing on co-occurrence in the same paragraph. Chambers and Jurafsky [46, 47] took advantage of co-occurrence at the level of documents to automatically construct narrative chains such as *"A search B ⇒ A arrest B ⇒ B is convicted ⇒ B is sentenced"* (notice that the arrows here denote a narrative chain relationship, which does not strictly correspond to entailment). While this latter work has not been utilized yet for textual inference, it seems to have interesting potential for supporting the learning of certain entailment rules, such as the rule that sentencing someone entails their conviction.

Weisman et al. [253] combine co-occurrence cues from both the sentence level and document level with distributional similarity information and use them as features for a supervised classifier that determines (directional) entailment for pairs of verbs. Notably, they introduce several linguistically motivated features, considering aspects such as discourse markers, verb polarity, tense ordering, dependency relations between clauses, verb classes, and relation-specific distributional similarity (such as for the verb-adverb dependency relation). Their results demonstrate improved performance for verb entailment prediction and show that information coming from each textual information source contributes to overall performance.

A different type of co-occurrence pattern that predicts verb entailment is proposed in [265]. The authors identify subject-verb constructions in which the subject is an agentive nominalization of another verb, such as *player wins*. They suggest that such constructions indicate likely entailment relations, where the verb in the construction entails the verb from which the nominalization was derived, like *win → play*. The validity of such candidate rules is assessed by a mutual-information style measure, based on overall corpus statistics for the participating elements. The authors report experiments for this method and its combination with related approaches, including some VerbOcean patterns.

5.3.3   ACQUISITION FROM PARALLEL AND COMPARABLE CORPORA

Most works on corpus-based acquisition of entailment-related semantic relations exploit standard monolingual corpora or use the web as a corpus, as described in the preceding two subsections. We now briefly review methods that exploit special types of corpora, including monolingual parallel corpora, monolingual comparable corpora, and bilingual parallel corpora. We note that given the symmetric structure of these corpora, which contain multiple texts that convey the same information, they have been used mostly for learning paraphrase rules, or bi-directional entailment rules.[12] This differs from the methods for learning directional entailment rules described previously, which have mostly been applied to single monolingual corpora.

Monolingual parallel corpora   Monolingual parallel corpora are created when the same source text is translated by several translators into the same target language, yielding multiple target-language versions of the same text. The advantage of such a corpus is that we readily obtain pairs of semantically equivalent sentences. This allows the extraction of paraphrase rules by directly aligning words and phrases across the two sentences, in a fashion similar to Statistical Machine Translation [15, 121, 184, 200]. However, monolingual parallel corpora are scarce, and so the amount of paraphrases that can be derived from such methods is quite limited, which prevents the construction of large-scale paraphrase resources based on such corpora.

Monolingual comparable corpora   A monolingual comparable corpus is composed of documents in the same language that overlap substantially in the information they convey: for instance, stories about the same events from different press agencies [13]. Monolingual comparable corpora are much more common than monolingual parallel corpora and so potentially can yield more entailment rules. On the other hand, parallelism between sentences is replaced by topical overlap at the level of documents. Thus, the task of aligning words and phrases from one document to the other becomes much more difficult. Consequently, methods that take advantage of comparable corpora either use matching Named Entities (NEs) in the pair of documents as alignment anchors for discovering paraphrase candidates [218] or develop more sophisticated coarse-grained alignment methods and leverage this alignment [14, 217]. While large comparable corpora could in theory be created by aligning news stories from multiple sources, such corpora have not yet become a commonly available resource. Consequently, knowledge acquisition methods that are based on parallel monolingual corpora have not yet been investigated extensively, nor yielded substantial rule-bases.

Bilingual parallel corpora   Unlike the limited exploitation of the above two types of corpora, paraphrase learning from bilingual parallel corpora has become an active research area. It has been largely facilitated by the prominence of such corpora in Statistical Machine Translation (SMT) research and by the adaptation and extension of SMT-related methods.

A bilingual parallel corpus contains a text alongside its translation into another language. As with monolingual parallel corpora, the advantage of bilingual parallel corpora is that sentences with equivalent semantics are aligned to one another. Paraphrase extraction from bilingual parallel corpora was proposed by Bannard and Callison-Burch [6]. They generated a bilingual phrase table (a statistically derived bilingual "dictionary") between a source and a target language using standard Statistical Machine Translation (SMT) techniques. They obtained paraphrases in the source language from this table by *pivoting*, that is, by looking for different phrases in the source language aligned in the phrase table to the same target phrase. Subsequent research extended this

---

[12]See the above mentioned survey on paraphrase generation by Madnani and Dorr [154] for further information about using these special corpus types.

idea by incorporating various types of syntactic information [39, 62, 153, 267, 268], extracting syntactic paraphrases [96] with Synchronous Context Free Grammars (SCFGs) [2], and employing more than just one pair of languages [134]. A certain weakness of acquisition methods based on bilingual parallel corpora is that they rely on somewhat noisy automatic alignments, which might limit accuracy. Still, bilingual parallel corpora constitute a rich source of information about semantic equivalence.

There have been few attempts to combine the information from bilingual parallel corpora and regular monolingual corpora. Chan et al. [48] and Ganitkevitch et al. [97] attempt to re-rank paraphrases extracted from a parallel bilingual corpus using distributional similarity computed over a monolingual corpus. From a general perspective, combining these two different types of corpora is attractive since they provide different types of information, and thus have the potential to improve state-of-the-art techniques that mostly use a single type of corpus.

5.4   INTEGRATING MULTIPLE SOURCES OF EVIDENCE

The various acquisition methods reviewed so far mostly focused on learning individual entailment rules (or related semantic relations) from an individual information source. Ultimately, though, it is desirable to integrate all related pieces of evidence in order to obtain the most reliable results. In this section we review two aspects of such integration: integrating different sources of information about a candidate entailment rule, and integrating information obtained about different entailment rules.

5.4.1   INTEGRATING MULTIPLE INFORMATION SOURCES

Naturally, combining information from manually created resources, distributional similarity, and co-occurrence-based methods is an appealing research direction, as these information sources are largely orthogonal and often complement one another.

Mirkin et al. [164] extract entailment rules between nouns based on both distributional similarity and Hearst patterns. The two sources of information are combined by encoding them as features in a supervised classification scheme. They show that the combination of methods outperforms each method in isolation as the two sources of information are largely complementary. Pennacchiotti and Pantel [192] present a richer *ensemble semantics* approach, which they apply to the related task of entity extraction. Like Mirkin et al. they incorporate pattern-based and distributional information, augmented with additional features gathered from a large web crawl and query logs. Hagiwara et al. [108] train a supervised classifier for the task of paraphrasing, combining thousands of distributional similarity and co-occurrence-based features. In a similar vein, Berant et al. [25] integrate a rich set of information sources as features for a supervised classifier that learns entailment rules for predicative templates. Their information sources include several of the methods reviewed earlier in this chapter: predicate-level and lexical-level distributional similarity, both symmetric and directional; the pattern-based VerbOcean resource; and several rule resources mined from manually created lexicographic resources, including WordNet, CATVAR, NOMLEX, and the FrameNet-based FRED resource.

It is worthwhile noting that two different training approaches may be used when combining information sources through feature-based supervised classification. One is *distant supervision*, described above within the supervised pattern-based learning approach of Snow et al. [224]. This approach relied on WordNet information to obtain positive and negative training examples for the target hyponymy relation (hyponyms as positive examples and pairs of non-related words as negative examples). A similar approach was used by Berant et al. [25] in experiments in which WordNet was not used as one of the information sources.

Note that when a resource like WordNet is integrated with other information sources used by the classifier via the feature representation, it is not possible to also use this resource for deriving positive and negative training examples in the distant supervision scheme. Thus, when choosing to exploit all available resources as features for the integrated classifier, it is necessary to independently obtain training examples, typically through manual annotation. This latter approach was also used by Berant et al., while applying a leave-one-out approach to best exploit the annotated gold standard dataset. Manual annotation of training examples was performed also in the work of Wiseman et al. [253], which was described above in the context of co-occurrence-based methods for verb entailment, but which combined distributional similarity features as well.

A different type of supervised model that integrates multiple information sources was proposed by Shnarch et al. in [221] and later extended in [222] and [220]. Rather than requiring training data that provides positive and negative examples for entailment rules, they use standard RTE datasets which contain T-H text pairs annotated for entailment (or non-entailment) at the full text level. To use such indirect supervision, they formulate a hidden probabilistic model that predicts overall entailment at the text level based on lexical-level entailment rules. The hidden model parameters reflect the reliability of various entailment rule resources, and are learned via the EM algorithm. The model then enables estimation of the reliability of lexical entailments that are supported by multiple information sources and which may be formed through rule chaining.

Szpektor and Dagan [234] combined lexicographic resources with distributional similarity in an unsupervised setting. They constructed a resource, termed *Argument-mapped WordNet (AmWN)*, which combines lexical entailment information for predicates obtained from Word-Net, including transitive chaining of WordNet relations, with argument mapping information obtained from Nomlex. Rules generated in this way were then verified using distributional similarity methods. A different unsupervised approach for integrating distributional similarity and WordNet information was proposed by Dinu and Wang [84], who extended the DIRT rule base by adding rules in which lexical items involved in an original DIRT rule are replaced with Word-Net synonyms. They also filtered out DIRT rules based on pairs of WordNet antonyms, removing rules in which the two rule sides are identical except for the occurrence of the antonymous words. Yates and Etzioni [257] identified synonymous predicates by combining distributional similarity information with string similarity in an unsupervised probabilistic framework. To compare strings that represent predicates they used the Levenshtein edit-distance metric [61].

5.4.2 SIMULTANEOUS GLOBAL LEARNING OF MULTIPLE RULES

The methods reviewed so far have focused on what may be termed *local learning*, that is, deciding individually for each pair of language elements whether the target semantic relation holds for that pair. In terms of entailment rule learning, a local learning method assesses the validity of each candidate rule independently of all other rules. In what we term *global learning*, the learning method considers the complete set of elements and tries to find simultaneously *all* element pairs for which the target relation holds. In terms of entailment rules, global learning allows joint consideration of all candidate rules, that is, deciding whether a certain rule is valid or not affects the decision regarding other rules. This setting allows consideration of global properties of the complete set of entailment rules, and as a result can capture rule dependencies. A prominent global property that has been the focus of much research in this area is transitivity. Textual entailment and related semantic relations like hyponymy are, to a large extent, transitive relations: having $x \rightarrow y$ and $y \rightarrow z$ implies (under certain circumstances) $x \rightarrow z$.

As advocated in [25] by Berant et al., global learning of a directed transitive relation can be naturally represented as the task of learning an optimal set of edges for a directed transitive graph. In this approach, the graph nodes are given in advance and correspond to the set of elements for which the relation should be learned; for example, a set of nouns for learning the hyponymy relation or a set of language expressions for which entailment rules should be identified. The graph edges represent the target semantic relation: that is, having a directed edge between two nodes x and y asserts that the relation holds for the corresponding language elements. In our examples, such an edge would assert that x is a hyponym of y, or that $x \rightarrow y$ is a valid entailment rule.

Under this formulation, the learning task is to find an optimal set of directed edges that connect the given graph nodes, which optimizes some target scoring function while respecting graph transitivity. Intuitively, the target optimization function should reward edges for which we have supporting evidence and penalize edges for which such evidence is lacking or for which negative evidence is available. For example, when learning entailment rules we would like to reward rules (edges) which are supported by any of the local rule learning methods and information sources reviewed in this chapter. On the other hand, we may want to penalize an entailment rule (an edge) that asserts that two known antonyms (say from WordNet) entail each other. Incorporating the global constraint of transitivity into the learning problem does, however, significantly reduce efficiency, since finding the optimal set of edges that respect transitivity is NP-hard in both directed and undirected graphs [25]. This efficiency challenge has been addressed in several ways, as described below.

A pioneering global learning model was proposed by Snow et al. [224] to learn a taxonomy graph of the hyponymy relation for a large set of nouns. Their model first assumes that a local probability estimate for each edge can be derived from some information source. Specifically, they employed the corpus-based hyponym classifier described earlier in Section 5.3.2 [224] to estimate this probability. Then, they seek the set of edges (hyponymy relations) that would maximize the overall likelihood of the corpus data.

Since the optimization problem is NP-hard, Snow et al. employ the following polynomial greedy hill-climbing optimization algorithm: at each step they go over all pairs of words (u, v) that are not in the hyponymy taxonomy yet, and try to add a single hyponymy relation between one of the pairs. Then, they calculate the set of relations S_{uv} that this relation will add to the taxonomy due to the transitivity constraint. Finally, they choose to add that set of relations S_{uv} that maximizes the likelihood of the observed corpus data out of all the possible S_{uv} candidates (corresponding to all (u, v) candidates that could be added to the taxonomy). This iterative process stops when the likelihood of the data given the current taxonomy edges starts dropping. Of course, as the problem is NP-hard, the taxonomy produced by the algorithm is not guaranteed to be globally optimal. The authors applied their algorithm at a large scale to augment the WordNet hyponymy hierarchy with 400,000 synsets, released as the *Augmented WordNet* resource.[13]

In a recent line of works [22, 23, 24, 25], Berant et al. focus on the problem of global learning of predicative entailment rules, taking the transitive graph learning perspective and progressively addressing optimization efficiency. In their setting, they consider an *entailment graph* in which nodes are predicative templates, such as *X relieves Y*, and edges correspond to entailment rules, such as *X relieves Y → X helps with Y*. Given a set of predicative templates extracted from a corpus (the graph nodes), their goal is to learn an optimal set of entailment rules for them (the graph edges) which respects the transitivity constraint.

Berant et al. first show that this optimization problem is NP-hard and then suggest finding an exact solution for it by formulating the problem as an Integer Linear Program (ILP) and applying a standard ILP solver [23, 25]. Their optimization objective is formulated both in terms of a score function and in terms of a probabilistic model that generalizes the Snow et al. model mentioned above [225]. These models rely on a local classifier that integrates multiple information sources in order to quantify the supporting evidence for each individual edge (entailment rule). The ILP formulation also allows additional information to be encoded as negative constraints, for example based on WordNet antonyms or on negation words [24]. The authors test their method over a set of manually annotated entailment graphs and demonstrate that learning graphs that respect the transitivity constraint significantly improves the quality of the learned rules. Since the optimization problem is NP-hard, the scalability of ILP solvers is inherently limited. Accordingly, in this first phase the authors apply their method to relatively small *focused entailment graphs*, each comprising several dozens of predicates that involve a particular argument of interest (applied to the medical domain, with arguments such as *asthma*, *chemotherapy*, and *alcohol*).

In subsequent work, Berant et al. develop methods for learning larger entailment graphs. Their first insight is that entailment graphs tend to be sparse—that is, most predicates do not entail one another. They showed that sparseness enables large graphs to be decomposed into several

---

[13]http://ai.stanford.edu/~rion/swn/augmented.html

smaller components, and each component to be exactly solved independently of the others [24]. A second type of scalability improvement is achieved by identifying a novel structural property of entailment graphs, namely, that they tend to have a "tree-like" structure. They formally define this notion and prove that it allows an efficient polynomial approximation algorithm to be devised that empirically scales to graphs containing tens of thousands of nodes [22]. Furthermore, the approximation algorithm compares favorably with an exact solution, when tested on cases in which the latter is still feasible. Learning open-domain large-scale graphs reveals an interesting limitation of state-of-the-art models, showing that in such graphs transitivity does not fully hold, mainly due to sense shifts and context sensitivity, calling for future work on these aspects. Recently, Berant has applied both local and global methods over an open domain web-scale data set and generated new publicly available knowledge resources containing hundreds of thousands and even millions of predicative entailment rules.[14]

Several other works have developed learning models for entailment-related knowledge which consider transitivity in a global manner. The probabilistic model proposed in [88] for taxonomy learning exploits the transitive network to induce the reliability of transitively-derived relations based on the reliability of pairs which were directly derived from corpus data. Yates and Etzioni [257] learn the symmetric transitive relation of *synonymy* between nouns and predicates. Since learning a symmetric transitive relation is equivalent to *clustering*, they propose a variant of greedy agglomerative clustering whose main benefit is scalability to very large data. Again, as the problem is NP-hard the solution they provide is not guaranteed to be optimal. Poon and Domingos [196, 197] use transitivity in the context of semantic parsing, in which they learn the transitive synonymy, hyponymy, and troponymy relations. Nakashole et al. [177] describe PATTY, a large resource for predicative textual patterns which are semantically typed and organized into a transitive subsumption taxonomy. They aim to construct a WordNet-style hierarchy for binary textual relations, and present efficient algorithms that identify predicate subsumptions and organize them in a directed acyclic graph (DAG). Applying their algorithms to the Wikipedia corpus, they have created a publicly available taxonomy of about 350,000 pattern synsets with reported precision of 84.7%.[15] Finally, it is worthwhile mentioning that the structural property of transitivity has also been investigated in other research areas in NLP, in related computational models. For example, Finkel and Manning [93] explore the co-reference relation, which is an undirected transitive relation between noun phrases, while Ling and Weld [146] explore the ordering of a sequence of events through time, which is also a directed transitive relation.

5.5   CONTEXT SENSITIVITY OF ENTAILMENT RULES

A fundamental property of entailment rules is that they are typically valid only in some "topical" contexts but not in others. For example, the rule *win* → *play* is valid in the context of games while

---

[14]http://u.cs.biu.ac.il/~nlp/downloads/ReverbLocalGlobal.html
[15]www.mpi-inf.mpg.de/yago-naga/patty/

win → *fight* is valid in the context of war, but not vice versa. Thus, to correctly apply each rule, an entailment system should verify that the given context is indeed valid for that rule.

To a limited extent, this context sensitivity of entailment rules may be mapped, or reduced, to the Word Sense Disambiguation (WSD) problem. For example, the two entailment rules *log* → *wood* and *log* → *record* correspond to two different senses of *log* in WordNet. Further, both rules may be identified in WordNet since each of *wood* and *record* is specified as a hypernym of the corresponding sense of *log*. Thus, to validate the application of these rules to an occurrence of the word *log* an entailment system might first disambiguate that occurrence using some WSD method and then check whether the rule corresponds to the identified sense. However, this reduction to the WSD task depends on two assumptions which very often do not hold. First, to use WSD we need to know the relevant senses of the words in the rule. This information may be obtained for rules derived from WordNet, or from other sources linked to it such as YAGO, but for most rule sources this information is not available. Second, and even more critically, in many cases the valid contexts of an entailment rule do not correspond to a distinct sense of the involved word. In the example above, the two different contexts for *win* correspond to the same WordNet sense (the first sense of *win*, both as a noun and as a verb). In such cases WSD will be useless, because it is needed to identify contexts that correspond to the individual rule rather than to a particular sense. Finally, even in cases where rule validation can be mapped to WSD, we would have to rely on the accuracy of state-of-the-art WSD systems, which might be solving a harder problem than needed for textual inference.

An early observation of this setting was presented by Dagan et al. [75], who proposed the task of *direct sense matching* as an alternative to WSD in lexical inference. Their key insight was that in order to infer the meaning of one word from another in a given context it is not necessary to *explicitly* identify the sense of the given word; rather, it suffices to verify that the senses of the two words match in the given context with respect to the expected inference relation between them, while leaving the identity of these senses implicit. A similar rationale underlies the introduction of the *lexical substitution* task by McCarthy and Navigli, at the SemEval-2007 evaluation campaign [156].

Pantel et al. [185] formally define the task of validating the applicability of a predicative inference rule given a particular argument instantiation, proposing a framework called *Inferential Selectional Preferences (ISP)*. Given rules such as *X charge Y* → *X accuses Y*, they learn for each rule a class-based representation describing the arguments that may instantiate the rule's variables. The rule may then be applied only in contexts where the arguments match that representation. For instance, in the above example 'Y' should be a person rather than an electrical appliance. Ritter et al. [204] construct a probabilistic representation for arguments that is based on *Latent Dirichlet Allocation (LDA)* [30] and demonstrate that this representation outperforms Pantel et al.'s approach in the task of filtering erroneous rule applications.

Szpektor et al. [235] substantially extend the specification of the target setting, proposing what they call *Contextual Preferences (CP)* as an encompassing framework for validating entailment inference in context. This framework is captured through a conceptual triangle that incorporates pairwise context matching for the three objects involved in inference: matching the Text and the inference rule, the rule and the Hypothesis, and direct matching of the Text and Hypothesis. To perform matching, the contexts of the Text and the Hypothesis, together with a specification of the valid contexts of the rule, should be represented consistently to allow compatibility assessments. Szpektor et al. present a combination of several unsupervised context representations and matching models as a concrete implementation of their framework. These include word-level, entity-type, and latent semantic representations, considering both predicate arguments and other locally related context words as well as words in a broader global context. Their evaluations demonstrate that considering context during rule application improves performance in an information extraction task. Later, Mirkin et al. [165] present another implementation of the Contextual Preferences framework that uses a classification-based model and show it leads to improved performance in a text classification task.

As implied above, validating the applicability of entailment rules in context relies on effective context representations for Texts, Hypotheses, and rules. Developing context matching models for inference may thus benefit from recent active research in the broader computational semantics field on generic context representations for words and phrases. For example, Dinu and Lapata [83] and later Van de Cruys et al. [242] suggest word meaning representations based on probability distributions over latent "senses," which are learned in an unsupervised manner using either LDA or *Non-negative Matrix Factorization (NMF)* [139]. They show that this representation is useful for assessing word similarity in context. Reisinger and Mooney represent the meaning of words as a set of vectors, where each vector corresponds to a different sense or context. Ó Séaghdha [182] develops a model that is similar to Ritter et al.'s, but rather than evaluating it in the framework of textual inference, he uses the model to judge the plausibility of predicate-argument combinations. Finally, it should be noted that while context validation for entailment rules is a different task than WSD, as explained above, the nature of the two tasks is similar and hence WSD context representations and matching methods may be useful for inference-oriented research and have indeed already influenced it.

While the issue of context sensitivity of inference rules has received some attention in recent years, as reviewed above, researchers have yet to converge on a specific approach. In fact, all the above works were evaluated in rather specific inference settings and to the best of our knowledge have not been incorporated yet into RTE systems and benchmarks. This immature state of affairs calls for further research on this topic and broader evaluations. Once some broadly effective context representations and matching methods emerge, their incorporation in entailment systems would require two implementation steps. First, available knowledge resources of inference rules should be augmented with proper context representations for the rules they contain, to make them amenable to context-sensitive inference. This should be accompanied by provision of corresponding computational modules that construct context representations for texts and match them with the rules' context representations at inference time.

5.6 CONCLUDING REMARKS AND FUTURE DIRECTIONS

As reviewed in this chapter, there is a large body of research on acquiring semantic knowledge that can be useful for entailment inference, and particularly that may be used in the form of entailment rules. Furthermore, quite a few relevant knowledge resources have been made publicly available. Indeed, as summarized in the RTE Knowledge Resources portal, a significant number of these resources have been incorporated into RTE systems in the RTE challenges, often improving system performance as reported in ablation tests.[16]

This past experience suggests certain practical conclusions regarding publicly available resources covered in this chapter. By far, the most widely used resource has been WordNet, which mostly yielded positive performance gains according to ablation tests. It should be noted, however, that there is no standard way of using WordNet information, as discussed in section 5.2.1. Therefore, the exact types of WordNet information which were leveraged and the methods by which they were exploited need to be traced within individual systems. Other resources that were used by several RTE systems each include Wikipedia, VerbOcean, and DIRT. Few systems exploited information in lexical-semantic resources such as VerbNet, FrameNet, and PropBank. Other resources which are worth mentioning as showing positive results in research papers include CATVAR and the directional similarity resource of Kotlerman et al. Overall, builders of inference systems are advised to consult the RTE Knowledge Resources portal, as well as recent publications that report usage of knowledge resources for inference, and investigate the best configuration of knowledge resources that fits their setting.[17]

While entailment rules and similar types of knowledge are a critical component of textual entailment architectures, it should be noticed that the impact of individual resources on overall system performance is usually small and is inconsistent across systems. This might indicate several weaknesses in the current state of the art with respect to both the acquisition of entailment knowledge and its utilization within RTE systems. First, it should be acknowledged that there are no clear definitions of the exact types of knowledge useful for entailment modeling. Such definitions have been proposed for lexical entailment rules [105, 167, 269], based on notions of substitutability and meaning reference, but these attempts did not seem to yield much impact. With respect to resource usage, a few information resources have been broadly adopted, as mentioned above, while most other resources have been used sporadically if at all. Furthermore, even for resources that are widely used, there is no clear consensus on *how* they should be used, as demonstrated by different systems using different subsets of information from WordNet, or mining Wikipedia information in different ways. An interesting investigation into how to use DIRT-based inference rules effectively for RTE, supported by data analysis, was presented by Dinu and Wang [84]. Many more investigations of this kind, which fall on the borderline between research on knowledge acquisi-

---

[16]As mentioned earlier, see http://aclweb.org/aclwiki/index.php?title=RTE_Knowledge_Resources for tables summarizing resource usage and ablation tests. More detailed presentations of ablation tests and resource impacts appear in the corresponding individual system reports.

[17]Two additional sites that continuously accumulate repositories of inference knowledge resources are http://www.cs.biu.ac.il/nlp/downloads and http://www.excitement-project.eu/ (the latter is expected to launch in 2013).

tion and research on knowledge use within RTE systems, are needed. Finally, it is apparent that the quality of available knowledge resources is typically mediocre from the perspective of textual inference, requiring further improvements in knowledge acquisition methods.

This current state of affairs suggests several directions for future research. From a methodological infrastructure perspective, two endeavors are desirable. The first is to obtain some theoretical foundations that specify the types of knowledge relevant for entailment reasoning, their constituents, and the roles they should play in entailment modeling. Until now, most RTE research has been guided by empirical performance while little attention has been devoted to analytical foundations. Hence further theoretical studies, guided by extensive data analyses, seem necessary. Second, better methodologies and practices are needed for the evaluation of knowledge resource quality on the one hand, and their utility in textual inference applications such as RTE on the other. Typically, developers of knowledge resources perform intrinsic evaluations of resource quality, but these do not necessarily predict well the actual resource utility for entailment inference. RTE system developers, on the other hand, perform indirect extrinsic evaluations of knowledge resources via ablation tests. However, such tests do not necessarily indicate resource quality, which may be masked by the impact of other system components or by inappropriate knowledge use by the RTE algorithm. Better objective evaluation methodologies are thus needed that can bridge these different perspectives and bring together the communities of knowledge creators and knowledge consumers. Such methodologies should lead to public benchmarks of knowledge resources—which are presently lacking—which may promote research on knowledge acquisition.

From the algorithmic and empirical points of view, further research is needed to extend and improve the quality of knowledge resources for entailment systems. A promising research direction is knowledge integration, extending the preliminary work described in Section 5.4. Ideally, an RTE system could use a single integrated knowledge resource of entailment rules, compared with the current situation where each system incorporates its own ad-hoc assemblage of available resources. To achieve this goal, further research is needed to identify additional broad-coverage sources of entailment rules and to develop better methods for assessing their validity based on integrating all available information, considering both the local (single-rule) and global (multiple-rule) levels. Also required to improve the effectiveness of entailment rules is to make them context-sensitive, as described in Section 5.5. As discussed there, each rule in the available knowledge resources should be augmented with a concrete representation of the contexts under which it is valid. In addition, corresponding modules should be provided that match the rule context representation against a given text at inference time. A related research challenge is to exploit context representations during rule *learning*, rather than during rule application at inference time (as discussed in Section 5.5). For example, distributional similarity methods typically consider a context vector for a word that mixes together all its typical contexts. Thus, when learning the rule *win* → *play* mentioned above, the context vector of *win* includes features that correspond to the fighting context and which are likely to mask the identified distributional similarity between *win* and *play*. It is therefore desirable to develop methods that distinguish different entailment contexts during rule learning. Finally, further quality improvements may be obtained by using humans to validate automatically acquired candidate rules, via crowdsourcing or games with a purpose, using simplified annotation procedures such as those proposed recently by Zeichner et al. [266].

Beyond improving the quality of current types of entailment knowledge, it is necessary to broaden the scope of entailment knowledge resources in several directions. One type of entailment rule that is currently missing in available knowledge resources pertains to capturing entailments that are based purely on generic syntactic structure. As a simple example, the sentence *John read a book* entails *The book was read by John*, since active and passive forms typically convey the same meaning. Similarly, *John and Mary went* entails *Mary went*, based on the conjunction structure. These inferences can be captured by entailment rules whose left-hand and right-hand sides specify generic syntactic templates, such as the structures of active and passive forms, which do not contain any specific content words (in contrast to all rule types reviewed earlier). Some inferences of this sort are often mentioned as being manually specified within entailment systems, e.g. [9, 207], but to date no public resource of such rules has been released. Further, it is necessary to develop learning methods that acquire such rules. A step in this direction was recently incorporated in the OLLIE Open IE system of Mausam et al. [155], whose algorithm for learning extraction patterns is capable of producing patterns that capture purely syntax-based inferences (in addition to learning lexicalized inference patterns). Such inference patterns may be useful not just for entailment inference, but also for canonicalization within rule learning algorithms, as proposed by Szpektor et al. [232].

A related type of entailment rules, for which public resources and learning algorithms are needed, relies on generic syntactic structures as well as on classes of lexical items. This type involves inferences based on factivity and implicativity properties of certain verb classes, as investigated by Nairn et al. [176]. Such knowledge would allow us to infer, for example, that *John managed to leave* entails *John left* where *John didn't manage to leave* entails *John didn't leave*, while the verb *fail* would imply the opposite entailments (see [151] for additional discussion of these phenomena under the *Natural Logic* framework). Acquiring this type of knowledge would involve identifying generic syntax-based entailment rules that match factivity and implicativity constructions, as well as learning the different lexical classes of factive and implicative verbs that imply different entailment patterns.

Another dimension in extending knowledge acquisition for textual entailment is providing the knowledge needed for modeling refined logic-style inference phenomena, of the types addressed within the *Natural Logic* framework, such as considering the effects of negation, monotonicity, and subset or part-of relations on entailment and contradiction relations. Addressing such phenomena requires more refined types of knowledge that go beyond the coarse notion of *entailment rules* discussed in this chapter (which reflects current typical modeling levels). For example, the sentence *Snoopy is a dog* entails *Snoopy is not a cat*, or equivalently, contradicts *Snoopy is a cat.* However, *John is a lawyer* does not contradict *John is a hunter*. To distinguish these inferences we need to know that *cat* and *dog* denote disjoint concepts while *lawyer* and *hunter* do not (as the same person may be both simultaneously). Another example concerns inferences that depend on predicate monotonicity and part-of or subset relations: *visiting Paris* entails *visiting France*, but *crossing Paris* does not entail *crossing France*. Distinguishing these inferences requires knowing that *Paris* is a meronym of *France*, and that with respect to monotonicity *visit* corresponds to existential quantification (visiting a region means visiting *some* part of it) while *cross* implies universal quantification (crossing a region means crossing *all* of it).

Some of the information needed for such refined inferences falls under classic notions in lexical semantics that can be found in available resources or that have been the target of automatic acquisition methods. This includes, for example, the relations of meronymy and antonymy, which is a special case of disjointness. However, most of the refined knowledge needed has not been acquired yet, or sufficiently addressed by research. Initial steps toward learning monotonicity properties, particularly learning downward-entailing (downward-monotonic) operators, were presented by Danescu-Niculescu-Mizil and Lee [77] and by Cheung and Penn [52]. A related area which has received relatively little attention so far is that of functional relations. For example, *John is my father* contradicts *Jim is my father*, because the relation *father of X* corresponds to a function, where only a single value can satisfy the relation for any given X. On the other hand, *John is my brother* does not contradict *Jim is my brother*, since *brother of X* is not a functional. Learning functional relations was addressed by Lin et al. [145], who also released a preliminary automatically created resource of candidates for such relations.[18] It should be noted that this kind of knowledge may be useful not only at inference time, but may also support entailment rule learning methods. For example, antonyms and co-hyponyms were used as negative features in the integrative classification-based entailment rule learning method of Berant et al. [25] mentioned earlier.

This chapter focused on acquiring the types of entailment-related knowledge needed at inference time, when recognizing entailment for given Text-Hypothesis pairs. As a final note we point at another line of work, which has received relatively little attention so far, which addresses the acquisition of Text-Hypothesis entailment corpora for system training and testing. So far RTE research has been driven mostly by the datasets of the RTE challenge main tasks, which were manually annotated specifically for the RTE task. As the size of these corpora is relatively small, training capacity is limited with respect to rich feature sets in entailment classification. A valuable direction in RTE dataset creation was pursued in the RTE KBP (Knowledge-base Population) Validation pilot task of RTE-6 and RTE-7, where the RTE datasets were derived automatically from the data of the independent KBP information extraction task of the Text Analysis Conference (TAC), including deriving the RTE gold standard annotations from the KBP annotations. This enabled the creation of much larger datasets, leveraging the large-scale annotations which were available for the KBP data. Being an RTE pilot task, the KBP Validation

---

[18]http://abstract.cs.washington.edu/~tlin/leibniz/

datasets have received little attention so far, but may have interesting potential for future research. A similar approach is being taken in the RTE-8 challenge,[19] which is a joint challenge between RTE and a Student Response Analysis benchmark. Here, the RTE task largely coincides with assessing whether a textual student answer to a question implies the known reference answer, while leveraging a large available dataset that was previously annotated for this task. This approach was also taken independently by several researchers who used available Question Answering passage retrieval datasets as a proxy for training and testing textual inference systems (e.g., [220] and references therein). This trend of exploiting existing application datasets seems worth pursuing further, based on the above and additional applications such as Machine Translation evaluation. It will promote research on scaling RTE training and data analysis, and has the potential to bring RTE research closer to the end applications from which such datasets are derived.

Even larger, though substantially less accurate, RTE datasets may be acquired fully automatically from corpora, possibly in tandem with a manual assessment of the obtained Text-Hypothesis pairs. Only a few works have pursued this direction, exploiting different types of information that may indicate whether the entailment relation does or does not hold for certain sentence pairs. Dolan et al. [87] created a paraphrase corpus by identifying lexically similar sentence pairs in a comparable monolingual corpus, followed by manual annotation of these candidate pairs. Burger and Ferro [38] collected entailing text-hypothesis pairs based on the observation that the title of a news story is very often entailed by the first sentence of the story text. This heuristic has been replicated by Hickl et al. [119], and further investigated and extended across languages and domains by Faruqui and Padó [89]. Hickl et al. also proposed heuristics for identifying non-entailing sentence pairs. One approach relies on the assumption that two sentences in the same document which mention the same named entity are likely to convey different information. The other heuristic for generating non-entailing pairs identifies sentences that are contrasted in the discourse, such as two consecutive sentences where the second sentence starts with the phrase "In contrast." Zanzotto et al. [263] investigate the use of the Wikipedia revision history to identify both entailing and non-entailing sentence pairs. These correspond to cases where revisions were introduced either to augment a previous version of a sentence or to modify it, which can often be distinguished based on the comment field which accompanies the revision. Hashimoto et al. [114] observe that multiple definition sentences for the same concept typically constitute paraphrases of each other. Based on this observation they develop a supervised learning method which they use to extract about 300,000 paraphrases from web documents, with a precision rate of about 94%. Overall, this line of research has important potential in providing effective information sources both for training and analyzing textual inference systems as well as for new variants of entailment-rule learning methods.

---

[19]Underway at the time of writing; see http://www.cs.york.ac.uk/semeval-2013/task7/.

CHAPTER 6

Research Directions in RTE

The task of Recognizing Textual Entailment is at the core of one of the most enduring goals of Artificial Intelligence and Natural Language Processing: it requires significant advances in Natural Language Understanding, building on progress in learning and inference. It is also, as shown in Chapter 1, a task that encompasses many other long-standing NLP challenges, and has begun to have an impact in other NLP research areas. However, there are many research problems to overcome to bring RTE to a performance level that facilitates more widespread inclusion in other applications and allows more widespread adoption of RTE technology.

The challenges facing researchers in Textual Entailment are similar to those in other complex NLP tasks like Machine Translation and Information Extraction: integration of diverse, non-homogeneous subsystems; design of efficient inference protocols for complex structured decisions; efficient generation of labeled data; and specification and incorporation of domain knowledge and linguistic knowledge to support aspects of the overall task. RTE also raises the need to work on problems for which current technology is either immature or non-existing, such as negation and modality, event co-reference and identifying implied arguments, discourse-semantics interface, numerical/temporal/spatial reasoning, and combinations of these. These are all important tasks that were somewhat marginal until now, and RTE exhibits and drives the essential need to advance these tasks. While some of these are often thought as preprocessing tasks, RTE highlights the additional need for both specialized and general purpose inference components that operate over these phenomena.

RTE thus shines a light on the progress and limitations of several directions in NLP, of which we highlight a few essential components:

- Knowledge: Despite significant knowledge acquisition efforts, so far there has been little success incorporating these effectively into natural language understanding tasks. Current ontologies and rule sets are too noisy, too fine-grained, too incomplete, or too hard to apply (or some combination of these).

- Preprocessing tools: Current tools do not provide complete coverage of linguistic phenomena, and may not be accurate enough to robustly support textual inference. For example, a state-of-the-art tool can provide around 90% F1 parsing on news articles, and 80% SRL core argument tagging for this genre of text. This sounds (and is) impressive, but poses severe limitations when used in a pipeline architecture as input to RTE—and few if any existing parsers can be used in any way other than as a pipeline. Other tools, like those for co-reference resolution and discourse analysis, have even lower accuracy. Moreover, it seems that current preprocessing tools do not address all phenomena that we need analyzed. For example, current SRL tools only analyze single sentences, and only with respect to verb predicates.

- Textual Inference: There is no question that RTE requires multiple forms of inference and there is a need for a more significant study of these issues, addressing, as a minimum, two key issues: (i) What kind of inference? Is there a need to resort to the old AI paradigm of converting text into a fully formalized meaning representation, followed by some form of logical or probabilistic inference; or can we make significant progress using textual representations (possibly richer, multi-faceted)? (ii) How can various capabilities be combined? It is clear that successful RTE systems will need to integrate a variety of methods, models, and knowledge sources, but we have not made enough progress on how to do this in the context of complex decision problems such as textual entailment.

This book has outlined in some detail the methods and models that have been developed so far in all these areas in pursuit of this ambitious goal, leaving aside system building issues. The work we have covered in the preceding chapters shows much promise, but the task of Recognizing Textual Entailment remains far from resolved. We next consider research goals we feel are important in continuing to push research in this critical research area.

6.1   DEVELOPMENT OF BETTER/MORE FLEXIBLE PREPROCESSING TOOL CHAIN

The problem of the NLP tool chain which we address here is clearly a general NLP problem; we discuss it because it is critical for RTE as well, and because RTE, being such a comprehensive task, highlights these issues more than most NLP tasks.

Pipeline models pose significant limitations when individual components of the pipeline are noisy, and it is widely recognized by the NLP community that it is hard to incorporate diverse NLP resources into new projects. There are a number of open source NLP toolkits and frameworks, but none has been widely adopted, and all impose some limitations on the user: to use a particular programming language, a particular source of NLP tools, a particular set of data structures. More problematic still is a lack of agreement on and adoption of comprehensive standards for key underlying NLP tasks such as sentence splitting and tokenization, which acts as a severe hindrance to developing a more generic interface.

In addition, as noted above, the performance of the majority of NLP tasks has significant limitations, yet many are considered more or less "solved" tasks. This may be because the perceived difficulty of achieving significant improvement beyond current levels is too great, or because the expense of generating new resources for supervised learning of these components in new domains is too prohibitive. As yet, unsupervised and semi-supervised models have provided some gains in adaptation to new domains, but limited contributions to maximum performance levels.

These problems suggest two profitable directions for NLP research: 1) better standards for core tasks like segmentation, and ideally, new standards for NLP tools to support easier integration by the community at large; and 2) an investment of research effort in pushing component performance to higher levels, stemming from recognition that without some well-formalized, robust recovery process, NLP components need to perform at almost 100% $F1$ to avoid severely constraining performance of complex downstream NLP applications.

This improvement in performance may come not just from further research focus on individual tasks like syntactic parsing, but also from research into problem formulations that seek better ways to chain tools, and optimize performance globally rather than at the level of the individual task. While there has been a lot of recent work on "relaxed" pipelines (e.g., [211] and work that followed up on it) such a direction will also require components engineered to support such joint inference, whatever form it may take.

6.2   KNOWLEDGE ACQUISITION AND SPECIFICATION

Semantic knowledge acquisition has been the subject of numerous research works in the last couple of decades. This body of research is scattered across several fields, such as lexical acquisition, terminology extraction, ontology learning, and learning semantic knowledge for various inference-related applications, such as question answering, information extraction, and machine translation. More recently, some works have addressed knowledge acquisition specifically for the purpose of textual entailment inference. Broadly speaking, these types of knowledge may be viewed, from a textual inference perspective, as specifying equivalence or entailment relations between language expressions.

Despite this substantial research, the goal of obtaining effective and sufficient knowledge for robust textual inference is far from being attained. This situation is evident from the lack of standard repositories for inference knowledge, the lack of consensus on methods for using such knowledge for inference purposes (e.g., how to best use WordNet for inference, let alone consensus on the use of diverse other resources), and the difficulty of showing substantial performance gains when using acquired knowledge. Hence, progress along several lines is needed to attain the ultimate goal stated above.

A first obvious obstacle is the vast diversity of schemes by which inference-related knowledge is currently represented. The goal of obtaining a unified representation for inference knowledge is difficult, though, since knowledge should not be tied to an over-specialized representation (e.g., one particular syntactic parsing formalism) that will hinder its broad use. Chosen representations should thus be sufficiently general and expressive, aiming to correspond as much as possible to "theory-neutral" natural language forms.

Another important aspect is knowledge integration. Information about the same entailment relation might be specified, or implied, by different knowledge resources. For example, WordNet may suggest that a word in a synset entails another word in its hypernym synset. However, their degree of distributional similarity might be low, as indicated by some corpus-based measure, suggesting that in most cases the entailment relation does not hold. Furthermore, entailment relations for different expressions (or words) might interact with each other, due to global properties such as transitivity. While there has been some interesting initial work on such aspects of knowledge integration, as reviewed in Section 5.4, substantial work is needed in order to actually derive integrative knowledge resources from the plethora of semantic resources that exist today.

The inference knowledge embedded in many current resources is specified in a context-independent manner. (As indicated in Chapter 5, Section 5.5, this is closely tied to the problem of Word Sense Disambiguation.) For example, the DIRT resource [142] and a lot of the work that followed up on it specify inference rules for pairs of predicate templates, but do not specify the contexts in which each rule is applicable. Other resources may provide some contextual information: for example, information about the contexts in which a pair of words are synonymous may be derived from the gloss of the corresponding synset or from adjacent synsets in WordNet. While there has been some work on specifying or using contextual information for inference, as reviewed in Section 5.5, further research is needed to augment inference knowledge resources with explicit context specifications and to develop standard methods for matching contextual information at inference time. More generally, substantial research is needed to develop generic methods for using knowledge in inference, which would address multiple aspects like context matching or modeling degree of confidence for various inferences.

So far, we have largely equated inference knowledge with knowledge *resources*, implying that such resources are being acquired and constructed off line to be readily available at inference time. However, it is unrealistic to expect that all needed knowledge can be acquired beforehand to cover all possible inferences. Therefore, methods should be developed to acquire needed missing knowledge on the fly, at inference time, in the spirit proposed in [85, 202] (for example, using some semi-structured resource to supplement gaps in structured knowledge resources). Finally, and crucially, proper evaluation methodologies are needed to facilitate research on knowledge acquisition and resources, which will effectively assess their utility for entailment inference (as discussed in section 1.4).

6.3   OPEN SOURCE PLATFORM FOR TEXTUAL ENTAILMENT

As described in this book, textual entailment research has yielded appealing inference algorithms and components, and a fairly good understanding of a range of problems. However, most technology has been developed so far within individual "in-house" systems, each using its own architecture, components, and representation. Furthermore, most current technology is language-dependent, targeting English. This state of affairs inevitably slows down progress and prevents reuse and interoperability of entailment technology across research groups and languages.

However, collaborative effort is particularly critical for the area of textual inference, where a broad spectrum of algorithms and components is required. While different inference algorithms may be applied to the task, all of them need largely the same set of components, such as knowledge of entailment relations between "atomic" text expressions (entailment rules), identification of negation and modality constructions, recognizing entailment between numerical expressions, and so on. Thus, developing entailment technology around a common *open platform*, creating and sharing a joint pool of components while experimenting with different inference algorithms, would substantially boost future progress. An excellent precedent for such a resource is the Moses platform for Statistical Machine Translation (SMT) [133], which provides core SMT components and algorithms and is constantly being extended and used for multiple languages by a large scientific and industrial community.

The challenge in setting up an open platform for textual entailment, and for textual inference in general, goes far beyond merely making a specific state-of-the-art system open source. Such a platform should be based on a sufficiently generic and easily configurable architecture, with flexible interfaces and knowledge representation schemes that will allow investigation of a rich space of inference approaches and components. Such a platform would have the potential to address the needs of different communities in the semantic-inference arena. Developers of core inference algorithms would be able to jump-start their effort by using the platform's inference components, knowledge resources, and standard representations, and to compare their performance to other inference algorithms under a common setting. Conversely, developers of knowledge resources and inference components would be able to plug them into multiple existing inference algorithms and measure the improvements they yield. Finally, developers of various semantic applications, in both research and industry, would be able to use complete, configurable entailment "engines" to improve semantic inference in their applications.

A first step in this direction has been the release of the EDITS RTE system [158], which was configured in a flexible manner to allow easy extension and experimentation. A much broader effort in the spirit outlined here is the recently launched EXCITEMENT project,[1] which aims to design a suitable architecture for such an open platform and to make it publicly available as open source.

6.4   TASK ELABORATION AND PHENOMENON-SPECIFIC RTE RESOURCES

While the task of Recognizing Textual Entailment has been recognized as important and of practical value by a significant portion of the research community, many are discouraged from active participation by the complexity of the task: there are many individual semantic phenomena to capture and solve in order to achieve robust entailment performance, yet finding a good solution to any individual phenomenon will yield only marginal improvement in performance on the standard RTE data sets. A number of researchers have tried to catalog significant knowledge requirements for good RTE performance (such as [60]), and more recently there have been efforts

[1]http://www.excitement-project.eu/

to use such analysis as a basis for specifying clear methods for generating RTE corpora that would allow more focused evaluation of specific semantic inference capabilities [18, 212]. For example, [212] provides a taxonomy of RTE phenomena along with annotation of the specific phenomena required for each RTE pair—for example, *{coreference, event-chain, numerical reasoning}* could be a phenomena/inference chain required for a given pair. Some effort is underway to develop this annotation scheme and apply it to a larger corpus. The generation of corpora that allow more direct evaluation of methods for handling specific entailment phenomena should encourage better sharing and reuse of component technologies. More importantly, it may encourage researchers with a more theoretical focus to address challenges identified within the context of RTE and to provide more principled solutions upon which component systems can be based.

6.5   LEARNING AND INFERENCE: EFFICIENT, SCALABLE ALGORITHMS

The issue of pre-processing tools was discussed above in the context of a pipeline architecture. However, it is clear that the multiple decisions required to support a textual entailment decision are highly interdependent: decisions about assigning roles to arguments of a verb predicate in a given sentence are affected by assignments made with respect to prepositions in that sentence; understanding discourse relations could depend on understanding the relation expressed by the preposition. Inference algorithms need to account for this. As reported in earlier chapters, there is increasing work in the NLP community, and even in the context of RTE, attempting to exploit these interdependencies to get around the lack of perfection of preprocessing tools [34, 51, 211], but a lot more is needed in order to make these decisions robustly.

As pointed out earlier, challenges in this area range from better theories for reconciling proposals made by multiple components (or, more generally, distributions over multiple proposals) to even deeper issues—to what extent it is necessary to map natural language to more abstract representations in order to support reasoning?

Related challenges arise when we attempt to learn better models for RTE. On one hand, it is clear that better decision models can be learned if feedback is supplied that is detailed enough for the learning algorithm to figure out what components of the structured decision are at fault. On the other hand, this level of feedback is unrealistically expensive. Models have been suggested, as described earlier, that are capable of propagating minimal indirect supervision at the output back to individual components, thus supporting learning better decision models at a component level. This seems to be an important direction to pursue if we want to learn better decision models without the need to provide very detailed supervision.

Finally, the efficiency of inference is another significant issue standing between current RTE technologies and the ability to support real time applications. We will have to develop ways that support both efficient evaluation of the deep preprocessing tools used in RTE decisions and the inference algorithms that make use of these. Better decomposition, together with indexing and caching of partial solutions, could help in achieving these goals.

6.6 CONCLUSION

Research on textual entailment has evolved over the last few years beyond simplistic assumptions about the text and the use of straightforward statistical and logical approaches, and has made use of more advanced NLP tools, addressing more advanced and focused tasks. At the same time, the RTE research community has begun finding applications for existing RTE systems and approaches, along with some understanding of the strengths and weaknesses of these approaches. Key emergent strands of RTE research that we have foregrounded in this book include the optimization-based models centered on alignment of the Text and Hypothesis, and the role of linguistic and world knowledge in RTE systems. The pressing need to reliably access the relevant information in the world's vast quantity of unstructured text data combined with the growing interest of researchers and funding agencies in the grand challenge of Natural Language Understanding make this a very interesting time for RTE researchers. The RTE task defines a conceptual component that is central to the grand challenge of Textual Inference, and beyond that, of Natural Language Understanding.

APPENDIX A

Entailment Phenomena

This appendix lists natural language phenomena relating to the inference needs for human performance of the Recognizing Textual Entailment task. They have been gathered from a number of sources. [31] lists key aspects of natural language utterances that need to be accounted for in a formal representation of meaning, while [70, 259] focus on a range of core inference phenomena relating to presupposition and implicature, and monotonicity in reasoning in the context of recognizing entailment. A number of researchers [18, 98, 212] have conducted analyses of the RTE inference process from various perspectives (alignment, syntactic, predicate-argument), while others have focused on a subset of phenomena [80, 81, 166, 240, 244]. Other research [60, 147] has tried to develop coarse taxonomies of knowledge required to determine entailment labels, or to evaluate the utility of existing resources such as FrameNet [37].

We provide the following lists of phenomena and simple examples simply to provide an indication to the interested reader of the breadth and scope of the textual inference problem. These phenomena—which we do not claim to be complete—and others are examined in detail in the linguistics literature, and an in-depth description is beyond the scope of this book.

COMPARISON

The phenomena listed in Table A.1 arise when comparing two different utterances to understand their relative meaning. They may require domain-specific knowledge, in addition to linguistic competence in the target language. We will use the term "concept" to denote a construction in an utterance that we have identified as a meaningful constituent—for example, a reference to an entity or group of entities such as "the Wigan soccer team"; and the term "predicate-argument structure" to denote a construction linking concepts in a way that expresses some interaction or relation between them, for example "Claudius was the fourth Roman Emperor of the Julio-Claudian dynasty".

ELLIPSIS

A key challenge of interpreting natural language utterances is knowing what has *not* been said. Humans constantly omit salient information, relying on contextual and syntactic cues to inform the hearer/reader of the intended meaning. The phenomena and examples in Table A.2 relate to this linguistic behavior. Elided elements in examples are marked with square brackets.

Table A.1: Comparison phenomena

Phenomenon	Description	Example(s)
Hypernymy	"IsA"	"Honda Civic" $\models$ "car"
Synonymy	"is often interchangeable with"	"beast" $\models$ "animal"
Metonymy	"can be used to represent"	"wheels" for "car"; "the suits at the bank awarded themselves a pay raise"
Antonymy	"opposite"	"rise" and "fall"
Scalar implicature	relative proportions and quantities	"3 in 10 doctors" $\models$ "some doctors" but not "most doctors"
Thematic Roles	for a given predicate, "who did what to whom"	"John broke the vase" $\models$ "The vase was broken by John"

INTERPRETATION

Tables A.3 and A.4 collect phenomena relating to the interpretation of utterances: what we explicitly understand based on the exact phrasing of an utterance.

BACKGROUND KNOWLEDGE

This section lists types of knowledge observed to occur multiple times in existing RTE data. Again, these are not intended to represent a definitive or exhaustive list of capabilities required for textual inference.

CORE CAPABILITIES/CONCEPTS

Core capabilities and concepts describe general reasoning capabilities that occur in many domains.

- set inclusion/group membership

- leadership/representation (e.g., when people's actions represent those of their organizations)

- functionality (exclusivity—e.g., states that cannot occur simultaneously)

- spatial reasoning

- numeric reasoning

- temporal reasoning

- causality and correlation

Table A.2: Ellipsis phenomena

Phenomenon	Example
Implicit argument	"Xavier arrived in America in 1932. Within a year he was running a fashionable hardware store [in America]."
Implicit predicate (e.g., comparisons)	"More people arrived than we thought [would arrive]"
Redundant head	"The fumigation process" $\models$ "The fumigation".
Implicit argument	"Mary arrived at the party at 8pm. John came [to the party] later."
Head drop	"Three [people] died and two [people] were injured in a car accident on the M1 today."
Noun compounds (implicit relations)	"Microcomp CEO Jeff Burns" $\models$ "Jeff Burns is the CEO of Microcomp"; "oatmeal cookie" $\models$ "cookie containing oatmeal"
Possessives	"Einstein's Theory of Relativity" $\models$ "Einstein discovered the Theory of Relativity"; "Michelangelo's *David*" $\models$ "Michelangelo created the artwork 'David'"
Implicit quantifiers	"[all] Government employees must submit expense reports."

- transitivity (e.g., if Mr. Putin supports the United Russia Party, and the United Russia Party supports Mr. Medvedev, we may infer that Mr. Putin supports Mr. Medvedev)

- intention (different ways of expressing planned actions)

- naming

- awareness (who plausibly knows about specific occurrences)

POPULAR DOMAINS

These knowledge categories describe subjects that appear relatively frequently in RTE examples.

- kinship

- exchange (e.g. buying, selling, trading, owning)

- typical event sequences, e.g. legal process, employment, life events

- competition (for example, in business, sports)

Table A.3: Interpretation phenomena part 1

Phenomenon	Example
Intersective modifiers	"French city" and "Dutch city"
Non-intersective modifiers	"tall daisies" and "short tulips"
Superlatives	"Death Valley is the hottest location in the United States." $\models$ "New York has lower temperatures than Death Valley (most of the time)."
Comparatives	"Most people file a 1040EZ. A *better* approach for many is to file a 1040A."
Multi-word Expressions (don't allow syntactic variation)	"in short order" $\models$ "quickly"
Phrasal verbs	"take in" (deceive), "put up with" (bear)
Idiomatic expressions (may allow variation)	"kick the bucket"; "twice in a blue moon"
Metaphor	"tech stocks caught fire" $\models$ "tech stocks rose in value"
Plurals—distributive vs. collective	"The boys did their homework." could mean "Each boy did his individual homework." or "The boys worked on their collective homework task."
Coordinating structures	"John and David Smith enjoy popular radio and TV shows" $\models$ "John Smith enjoys popular radio shows"
Anaphora	"John helped his father, then he went home." $\models$ "John went home"
Bridging reference	"There were two especially popular US presidents. John F. Kennedy was a former Democratic representative..." $\models$ "John F. Kennedy was a US president".
Pleonastic "it", "that", "they"	"The city was bleak and gray. It was raining steadily as Anna left the building." does NOT entail "The city was raining."
One-anaphora	"John had a red shirt; Jenny had a blue one." $\models$ "Jenny had a blue shirt."
Events and states; temporal interpretation	"John worked at the New School for four years" implies a state, while "John visited the New School four years ago" implies an individual event

Table A.4: Interpretation phenomena part 2

Phenomenon	Example
Generics and habituals	"When John was working, he liked to smoke." (habitual); "Elephants prefer to eat grass." (generic); "Jill was working when her friend came in" (neither)
Conditionals and counterfactuals	"*If* John had won the bet, [*then*] you know he'd be talking about it"; "If Lily hadn't arrived just then, the boy would undoubtedly have died."
States of belief	"Alicia *thinks/believes/knows/hopes/says* that New York is a friendly place."
Light verb constructions	"made their getaway" $\models$ "got away"; "The Peeler-Juicer was Pelzer's invention" $\models$ "Pelzer invented the Peeler-Juicer"
Presupposition/implicature	"John forgot to close the door" $\models$ "the door was open";
Modal constructions	"*It is likely that* Mr. Franken will run for office."; "*Maybe* the President won't come here after all."
Negation	"*No* police officer fired their weapon"; "Bill Smith *did not* lie."
Factivity/veridicality	"The report *failed to mention* the final cost"; "Mary *managed to escape* the terrible conversation."

- name alternation (different conventions for expressing the same name, e.g. nicknames, initials, acronyms)

- origin, e.g. citizenship, place of birth

- preconditions and simultaneous conditions

- medical conditions and treatments

- harming/being harmed (killing, injury, death)

Bibliography

[1] Rod Adams. Textual entailment through extended lexical overlap. In *Proceedings of the Second PASCAL Challenges Workshop on Recognizing Textual Entailment*, 2006. 29, 34, 43

[2] Alfred V. Aho, Michael R. Garey, and Jeffrey D. Ullman. The transitive reduction of a directed graph. *SIAM Journal on Computing*, 1(2):131–137, 1972. DOI: 10.1137/0201008. 144

[3] Elena Akhmatova. Textual entailment resolution via atomic propositions. In *Proceedings of the First PASCAL Challenges Workshop on Recognizing Textual Entailment*, 2005. 36

[4] Ion Androutsopoulos and Prodromos Malakasiotis. A survey of paraphrasing and textual entailment methods. *Journal of Artificial Intelligence Research*, 38, 2010. DOI: 10.1613/jair.2985. 6, 131

[5] Colin Baker, Charles Fillmore, and John Lowe. The Berkeley Framenet project. In *Proceedings of the Annual Meeting of the Association for Computational Linguistics and International Conference on Computational Linguistics (ACL-COLING)*, Montreal, Canada, 1998. Association for Computational Linguistics. DOI: 10.3115/980845.980860. 30, 128

[6] Colin J. Bannard and Chris Callison-Burch. Paraphrasing with bilingual parallel corpora. In *Proceedings of the Annual Meeting of the Association for Computational Linguistics*, 2005. DOI: 10.3115/1219840.1219914. 143

[7] Roy Bar-Haim, Jonathan Berant, Ido Dagan, Iddo Greenthal, Shachar Mirkin, Eyal Shnarch, and Idan Szpektor. Efficient semantic deduction and approximate matching over compact parse forests. In *Proceedings of the Second Text Analysis Conference (TAC 2009)*, 2009. 92, 96

[8] Roy Bar-Haim, Ido Dagan, Bill Dolan, Lisa Ferro, Danilo Giampiccolo, Bernardo Magnini, and Idan Szpektor. The second PASCAL recognising textual entailment challenge. In *Proceedings of the Second PASCAL Challenges Workshop on Recognising Textual Entailment*. Venice, Italy, 2006. 3, 16

[9] Roy Bar-Haim, Ido Dagan, Iddo Greental, and Eyal Shnarch. Semantic inference at the lexical-syntactic level. In *Proceedings of the National Conference on Artificial Intelligence (AAAI)*, pages 871–876, 2007. 6, 12, 22, 42, 92, 153

[10] Roy Bar-Haim, Ido Dagan, Iddo Greental, Idan Szpektor, and Moshe Friedman. Semantic inference at the lexical-syntactic level for textual entailment recognition. In *Proceedings of the ACL-PASCAL Workshop on Textual Entailment and Paraphrasing*, pages 131–136, Prague, June 2007. Association for Computational Linguistics. 43, 92

[11] Roy Bar-Haim, Idan Szpektor, and Oren Glickman. Definition and analysis of intermediate entailment levels. In *Proceedings of the ACL Workshop on Empirical Modeling of Semantic Equivalence and Entailment*, pages 55–60. Association for Computational Linguistics, Ann Arbor, Michigan, June 2005. DOI: 10.3115/1631862.1631872. 10

[12] Roy Bar-Haim, Idan Szpektor, and Oren Glickman. Definition and analysis of intermediate entailment levels. In *Proceedings of the ACL Workshop on Empirical Modeling of Semantic Equivalence and Entailment*, pages 55–60, Ann Arbor, Michigan, June 2005. Association for Computational Linguistics. DOI: 10.3115/1631862.1631872. 125

[13] Regina Barzilay and Noemie Elhadad. Sentence alignment for monolingual comparable corpora. In *Proceedings of the Conference on Empirical Methods for Natural Language Processing (EMNLP)*, 2003. DOI: 10.3115/1119355.1119359. 143

[14] Regina Barzilay and Lillian Lee. Learning to paraphrase: An unsupervised approach using multiple-sequence alignment. In *Proceedings of the Human Language Technology Conference of the North American Chapter of the Association for Computational Linguistics (HLT-NAACL)*, 2003. DOI: 10.3115/1073445.1073448. 143

[15] Regina Barzilay and Kathleen McKeown. Extracting paraphrases from a parallel corpus. In *Proceedings of the Annual Meeting of the Association for Computational Linguistics*, pages 50–57, 2001. DOI: 10.3115/1073012.1073020. 143

[16] Samuel Bayer, John Burger, Lisa Ferro, John Henderson, and Alexander Yeh. Mitre's submissions to the EU PASCAL RTE challenge. In *Proceedings of the First PASCAL Challenges Workshop on Recognizing Textual Entailment*, 2005. 36, 39, 87

[17] Roni Ben Aharon, Idan Szpektor, and Ido Dagan. Generating entailment rules from FrameNet. In *Proceedings of the 48th Annual Meeting of the Association for Computational Linguistics, Short Papers*, pages 241–246, Uppsala, Sweden, July 2010. Association for Computational Linguistics. 128

[18] Luisa Bentivogli, Elena Cabrio, Ido Dagan, Danilo Giampiccolo, Medea Lo Leggio, and Bernardo Magnini. Building textual entailment specialized data sets: a methodology for isolating linguistic phenomena relevant to inference. In Nicoletta Calzolari (Conference Chair), Khalid Choukri, Bente Maegaard, Joseph Mariani, Jan Odijk, Stelios Piperidis, Mike Rosner, and Daniel Tapias, editors, *Proceedings of the International Conference on Language Resources and Evaluation*, Valletta, Malta, May 2010. European Language Resources Association (ELRA). 23, 121, 162, 165

[19] Luisa Bentivogli, Peter Clark, Ido Dagan, Hoa T. Dang, and Danilo Giampiccolo. The sixth PASCAL recognizing textual entailment challenge. In *Proceedings of the Third Text Analysis Conference (TAC 2010)*, 2010. 16, 19

[20] Luisa Bentivogli, Peter Clark, Ido Dagan, Hoa T. Dang, and Danilo Giampiccolo. The seventh PASCAL recognizing textual entailment challenge. In *Proceedings of the Fourth Text Analysis Conference (TAC 2011)*, 2011. 16, 19

[21] Luisa Bentivogli, Ido Dagan, Hoa T. Dang, Danilo Giampiccolo, and Bernardo Magnini. The fifth PASCAL recognizing textual entailment challenge. In *Proceedings of the Second Text Analysis Conference (TAC 2009)*, 2009. 16

[22] Jonathan Berant, Ido Dagan, Meni Adler, and Jacob Goldberger. Efficient tree-based approximation for entailment graph learning. In *Proceedings of ACL*, 2012. 147, 148

[23] Jonathan Berant, Ido Dagan, and Jacob Goldberger. Global learning of focused entailment graphs. In *Proceedings of the 48th Annual Meeting of the Association for Computational Linguistics*, pages 1220–1229, Uppsala, Sweden, July 2010. Association for Computational Linguistics. 147

[24] Jonathan Berant, Ido Dagan, and Jacob Goldberger. Global learning of typed entailment rules. In *Proceedings of ACL*, Portland, OR, 2011. 147, 148

[25] Jonathan Berant, Ido Dagan, and Jacob Goldberger. Learning entailment relations by global graph structure optimization. *Computational Linguistics*, 38(1):73–111, 2012. DOI: 10.1162/COLI_a_00085. 144, 145, 146, 147, 154

[26] Richard Bergmair. A proposal on evaluation measures for RTE. In *Proceedings of the Workshop on Applied Textual Inference (TextInfer)*, pages 10–17, Suntec, Singapore, August 2009. Association for Computational Linguistics. DOI: 10.3115/1708141.1708144. 19

[27] Matthew Berland and Eugene Charniak. Finding parts in very large corpora. In *Proceedings of ACL*, pages 57–64, College Park, Maryland, USA, 1999. DOI: 10.3115/1034678.1034697. 139

[28] Rahul Bhagat, Patrick Pantel, and Eduard Hovy. LEDIR: An unsupervised algorithm for learning directionality of inference rules. In *Proceedings of the Joint Conference on Empirical Methods in Natural Language Processing and Computational Natural Language (EMNLP-CoNLL)*, pages 161–170, 2007. 134

[29] Rahul Bhagat and Deepak Ravichandran. Large scale acquisition of paraphrases for learning surface patterns. In *Proceedings of the Annual Meeting of the Association for Computational Linguistics: Human Language Technologies (ACL-HLT)*, pages 674–682, Columbus, Ohio, June 2008. Association for Computational Linguistics. 132

[30] David M. Blei, Andrew Y. Ng, and Michael I. Jordan. Latent dirichlet allocation. *Journal of Machine Learning Research*, 3:993–1022, 2003. 149

[31] Johan Bos. Let's not argue about semantics. In *Proceedings of the International Conference on Language Resources and Evaluation*, 2008. 165

[32] Johan Bos and Katja Markert. Recognizing textual entailment with logical inference. In *Proceedings of the Human Language Technology Conference and the Conference on Empirical Methods in Natural Language Processing*, pages 628–635, Vancouver, 2005. DOI: 10.3115/1220575.1220654. 43, 85, 88

[33] Johan Bos and Katja Markert. When logical inference helps determining textual entailment (and when it doesn't). In *Proceedings of the Second PASCAL Challenges Workshop on Recognizing Textual Entailment*, 2006. 36, 48, 88

[34] Rodrigo de Salvo Braz, Roxana Girju, Vasin Punyakanok, Dan Roth, and Mark Sammons. An inference model for semantic entailment in natural language. In *Proceedings of the National Conference on Artificial Intelligence (AAAI)*, pages 1678–1679, 2005. DOI: 10.1007/11736790_15. 41, 90, 93, 162

[35] Chris Brockett. Aligning the RTE 2006 corpus. Technical Report MSR-TR-2007-77, Microsoft Research, 2007. 103

[36] Alexander Budanitsky and Graeme Hirst. Evaluating WordNet-based measures of lexical semantic relatedness. *Computational Linguistics*, 32(1):13–47, 2006. DOI: 10.1162/coli.2006.32.1.13. 127

[37] Aljoscha Burchardt and Marco Pennacchiotti. FATE: a FrameNet-annotated corpus for textual entailment. In *Proceedings of the International Conference on Language Resources and Evaluation*, Marrakech, Morocco, 2008. LREC. 165

[38] John Burger and Lisa Ferro. Generating an entailment corpus from news headlines. In *Proceedings of the ACL Workshop on Empirical Modeling of Semantic Equivalence and Entailment*, pages 49–54. Association for Computational Linguistics, Ann Arbor, Michigan, June 2005. DOI: 10.3115/1631862.1631871. 155

[39] Chris Callison-Burch. Syntactic constraints on paraphrases extracted from parallel corpora. In *Proceedings of the Conference on Empirical Methods for Natural Language Processing (EMNLP)*, pages 196–205, 2008. DOI: 10.3115/1613715.1613743. 144

[40] Chris Callison-Burch, Philipp Koehn, and Miles Osborne. Improved statistical machine translation using paraphrases. In *Proceedings of the Human Language Technology Conference of the North American Chapter of the Association for Computational Linguistics (HLT-NAACL)*, pages 17–24, New York City, USA, June 2006. Association for Computational Linguistics. DOI: 10.3115/1220835.1220838. 15

[41] Sharon A. Caraballo. Automatic construction of a hypernym-labeled noun hierarchy from text. In *Proceedings of the Annual Meeting of the Association for Computational Linguistics*, 1999. DOI: 10.3115/1034678.1034705. 139

[42] Jean Carletta. Assessing agreement on classification tasks: The Kappa statistic. *Computational Linguistics*, 22(2):249–254, 1996. 18

[43] Andrew Carlson, Justin Betteridge, Bryan Kisiel, Burr Settles, Estevam R. Hruschka Jr., and Tom M. Mitchell. Toward an architecture for never-ending language learning. In *Proceedings of the National Conference on Artificial Intelligence (AAAI)*, 2010. 136

[44] Xavier Carreras and Lluís Màrquez. Introduction to the CoNLL-2005 Shared Task: Semantic Role Labeling. In *Proceedings of the Annual Conference on Computational Natural Language Learning (CoNLL)*, pages 152–164, Ann Arbor, Michigan, June 2005. Association for Computational Linguistics. DOI: 10.3115/1706543.1706571. 2

[45] Asli Celikyilmaz, Marcus Thint, and Zhiheng Huang. A graph-based semi-supervised learning for question-answering. In *Proceedings of the Annual Meeting of the Association for Computational Linguistics*, pages 719–727, Suntec, Singapore, August 2009. Association for Computational Linguistics. 11

[46] Nathanael Chambers and Dan Jurafsky. Unsupervised learning of narrative schemas and their participants. In *Proceedings of the Joint Conference of the Annual Meeting of the Association for Computational Linguistics and the International Joint Conference on Natural Language Processing of the Asian Federation of Natural Language Processing*, pages 602–610, 2009. 142

[47] Nathanael Chambers and Daniel Jurafsky. Unsupervised learning of narrative event chains. In *Proceedings of the Annual Meeting of the Association for Computational Linguistics*, pages 789–797, 2008. 142

[48] Tsz Ping Chan, Chris Callison-Burch, and Benjamin Van Durme. Reranking bilingually extracted paraphrases using monolingual distributional similarity. In *Proceedings of the GEMS 2011 Workshop on GEometrical Models of Natural Language Semantics*, pages 33–42, Edinburgh, UK, July 2011. Association for Computational Linguistics. 144

[49] Ming-Wei Chang, Dan Goldwasser, Dan Roth, and Vivek Srikumar. Discriminative learning over constrained latent representations. In *Proceedings of the Annual Meeting of the North American Association of Computational Linguistics (NAACL)*, 6 2010. 110

[50] Ming-Wei Chang, Lev Ratinov, and Dan Roth. Constraints as prior knowledge. In *ICML Workshop on Prior Knowledge for Text and Language Processing*, pages 32–39, July 2008. 111

[51] Ming-Wei Chang, Vivek Srikumar, Dan Goldwasser, and Dan Roth. Structured output learning with indirect supervision. In *Proceedings of the International Conference on Machine Learning (ICML)*, 2010. 56, 78, 162

[52] Jackie Chi Kit Cheung and Gerald Penn. Unsupervised detection of downward-entailing operators by maximizing classification certainty. In Walter Daelemans, Mirella Lapata, and Lluís Màrquez, editors, *Proceedings of the European Chapter of the Association for Computational Linguistics*, pages 696–705. The Association for Computer Linguistics, 2012. 154

[53] Gennaro Chierchia and Sally McConnell-Ginet. *Meaning and Grammar: An introduction to Semantics*. MIT press, Cambridge, MA, 2001. 7

[54] Timothy Chklovski and Patrick Pantel. VerbOcean: Mining the Web for Fine-Grained Semantic Verb Relations. In *Proceedings of the Conference on Empirical Methods for Natural Language Processing (EMNLP)*, pages 33–40, 2004. 40, 48, 82, 105, 141

[55] Martin S. Chodorow, Roy J. Byrd, and George E. Heidorn. Extracting semantic hierarchies from a large on-line dictionary. In *Proceedings of the Annual Meeting of the Association for Computational Linguistics*, pages 299–304, 1985. DOI: 10.3115/981210.981247. 129

[56] Noam Chomsky. *Aspect of Syntax Theory*. MIT Press, Cambridge, Massachussetts, 1957. 64

[57] Philipp Cimiano, Andreas Hotho, and Steffen Staab. Comparing conceptual, divise and agglomerative clustering for learning taxonomies from text. In *Proceedings of the European Conference on Artificial Intelligence*, pages 435–439, 2004. 139

[58] Philipp Cimiano, Andreas Hotho, and Steffen Staab. Learning concept hierarchies from text corpora using formal concept analysis. *Journal of Artificial Intelligence Research*, 24:305–339, 2005. DOI: 10.1613/jair.1648. 134

[59] Peter Clark and Phil Harrison. An inference-based approach to recognizing entailment. In *Proceedings of the Second Text Analysis Conference (TAC 2009)*, pages 63–72, 2009. 86, 88, 90

[60] Peter Clark, Phil Harrison, John Thompson, William Murray, Jerry Hobbs, and Christiane Fellbaum. On the role of lexical and world knowledge in RTE3. In *Proceedings of the ACL-PASCAL Workshop on Textual Entailment and Paraphrasing*, pages 54–59, Prague, June 2007. Association for Computational Linguistics. 10, 161, 165

[61] William W. Cohen, Pradeep D. Ravikumar, and Stephen E. Fienberg. A comparison of string distance metrics for name-matching tasks. In *Proceedings of the IJCAI Workshop on Information Integration on the Web*, pages 73–78, 2003. 146

[62] Trevor Cohn and Mirella Lapata. Sentence compression beyond word deletion. In *Proceedings of the International Conference on Computational Linguistics (COLING)*. Coling 2008 Organizing Committee, 2008. DOI: 10.3115/1599081.1599099. 144

[63] Michael Collins. Discriminative training methods for Hidden Markov Models: Theory and experiments with perceptron algorithms. In *Proceedings of the Conference on Empirical Methods for Natural Language Processing (EMNLP)*, 2002. DOI: 10.3115/1118693.1118694. 102

[64] Michael Collins and Nigel Duffy. New ranking algorithms for parsing and tagging: Kernels over discrete structures, and the voted perceptron. In *Proceedings of the Annual Meeting of the Association for Computational Linguistics*. 2002. DOI: 10.3115/1073083.1073128. 62, 64, 66

[65] Robin Cooper, Dick Crouch, Jan Van Eijck, Chris Fox, Johan Van Genabith, Jan Jaspars, Hans Kamp, David Milward, Manfred Pinkal, Massimo Poesio, and Steve Pulman. Using the framework. Technical report, 1996. 99

[66] Courtney Corley and Rada Mihalcea. Measuring the semantic similarity of texts. In *Proceedings of the ACL Workshop on Empirical Modeling of Semantic Equivalence and Entailment*, pages 13–18. Association for Computational Linguistics, Ann Arbor, Michigan, June 2005. DOI: 10.3115/1631862.1631865. 60, 61

[67] Corinna Cortes and Vladimir Vapnik. Support Vector Networks. *Machine Learning*, 20:1–25, 1995. DOI: 10.1023/A:1022627411411. 71

[68] Bob Coyne and Owen Rambow. LexPar: A freely available English paraphrase lexicon automatically extracted from FrameNet. In *Proceedings of IEEE International Conference on Semantic Computing*, pages 53–58, 2009. DOI: 10.1109/ICSC.2009.56. 128

[69] K. Crammer and Y. Singer. Ultraconservative online algorithms for multiclass problems. *Machine Learning Research*, 3:951–991, 2003. DOI: 10.1162/jmlr.2003.3.4-5.951. 102

[70] Richard Crouch, Cleo Condoravdi, Valeria de Paiva, Reinhard Stolle, and Daniel G. Bobrow. Entailment, intensionality and text understanding. In *Proceedings of the Workshop on Text Meaning, Human Language Technology Conference (HLT-NAACL-2003)*, Edmonton, Canada, May 2003. DOI: 10.3115/1119239.1119245. 165

[71] Chad Cumby and Dan Roth. On kernel methods for relational learning. In *Proceedings of the International Conference on Machine Learning (ICML)*, pages 107–114, 2003. 70, 71

[72] Hamish Cunningham, Diana Maynard, Kalina Bontcheva, and Valentin Tablan. GATE: A Framework and Graphical Development Environment for Robust NLP Tools and Applications. In *Proceedings of the Annual Meeting of the Association for Computational Linguistics*, 2002. 104

[73] Ido Dagan, Bill Dolan, Bernardo Magnini, and Dan Roth. Recognizing textual entailment: Rational, evaluation and approaches. *Natural Language Engineering*, 15(Special Issue 04):i–xvii, 2009. DOI: 10.1017/S1351324909990209. 1, 17

[74] Ido Dagan and Oren Glickman. Probabilistic textual entailment: Generic applied modeling of language variability. In *PASCAL Workshop on Learning Methods for Text Understanding and Mining*, Grenoble, France, 2004. 1

[75] Ido Dagan, Oren Glickman, Alfio Gliozzo, Efrat Marmorshtein, and Carlo Strapparava. Direct word sense matching for lexical substitution. In *Proceedings the International Conference on Computational Linguistics and Annual Meeting of the Association for Computational Linguistics (COLING-ACL)*, pages 449–456, Sydney, Australia, July 2006. Association for Computational Linguistics. DOI: 10.3115/1220175.1220232. 149

[76] Ido Dagan, Oren Glickman, and Bernardo Magnini. The PASCAL recognising textual entailment challenge. In Quiñero-Candela et al., editor, *First PASCAL Machine Learning Challenges Workshop*, pages 177–190. Springer-Verlag, 2006. 1, 3, 16

[77] Cristian Danescu-Niculescu-Mizil and Lillian Lee. Don't 'have a clue'? unsupervised co-learning of downward-entailing operators. In *Proceedings of the Annual Meeting of the Association for Computational Linguistics*, pages 247–252, Uppsala, Sweden, July 2010. Association for Computational Linguistics. 154

[78] Marie-Catherine de Marneffe, Trond Grenager, Bill MacCartney, Daniel Cer, Daniel Ramage, Chloé Kiddon, and Christopher D. Manning. Aligning semantic graphs for textual inference and machine reading. In *AAAI Spring Symposium at Stanford 2007*, 2007. 35, 56, 102

[79] Marie-Catherine de Marneffe, Bill MacCartney, Trond Grenager, Daniel Cer, Anna Rafferty, and Christopher D. Manning. Learning to distinguish valid textual entailments. In Bernardo Magnini and Ido Dagan, editors, *Proceedings of the Second PASCAL Recognizing Textual Entailment Challenge*, Venice, Italy, 2006. Springer-Verlag. 68

[80] Marie-Catherine de Marneffe, Sebastian Padó, and Christopher D. Manning. Multiword expressions in textual inference: Much ado about nothing? In *Proceedings of the 2009 Workshop on Applied Textual Inference*, pages 1–9, Suntec, Singapore, August 2009. Proceedings of the Annual Meeting of the Association for Computational Linguistics. DOI: 10.3115/1708141.1708143. 165

[81] Marie-Catherine de Marneffe, Anna N. Rafferty, and Christopher D. Manning. Finding contradictions in text. In *Proceedings of the Annual Meeting of the Association for Computational Linguistics: Human Language Technologies (ACL-HLT)*, pages 1039–1047, Columbus, Ohio, June 2008. Association for Computational Linguistics. 9, 46, 165

[82] Lee R. Dice. Measures of the amount of ecologic association between species. *Journal of Ecology*, 26:297–302, 1945. 110

[83] Georgiana Dinu and Mirella Lapata. Measuring distributional similarity in context. In *Proceedings of the Conference on Empirical Methods for Natural Language Processing (EMNLP)*, pages 1162–1172, 2010. 150

[84] Georgiana Dinu and Rui Wang. Inference rules and their application to recognizing textual entailment. In *Proceedings of the European Chapter of the Association for Computational Linguistics*, 2009. 125, 145, 151

[85] Quang Do and Dan Roth. Constraints based taxonomic relation classifier. In *Proceedings of the Conference on Empirical Methods for Natural Language Processing (EMNLP)*, Massachussetts, USA, 10 2010. 57, 130, 160

[86] Quang Do, Dan Roth, Mark Sammons, Yuancheng Tu, and V.G.Vinod Vydiswaran. Robust, Light-weight Approaches to compute Lexical Similarity. Computer Science Research and Technical Reports, University of Illinois, 2010. http://L2R.cs.uiuc.edu/~danr/Papers/DRSTV10.pdf. 52, 57, 60, 61, 111

[87] Bill Dolan, Chris Quirk, and Chris Brockett. Unsupervised construction of large paraphrase corpora: Exploiting massively parallel news sources. In *Proceedings of the International Conference on Computational Linguistics (COLING)*, pages 350–356. COLING, Geneva, Switzerland, Aug 23–Aug 27 2004. DOI: 10.3115/1220355.1220406. 155

[88] Franscesca Falluchi and Fabio Massimo Zanzotto. Inductive probabilistic taxonomy learning using singular value decomposition. *Natural Language Engineering*, 17(01):71–94, 2011. DOI: 10.1017/S1351324910000197. 148

[89] Manaal Faruqui and Sebastian Padó. Acquiring entailment pairs across languages and domains: a data analysis. In *Proceedings of the Ninth International Conference on Computational Semantics*, IWCS '11, pages 95–104, Stroudsburg, PA, USA, 2011. Association for Computational Linguistics. 155

[90] Christiane Fellbaum, editor. *WordNet: An Electronic Lexical Database*. MIT Press, Cambridge, MA, 1998. 1, 37, 48, 82, 125

[91] Óscar Ferrández, Christian Spurk, Milen Kouylekov, Iustin Dornescu, Sergio Ferrández, Matteo Negri, Rubén Izquierdo, David Tomás, Constantin Orasan, Guenter Neumann, Bernardo Magnini, and Jose Luis Vicedo. The QALL-ME Framework: A specifiable-domain multilingual Question Answering architecture. *Web Semantics: Science, Services and Agents on the World Wide Web*, 9(2):137 – 145, 2011. DOI: 10.1016/j.websem.2011.01.002. 11

[92] Charles John Fillmore, Christopher R. Johnson, and M. R. L. Petruck. Background to FrameNet. *International Journal of Lexicography*, 16(3):235–250, 2003. DOI: 10.1093/ijl/16.3.235. 1

[93] Jenny R. Finkel and Christopher D. Manning. Enforcing transitivity in coreference reso-lution. In *Proceedings of the Annual Meeting of the Association for Computational Linguistics: Human Language Technologies (ACL-HLT)*, pages 45–48, 2008. 148

[94] Abraham Fowler, Bob Hauser, Daniel Hodges, Ian Niles, Adrian Novischi, and Jans Stephan. Applying cogex to recognize textual entailment. In *Proceedings of the First PAS-CAL Challenges Workshop*, 2005. DOI: 10.1007/11736790_24. 48, 84, 87

[95] Katrin Fundel, Robert Küffner, and Ralf Zimmer. Relex - relation extraction using de-pendency parse trees. *Bioinformatics*, 23(3):365–371, 2007. DOI: 10.1093/bioinformat-ics/btl616. 139

[96] Juri Ganitkevitch, Chris Callison-Burch, Courtney Napoles, and Benjamin Van Durme. Learning sentential paraphrases from bilingual parallel corpora for text-to-text genera-tion. In *Proceedings of the Conference on Empirical Methods for Natural Language Processing (EMNLP)*, pages 1168–1179, 2011. 144

[97] Juri Ganitkevitch, Benjamin Van Durme, and Chris Callison-Burch. Monolingual distri-butional similarity for text-to-text generation. In *Joint Conference on Lexical and Compu-tational Semantics*, 2012. 144

[98] Konstantina Garoufi. Towards a better understanding of applied textual entailment: An-notation and evaluation of the RTE-2 dataset. Master's thesis, Saarland University, Ger-many, 2008. 10, 165

[99] Thomas Gärtner. A survey of kernels for structured data. *SIGKDD Explorations*, 2003. DOI: 10.1145/959242.959248. 62, 63

[100] Maayan Geffet and Ido Dagan. The distributional inclusion hypotheses and lexical entail-ment. In *Proceedings of the Annual Meeting of the Association for Computational Linguistics*, 2005. DOI: 10.3115/1219840.1219854. 134

[101] Danilo Giampiccolo, Hoa T. Dang, Bernardo Magnini, Ido Dagan, and Bill Dolan. The fourth PASCAL recognizing textual entailment challenge. In *Proceeedings of the First Text Analysis Conference (TAC 2008)*, 2008. 16

[102] Danilo Giampiccolo, Bernardo Magnini, Ido Dagan, and Bill Dolan. The third PASCAL recognizing textual entailment challenge. In *Proceedings of the ACL-PASCAL Workshop on Textual Entailment and Paraphrasing*, pages 1–9. Association for Computational Linguis-tics, Prague, June 2007. 16

[103] Roxana Girju, Adriana Badulescu, and Dan I. Moldovan. Automatic discov-ery of part-whole relations. *Computational Linguistics*, 32(1):83–135, 2006. DOI: 10.1162/089120106776173075. 139

[104] Oren Glickman, Ido Dagan, and Moshe Koppel. A lexical alignment model for probabilistic textual entailment. In Joaquin Quiñonero Candela, Ido Dagan, Bernardo Magnini, and Florence d'Alché Buc, editors, *First PASCAL Machine Learning Challenges Workshop*, volume 3944 of *Lecture Notes in Computer Science*, pages 287–298. Springer, 2005. 8

[105] Oren Glickman, Eyal Shnarch, and Ido Dagan. Lexical reference: a semantic matching subtask. In *Proceedings of the Conference on Empirical Methods for Natural Language Processing (EMNLP)*, pages 172–179, Sydney, Australia, July 2006. Association for Computational Linguistics. 151

[106] Yoav Goldberg and Michael Elhadad. An efficient algorithm for easy-first non-directional dependency parsing. In *Proceedings of the Annual Meeting of the North American Association of Computational Linguistics (NAACL)*. Association for Computational Linguistics, 2010. 29

[107] Nizar Habash and Bonnie Dorr. A categorial variation database for english. In *Proceedings of the Human Language Technology Conference of the North American Chapter of the Association for Computational Linguistics (HLT-NAACL)*, NAACL '03, pages 17–23, Edmonton, Canada, 2003. 128

[108] Masato Hagiwara, Yasuhiro Ogawa, and Katsuhiko Toyama. Supervised synonym acquisition using distributional features and syntactic patterns. *Journal of Natural Language Processing*, 16(2):59–83, 2009. DOI: 10.5715/jnlp.16.2_59. 144

[109] Sanda Harabagiu and Andrew Hickl. Methods for Using Textual Entailment in Open-Domain Question Answering. In *Proceedings the International Conference on Computational Linguistics and Annual Meeting of the Association for Computational Linguistics (COLING-ACL)*, pages 905–912, Sydney, Australia, July 2006. Association for Computational Linguistics. DOI: 10.3115/1220175.1220289. 2, 11

[110] Sanda Harabagiu, Andrew Hickl, and Finley Lacatusu. Satisfying information needs with multi-document summaries. *Information Processing & Management*, 43(6):1619 – 1642, 2007. Text Summarization. DOI: 10.1016/j.ipm.2007.01.004. 2, 13

[111] Stefan Harmeling. Inferring textual entailment with a probabilistically sound calculus. *Natural Language Engineering*, 20(4):459–477, 2009. DOI: 10.1017/S1351324909990118. 94

[112] Zellig Harris. Distributional structure. *Word*, 10(23):146–162, 1954. 131

[113] Phil Harrison and Michael Maxwell. A new implementation of gpsg. In *Proceedings of the 6th Canadian Conference on AI (CSCSI'86)*, pages 78–83, 1986. 89

[114] Chikara Hashimoto, Kentaro Torisawa, Stijn De Saeger, Jun'ichi Kazama, and Sadao Kurohashi. Extracting paraphrases from definition sentences on the web. In *Proceedings of the Annual Meeting of the Association for Computational Linguistics: Human Language Technologies (ACL-HLT)*, pages 1087–1097, Portland, Oregon, USA, June 2011. Association for Computational Linguistics. 155

[115] Marti Hearst. Automatic acquisition of hyponyms from large text corpora. In *Proceedings of the International Conference on Computational Linguistics (COLING)*. COLING, 1992. DOI: 10.3115/992133.992154. 139

[116] Michael Heilman and Noah A. Smith. Tree edit models for recognizing textual entailments, paraphrases, and answers to questions. In *Proceedings of the Human Language Technology Conference of the North American Chapter of the Association for Computational Linguistics (HLT-NAACL)*, pages 1011–1019, Los Angeles, California, June 2010. Association for Computational Linguistics. 34, 82, 119

[117] Andrew Hickl. Using discourse commitments to recognize textual entailment. In *Proceedings of the International Conference on Computational Linguistics (COLING)*. Coling 2010 Organizing Committee, 2008. DOI: 10.3115/1599081.1599124. 6, 110, 120

[118] Andrew Hickl and Jeremy Bensley. A Discourse Commitment-Based Framework for Recognizing Textual Entailment. In *Proceedings of the ACL-PASCAL Workshop on Textual Entailment and Paraphrasing*, pages 171–176, 2007. 107, 108, 121

[119] Andrew Hickl, John Williams, Jeremy Bensley, Kirk Roberts, Bryan Rink, and Ying Shi. Recognizing textual entailment with LCC's GROUNDHOG system. In Bernardo Magnini and Ido Dagan, editors, *Proceedings of the Second PASCAL Recognizing Textual Entailment Challenge*, Venice, Italy, 2006. Springer-Verlag. 13, 155

[120] Jerry R. Hobbs, Mark Stickel, Paul Martin, and Douglas Edwards. Interpretation as abduction. In *Proceedings of the Annual Meeting of the Association for Computational Linguistics*, pages 95–103, 1988. DOI: 10.1016/0004-3702(93)90015-4. 36

[121] Ali Ibrahim, Boris Katz, , and Jimmy Lin. Extracting structural paraphrases from aligned monolingual corpora. In *Proceedings of the International Workshop on Paraphrasing*, 2003. DOI: 10.3115/1118984.1118992. 143

[122] Nancy Ide and Jean Véronis. Extracting knowledge bases from machine-readable dictionaries: Have we wasted our time? In *Proceedings of KB and KS Workshop*, pages 257–266, 1993. 129

[123] Adrian Iftene. UAIC participation at RTE4. In *Proceedings of the First Text Analysis Conference (TAC 2008)*, 2008. 35, 104, 105

[124] Adrian Iftene and Alexandra Balahur-Dobrescu. Hypothesis transformation and semantic variability rules used in recognizing textual entailment. In *ACL-PASCAL Workshop on Textual Entailment and Paraphrasing*, pages 125–130, 2007. 104, 105

[125] Adrian Iftene and Mihai-Alex Moruz. UAIC participation at RTE5. In *Proceedings of the Second Text Analysis Conference (TAC 2009)*, pages 367–376, 2009. 43, 104, 105

[126] Jay J. Jiang and David W. Conrath. Semantic similarity based on corpus statistics and lexical taxonomy. In *Proceedings of the Conference on Computational Linguistics and Speech Processing*, pages 132–139. Tapei, Taiwan, 1997. 61

[127] Valentin Jijkoun and Maarten de Rijke. Recognizing textual entailment using lexical similarity. In *Proceedings of the First PASCAL Challenges Workshop*, Southampton, UK, 2005. 56

[128] Hans Kamp and Uwe Reyle. A calculus for first order discourse representation structures. *Logic, Language and Information*, 5:297–348, 1996. DOI: 10.1007/BF00159343. 85

[129] Jun'ichi Kazama and Kentaro Torisawa. Exploiting Wikipedia as external knowledge for named entity recognition. In *Proceedings of the Joint Conference on Empirical Methods in Natural Language Processing and Computational Natural Language (EMNLP-CoNLL)*, pages 698–707, 2007. 129

[130] Roni Khardon, Dan Roth, and Rocco A. Servedio. Efficiency versus convergence of boolean kernels for on-line learning algorithms. *Journal of Machine Learning Research*, 24:341–356, 2005. DOI: 10.1613/jair.1655. 70, 71

[131] Paul Kingsbury, Martha Palmer, and Mitch Marcus. Adding semantic annotation to the Penn treebank. In *Proceedings of the 2002 Human Language Technology conference (HLT)*, San Diego, CA, 2002. 30, 128

[132] Dan Klein and Chris Manning. Accurate unlexicalized parsing. In *Proceedings of the Annual Meeting of the Association for Computational Linguistics*. Association for Computational Linguistics, 22003. DOI: 10.3115/1075096.1075150. 29

[133] Philipp Koehn, Hieu Hoang, Alexandra Birch, Chris Callison-Burch, Marcello Federico, Nicola Bertoldi, Brooke Cowan, Wade Shen, Christine Moran, Richard Zens, Chris Dyer, Ondřej Bojar, Alexandra Constantin, and Evan Herbst. Moses: open source toolkit for statistical machine translation. In *Proceedings of the Annual Meeting of the Association for Computational Linguistics*, pages 177–180, Morristown, NJ, USA, 2007. Association for Computational Linguistics. 161

[134] Stanley Kok and Chris Brockett. Hitting the right paraphrases in good time. In *Proceedings of the GEMS 2011 Workshop on GEometrical Models of Natural Language Semantics*.

Proceedings of the Annual Meeting of the North American Association of Computational Linguistics (NAACL), 2010. 144

[135] Lili Kotlerman, Ido Dagan, Idan Szpektor, and Maayan Zhitomirsky-Geffet. Directional distributional similarity for lexical inference. *Natural Language Engineering*, 16:359–389, 2010. DOI: 10.1017/S1351324910000124. 135

[136] Milen Koulyekov and Bernardo Magnini. Recognizing textual entailment with tree edit distance algorithms. In *Proceedings of the First PASCAL Challenges Workshop*, 2005. 82

[137] Zornitsa Kozareva, Eduard H. Hovy, and Ellen Riloff. Learning and evaluating the content and structure of a term taxonomy. In *AAAI Spring Symposium: Learning by Reading and Learning to Read'09*, pages 50–57, 2009. 139, 140

[138] Zornitsa Kozareva, Ellen Riloff, and Eduard Hovy. Semantic class learning from the web with hyponym pattern linkage graphs. In *Proceedings of the Annual Meeting of the Association for Computational Linguistics: Human Language Technologies (ACL-HLT)*, pages 1048–1056, Columbus, Ohio, June 2008. Association for Computational Linguistics. 139

[139] Daniel D. Lee and H. Sebastian Seung. Algorithms for non-negative matrix factorization. In *Proceedings of the Conference on Advances in Neural Information Processing Systems (NIPS)*, pages 556–562, 2000. 150

[140] Lillian Lee. Measures of distributional similarity. In *Proceedings of the Annual Meeting of the Association for Computational Linguistics*, pages 25–32, 1999. DOI: 10.3115/1034678.1034693. 132

[141] Dekang Lin. Automatic retrieval and clustering of similar words. In *Proceedings the International Conference on Computational Linguistics and Annual Meeting of the Association for Computational Linguistics (COLING-ACL)*, pages 768–774, Montreal, Canada, 1998. Association for Computational Linguistics. DOI: 10.3115/980691.980696. 1, 132

[142] Dekang Lin and Patrick Pantel. DIRT: discovery of inference rules from text. In *Proceedings of the ACM SIGKDD Conference on Knowledge Discovery and Data Mining*, pages 323–328, 2001. DOI: 10.1145/502512.502559. 40, 160

[143] Dekang Lin and Patrick Pantel. Discovery of inference rules for question answering. *Natural Language Engineering*, 7(4):343–360, 2001. DOI: 10.1017/S1351324901002765. 1, 133

[144] Dekang Lin and Patrick Pantel. Induction of semantic classes from natural language text. In *Proceedings of the ACM SIGKDD Conference on Knowledge Discovery and Data Mining*, pages 317–322, 2001. DOI: 10.1145/502512.502558. 48

[145] Thomas Lin, Mausam, and Oren Etzioni. Identifying functional relations in web text. In *Proceedings of the Conference on Empirical Methods for Natural Language Processing (EMNLP)*, pages 1266–1276, Cambridge, MA, October 2010. Association for Computational Linguistics. 154

[146] Xiao Ling and Daniel S. Weld. Temporal information extraction. In *Proceedings of the National Conference on Artificial Intelligence (AAAI)*, 2010. 148

[147] Peter LoBue and Alexander Yates. Types of common-sense knowledge needed for recognizing textual entailment. In *Proceedings of the Annual Meeting of the Association for Computational Linguistics: Human Language Technologies (ACL-HLT)*, pages 329–334, Portland,Oregon,USA, June 2011. Proceedings of the Annual Meeting of the Association for Computational Linguistics. 121, 165

[148] Bill MacCartney. *Natural Language Inference*. PhD thesis, Stanford University, 2009. 96

[149] Bill MacCartney, Michel Galley, and Christopher D. Manning. A phrase-based alignment model for natural language inference. In *Proceedings of the Conference on Empirical Methods for Natural Language Processing (EMNLP)*, 2008. DOI: 10.3115/1613715.1613817. 56, 102

[150] Bill MacCartney, Trond Grenager, and Marie-Catherine de Marneffe. Learning to recognize features of valid textual entailments. In *Proceedings of the Human Language Technology Conference of the North American Chapter of the Association for Computational Linguistics (HLT-NAACL)*, 2006. DOI: 10.3115/1220835.1220841. 100

[151] Bill MacCartney and Christopher D. Manning. An extended model of natural logic. In *Proceedings of the Eighth International Conference on Computational Semantics*, IWCS-8 '09, pages 140–156, Stroudsburg, PA, USA, 2009. Association for Computational Linguistics. 10, 96, 126, 153

[152] Catherine Macleod, Ralph Grishman, Adam Meyers, Leslie Barrett, and Ruth Reeves. NOMLEX: A lexicon of nominalizations. In *Proceedings of the European Association for Lexicography (EURALEX)*, 1998. 128

[153] Nitin Madnani, Necip Fazil Ayan, Philip Resnik, and Bonnie Dorr. Using paraphrases for parameter tuning in statistical machine translation. In *Proceedings of the NAACL Workshop on Machine Translation*, 2007. 144

[154] Nitin Madnani and Bonnie J. Dorr. Generating phrasal and sentential paraphrases: A survey of data-driven methods. *Computational Linguistics*, 36, 2010. DOI: 10.1162/coli_a_00002. 131, 143

[155] M.S. Mausam, Michael Schmitz, Stephen Soderland, Robert Bart, and Oren Etzioni. Open language learning for information extraction. In *Proceedings of the Joint Conference on Empirical Methods in Natural Language Processing and Computational Natural Language (EMNLP-CoNLL)*, pages 523–534, Jeju Island, Korea, July 2012. Association for Computational Linguistics. 153

[156] Diana McCarthy and Roberto Navigli. Semeval-2007 task 10: English lexical substitution task. In *Proceedings of the Fourth International Workshop on Semantic Evaluations (SemEval-2007)*, pages 48–53, Prague, Czech Republic, June 2007. Association for Computational Linguistics. DOI: 10.3115/1621474.1621483. 149

[157] David McClosky, Eugene Charniak, and Mark Johnson. Effective self-training for parsing. In *Proceedings of the Human Language Technology Conference of the North American Chapter of the Association for Computational Linguistics (HLT-NAACL)*, 2006. DOI: 10.3115/1220835.1220855. 29

[158] Yashar Mehdad, Matteo Negri, Elena Cabrio, Milen Kouylekov, and Bernardo Magnini. Edits: An open source framework for recognizing textual entailment. In *Proceedings of the Second Text Analysis Conference (TAC 2009)*, pages 169–178, 2009. 34, 43, 82, 84, 161

[159] Yashar Mehdad, Matteo Negri, and Marcello Federico. Towards cross-lingual textual entailment. In *Proceedings of the Human Language Technology Conference of the North American Chapter of the Association for Computational Linguistics (HLT-NAACL)*, pages 321–324. Association for Computational Linguistics, 2010. 2

[160] Yashar Mehdad, Fabio Massimo Zanzotto, and Alessandro Moschitti. Semker: Syntactic/semantic kernels for recognizing textual entailment. In *Proceedings of the Second Text Analysis Conference (TAC 2009)*, pages 259–265, 2009. 113

[161] Adam Meyers, Ruth Reeves, Catherine Macleod, Rachel Szekeley, Veronika Zielinska, and Brian Young. The cross-breeding of dictionaries. In *Proceedings of the International Conference on Language Resources and Evaluation*, 2004. 128

[162] George A. Miller. WordNet: A lexical database for English. *Communications of the ACM*, 38(11):39–41, November 1995. DOI: 10.1145/219717.219748. 61

[163] Shachar Mirkin, Jonathan Berant, Roy Bar-Haim, Eyal Shnarch, Asher Stern, and Idan Szpektor. Addressing discourse and document structure in the RTE search task. In *Proceedings of the Second Text Analysis Conference (TAC 2009)*, 2009. 92

[164] Shachar Mirkin, Ido Dagan, and Maayan Gefet. Integrating pattern-based and distributional similarity methods for lexical entailment acquisition. In *Proceedings the International*

Conference on Computational Linguistics and Annual Meeting of the Association for Computational Linguistics (COLING-ACL), pages 579–586. Association for Computational Linguistics, 2006. 144

[165] Shachar Mirkin, Ido Dagan, Lili Kotlerman, and Idan Szpektor. Classification-based contextual preferences. In *Proceedings of the Workshop on Textual Entailment (TextInfer)*, Edinburgh, Scotland, UK, August 2011. 150

[166] Shachar Mirkin, Ido Dagan, and Sebastian Pado. Assessing the role of discourse references in entailment inference. In *Proceedings of the Annual Meeting of the Association for Computational Linguistics*, pages 1209–1219, Uppsala, Sweden, July 2010. Association for Computational Linguistics. 10, 20, 165

[167] Shachar Mirkin, Ido Dagan, and Eyal Shnarch. Evaluating the inferential utility of lexical-semantic resources. In *Proceedings of the European Chapter of the Association for Computational Linguistics*, pages 558–566, Athens, Greece, March 2009. Association for Computational Linguistics. 125, 131, 132, 151

[168] Shachar Mirkin, Lucia Specia, Nicola Cancedda, Ido Dagan, Marc Dymetman, and Idan Szpektor. Source-language entailment modeling for translating unknown terms. In *Proceedings of the Joint Conference of the Annual Meeting of the Association for Computational Linguistics and the International Joint Conference on Natural Language Processing of the Asian Federation of Natural Language Processing*, pages 791–799, Suntec, Singapore, August 2009. Association for Computational Linguistics. 2, 15

[169] Dan Moldovan, Christine Clark, Sanda Harabagiu, and Steve Maiorano. Cogex: A logic prover for question answering. 2003. 36

[170] Dan Moldovan and Adrian Novischi. Lexical chains for question answering. In *Proceedings of the International Conference on Computational Linguistics (COLING)*. COLING, 2002. DOI: 10.3115/1072228.1072395. 127

[171] Dan Moldovan and Vasile Rus. Logic form transformation of WordNet and its applicability to question answering. In *Proceedings of the Annual Meeting of the Association for Computational Linguistics*, pages 394–401, 2001. DOI: 10.3115/1073012.1073064. 127, 129

[172] Alessandro Moschitti. Making tree kernels practical for natural language learning. In *Proceedings of the European Chapter of the Association for Computational Linguistics*. Trento, Italy, 2006. 66

[173] Alessandro Moschitti and Fabio Massimo Zanzotto. Fast and effective kernels for relational learning from texts. In Zoubin Ghahramani, editor, *Proceedings of the Interna-*

tional Conference on Machine Learning (ICML), pages 649–656. Omnipress, 2007. DOI: 10.1145/1273496. 113

[174] S. Muggleton. Inverse entailment and Progol. *New Generation Computing, Special issue on Inductive Logic Programming*, 13(3-4):245–286, 1995. DOI: 10.1007/BF03037227. 136

[175] Arcady Mushegian and Eugene Koonin. A minimal gene set for cellular life derived by comparison of complete bacterial genomes. In *Proceedings of the National Academies of Science*, volume 93, pages 10268–10273, 2005. 110

[176] Rowan Nairn, Cleo Condoravdi, and Lauri Karttunen. Computing relative polarity for textual inference. In *Proceedings of ICoS-5 (Inference in Computational Semantics)*, Buxton, UK, 2006. 96, 153

[177] Ndapandula Nakashole, Gerhard Weikum, and Fabian Suchanek. Patty: A taxonomy of relational patterns with semantic types. In *Proceedings of the Joint Conference on Empirical Methods in Natural Language Processing and Computational Natural Language (EMNLP-CoNLL)*, pages 1135–1145, Jeju Island, Korea, July 2012. Association for Computational Linguistics. 148

[178] Roberto Navigli and Paola Velardi. Structural semantic interconnections: a knowledge-based approach to word sense disambiguation. 27(7):1075–1088, 2005. 34

[179] Eamonn Newman, Nicola Stokes, John John Dunnion, and Joe Carthy. Ucd iirg approach to the textual entailment challenge. In *Proceedings of the First PASCAL Challenges Workshop*, Southampton, UK, 2005. 61

[180] Eric Nichols, Francis Bond, and Daniel Flickinger. Robust ontology acquisition from machine-readable dictionaries. In *Proceedings of the International Joint Conference on Artificial Intelligence (IJCAI)*, pages 1111–1116, 2005. 129

[181] Rodney d. Nielsen, Wayne Ward, and James h. Martin. Recognizing entailment in intelligent tutoring systems*. *Natural Language Engineering*, 15:479–501, October 2009. DOI: 10.1017/S135132490999012X. 2, 14

[182] Diarmuid Ó Séaghdha. Latent variable models of selectional preference. In *Proceedings of the Annual Meeting of the Association for Computational Linguistics*, pages 435–444, Uppsala, Sweden, July 2010. Association for Computational Linguistics. 150

[183] Sebastian Padó, Michel Galley, Dan Jurafsky, and Chris Manning. Robust machine translation evaluation with entailment features. In *Proceedings of the Joint Conference of the Annual Meeting of the Association for Computational Linguistics and the International Joint Conference on Natural Language Processing of the Asian Federation of Natural Language Processing*, ACL '09, pages 297–305, Stroudsburg, PA, USA, 2009. Association for Computational Linguistics. 2, 14

[184] Bo Pang, Kevin Knight, and Daniel Marcu. syntax-based alignment of multiple transla-tions: Extracting paraphrases and generating new sentences. In *Proceedings of the Human Language Technology Conference of the North American Chapter of the Association for Compu-tational Linguistics (HLT-NAACL)*, 2003. DOI: 10.3115/1073445.1073469. 143

[185] Patrick Pantel, Rahul Bhagat, Bonaventura Coppola, Timothy Chklovski, and Eduard H. Hovy. Isp: Learning inferential selectional preferences. In *Proceedings of the Human Lan-guage Technology Conference of the North American Chapter of the Association for Computa-tional Linguistics (HLT-NAACL)*, pages 564–571, 2007. 149

[186] Patrick Pantel and Marco Pennacchiotti. Espresso: Leveraging generic patterns for au-tomatically harvesting semantic relations. In *Proceedings the International Conference on Computational Linguistics and Annual Meeting of the Association for Computational Linguis-tics (COLING-ACL)*, pages 113–120. Association for Computational Linguistics, Sydney, Australia, July 2006. DOI: 10.3115/1220175.1220190. 138

[187] Marius Pasca and Péter Dienes. Aligning needles in a haystack: Paraphrase acquisition across the web. In *Proceedings of the International Joint Conference on Natural Language Processing (IJCNLP)*, pages 119–130, 2005. DOI: 10.1007/11562214_11. 132

[188] Ted Pedersen, Siddharth Patwardhan, and Jason Michelizzi. Word-net::similarity - mea-suring the relatedness of concepts. In *Proceedings of the Nineteenth National Conference on Arti- ficial Intelligence*, San Jose, CA, 2004. Proceedings of the National Conference on Artificial Intelligence (AAAI). 110, 127

[189] Viktor Pekar. Discovery of event entailment knowledge from text corpora. *Computer Speech & Language*, 22(1):1–16, 2008. DOI: 10.1016/j.csl.2007.05.001. 142

[190] Anselmo Peñas, Álvaro Rodrigo, Valentín Sama, and Felisa Verdejo. Overview of the answer validation exercise 2006. volume 4730 of *Lecture Notes in Computer Science*, pages 257–264. Springer, 2006. DOI: 10.1007/978-3-540-74999-8_32. 2, 21

[191] Anselmo Peñas, Álvaro Rodrigo, and Felisa Verdejo. Overview of the answer validation exercise 2007. volume 5152 of *Lecture Notes in Computer Science*, pages 237–248. Springer, 2007. DOI: 10.1007/978-3-540-74999-8_32. 21

[192] Marco Pennacchiotti and Patrick Pantel. Entity extraction via ensemble semantics. In *Pro-ceedings of the Conference on Empirical Methods for Natural Language Processing (EMNLP)*, pages 238–247, 2009. 144

[193] Marco Pennacchiotti and Fabio Massimo Zanzotto. Learning shallow semantic rules for textual entailment. In *Proceedings of the International Conference on Recent Advances in Natural Language Processing*, 2007. 113

[194] Slav Petrov and Dan Klein. Discriminative log-linear grammars with latent variables. In J.C. Platt, D. Koller, Y. Singer, and S. Roweis, editors, *Proceedings of the Conference on Advances in Neural Information Processing Systems (NIPS)*, pages 1153–1160, Cambridge, MA, 2008. MIT Press. 29

[195] Simone Paolo Ponzetto and Michael Strube. Deriving a large scale taxonomy from Wikipedia. In *Proceedings of the National Conference on Artificial Intelligence (AAAI)*, pages 1440–1447, Vancouver, B.C., 2007. 130

[196] Hoihung Poon and Pedro Domingos. Unsupervised semantic parsing. In *Proceedings of the Conference on Empirical Methods for Natural Language Processing (EMNLP)*, 2009. 148

[197] Hoihung Poon and Pedro Domingos. Unsupervised ontology induction from text. In *Proceedings of the Annual Meeting of the Association for Computational Linguistics*, 2010. 148

[198] Vasin Punyakanok, Dan Roth, and Wen-Tau Yih. Natural language inference via dependency tree mapping: An application to question answering. In submission, 2004. 82

[199] J. Ross Quinlan. Learning logical definitions from relations. *Machine Learning*, 5:239–266, 1990. DOI: 10.1007/BF00117105. 136

[200] Chris Quirk, Chris Brockett, and William Dolan. Monolingual machine translation for paraphrase generation. In *Proceedings of the Conference on Empirical Methods for Natural Language Processing (EMNLP)*, 2004. 143

[201] Rajat Raina, Andrew Y. Ng, and Chris Manning. Robust textual inference via learning and abductive reasoning. In *Proceedings of the National Conference on Artificial Intelligence (AAAI)*, 2005. 36, 37, 78, 85, 86, 96, 120

[202] Lev Ratinov, Dan Roth, Doug Downey, and Mike Anderson. Local and global algorithms for disambiguation to Wikipedia. In *Proceedings of the Annual Meeting of the Association for Computational Linguistics*, 2011. 160

[203] Deepak Ravichandran and Eduard Hovy. Learning surface text patterns for a question answering system. In *Proceedings of the Annual Meeting of the Association for Computational Linguistics*. Philadelphia, Pennsilvania, 2002. DOI: 10.3115/1073083.1073092. 138

[204] Alan Ritter, Mausam, and Oren Etzioni. A latent dirichlet allocation method for selectional preferences. In *Proceedings of the Annual Meeting of the Association for Computational Linguistics*, pages 424–434, 2010. 149

[205] Álvaro Rodrigo, Anselmo Peñas, and Felisa Verdejo. Evaluating question answering validation as a classification problem. *Language Resources and Evaluation*, pages 1–9, March 2011. DOI: 10.1007/s10579-011-9143-2. 21

[206] Álvaro Rodrigo, Anselmo Peñas, and Felisa Verdejo. Overview of the answer validation exercise 2008. volume 5706 of *Lecture Notes in Computer Science*, pages 296–313. Springer, 2008. DOI: 10.1007/978-3-642-04447-2_35. 21

[207] Lorenza Romano, Milen Kouylekov, Idan Szpektor, Ido Dagan, and Alberto Lavelli. Investigating a generic paraphrase-based approach for relation extraction. In *Proceedings of the European Chapter of the Association for Computational Linguistics*, 2006. 2, 12, 22, 137, 153

[208] Frank Rosenblatt. The perceptron: A probabilistic model for information storage and organization in the brain. *Psych. Rev.*, 65:386–407, 1958. (Reprinted in *Neurocomputing* (MIT Press, 1988).). DOI: 10.1037/h0042519. 70, 71

[209] Dan Roth and Mark Sammons. Semantic and logical inference model for textual entailment. In *Proceedings of the ACL-PASCAL Workshop on Textual Entailment and Paraphrasing*, pages 107–112, Prague, Czech Republic, June 2007. Association for Computational Linguistics. 121

[210] Dan Roth, Mark Sammons, and V.G.Vinod Vydiswaran. A Framework for Entailed Relation Recognition. In *Proceedings of the Annual Meeting of the Association for Computational Linguistics*, Singapore, August 2009. Association for Computational Linguistics. 6, 13

[211] Dan Roth and Wen-Tau Yih. Global inference for entity and relation identification via a linear programming formulation. In Lise Getoor and Ben Taskar, editors, *Introduction to Statistical Relational Learning*. MIT Press, 2007. 111, 159, 162

[212] Mark Sammons, V.G.Vinod Vydiswaran, and Dan Roth. "Ask not what Textual Entailment can do for you...". In *Proceedings of the Annual Meeting of the Association for Computational Linguistics*, Uppsala, Sweden, July 2010. Association for Computational Linguistics. 23, 121, 162, 165

[213] Mark Sammons, V.G.Vinod Vydiswaran, Timothy Vieira, Nikhil. Johri, Ming-Wei Chang, Dan Goldwasser, Vivek Srikumar, Gourab Kundu, Yuancheng Tu, Kevin Small, Joshua Rule, Quang Do, and Dan Roth. Relation Alignment for Textual Entailment Recognition. In *Proceedings of the Second Text Analysis Conference (TAC 2009)*, 2009. 43, 56, 105

[214] Erik F. Tjong Kim Sang and Fien De Meulder. Introduction to the coNLL-2003 shared task: Language-independent named entity recognition. In *Proceedings of the Annual Conference on Computational Natural Language Learning (CoNLL)*, pages 142–147, 2003. DOI: 10.3115/1119176.1119195. 2

[215] Stefan Schoenmackers, Jesse Davis, Oren Etzioni, and Daniel S. Weld. Learning first-order horn clauses from web text. In *Proceedings of the Conference on Empirical Methods for Natural Language Processing (EMNLP)*, pages 1088–1098, 2010. 135

[216] Stefan Schoenmackers, Oren Etzioni, and Daniel S. Weld. Scaling textual inference to the web. In *Proceedings of the Conference on Empirical Methods for Natural Language Processing (EMNLP)*, pages 79–88, 2008. DOI: 10.3115/1613715.1613727. 135

[217] Siwei Shen, Dragomir R. Radev, Agam Patel, and Gunes Erkan. Adding syntax to dynamic programming for aligning comparable texts for the generation of paraphrases. In *Proceedings of the Annual Meeting of the Association for Computational Linguistics and International Conference on Computational Linguistics (ACL-COLING)*. Association for Computational Linguistics, 2006. 143

[218] Yusuke Shinyama, Satoshi Sekine, and Kiyoshi Sudo. Automatic paraphrase acquisition from news articles. In *Proceedings of the 2002 Human Language Technology conference (HLT)*, 2002. 143

[219] Eyal Shnarch, Libby Barak, and Ido Dagan. Extracting lexical reference rules from Wikipedia. In *Proceedings of the Annual Meeting of the Association for Computational Linguistics*, 2009. 129

[220] Eyal Shnarch, Ido Dagan, and Jacob Goldberger. A probabilistic lexical model for ranking textual inferences. In *Joint Conference on Lexical and Computational Semantics*, pages 237–245, Montréal, Canada, 7-8 June 2012. Association for Computational Linguistics. 127, 145, 155

[221] Eyal Shnarch, Jacob Goldberger, and Ido Dagan. A probabilistic modeling framework for lexical entailment. In *Proceedings of the Annual Meeting of the Association for Computational Linguistics: Human Language Technologies (ACL-HLT)*, pages 558–563, Portland, Oregon, USA, June 2011. Association for Computational Linguistics. 145

[222] Eyal Shnarch, Jacob Goldberger, and Ido Dagan. Towards a probabilistic model for lexical entailment. In *Proceedings of the Workshop on Textual Entailment (TextInfer)*, pages 10–19, Edinburgh, Scottland, UK, July 2011. Association for Computational Linguistics. 127, 128, 145

[223] Reda Siblini and Leila Kosseim. Using ontology alignment for the TAC RTE challenge. In *Proceedings of the First Text Analysis Conference (TAC 2008)*, 2008. 57

[224] Rion Snow, Daniel Jurafsky, and Andrew Y. Ng. Learning syntactic patterns for automatic hypernym discovery. In *Proceedings of the Conference on Advances in Neural Information Processing Systems (NIPS)*, Vancouver, Canada, 2005. 140, 145, 146, 147

[225] Rion Snow, Daniel Jurafsky, and Andrew Y. Ng. Semantic taxonomy induction from heterogenous evidence. In *Proceedings of the Annual Meeting of the Association for Computational Linguistics*, pages 801–808, 2006. 147

[226] Rion Snow, Brendan O'Connor, Daniel Jurafsky, and Andrew Y. Ng. Cheap and fast—but is it good?: evaluating non-expert annotations for natural language tasks. In *Proceedings of the Conference on Empirical Methods for Natural Language Processing (EMNLP)*, EMNLP '08, pages 254–263, Stroudsburg, PA, USA, 2008. Association for Computational Linguistics. DOI: 10.3115/1613715.1613751. 18

[227] Asher Stern and Ido Dagan. A confidence model for syntactically-motivated entailment proofs. In *Proceedings of the International Conference on Recent Advances in Natural Language Processing*, 2011. 96

[228] Asher Stern, Amnon Lotan, Shachar Mirkin, Eyal Shnarch, Lili Kotlerman, Jonathan Berant, and Ido Dagan. Knowledge and tree-edits in learnable entailment proofs. In *Proceedings of the Fourth Text Analysis Conference (TAC 2011)*, 2011. 130, 135

[229] Asher Stern, Roni Stern, Ido Dagan, and Ariel Felner. Efficient search for transformation-based inference. In *Proceedings of the Annual Meeting of the Association for Computational Linguistics*, Jeju, Korea, 2012. 96, 120

[230] Fabian M. Suchanek, Gjergji Kasneci, and Gerhard Weikum. Yago: A core of semantic knowledge - unifying WordNet and Wikipedia. In *Proceedings of the 16th International World Wide Web Conference (WWW07)*, pages 1440–1447, Banff, Canada, 2007. DOI: 10.1145/1242572.1242667. 1, 130

[231] Jana Z. Sukkarieh and Svetlana Stoyanchev. Automating model building in c-rater. In *Proceedings of the Workshop on Applied Textual Inference (TextInfer)*, TextInfer '09, pages 61–69, Stroudsburg, PA, USA, 2009. Association for Computational Linguistics. DOI: 10.3115/1708141.1708153. 14

[232] Idan Szpektor and Ido Dagan. Learning canonical forms of entailment rules. In *Proceedings of the International Conference on Recent Advances in Natural Language Processing*, 2007. 153

[233] Idan Szpektor and Ido Dagan. Learning entailment rules for unary templates. In *Proceedings of the International Conference on Computational Linguistics (COLING)*, pages 849–856, Manchester, UK, August 2008. Coling 2008 Organizing Committee. DOI: 10.3115/1599081.1599188. 22, 23, 134, 136

[234] Idan Szpektor and Ido Dagan. Augmenting WordNet-based inference with argument mapping. In *Proceedings of the Workshop on Applied Textual Inference (TextInfer)*, pages 27–35, 2009. DOI: 10.3115/1708141.1708147. 127, 128, 145

[235] Idan Szpektor, Ido Dagan, Roy Bar-Haim, and Jacob Goldberger. Contextual prefer-
ences. In *Proceedings of the Annual Meeting of the Association for Computational Linguistics:
Human Language Technologies (ACL-HLT)*, pages 683–691, Columbus, Ohio, June 2008.
Association for Computational Linguistics. 22, 23, 149

[236] Idan Szpektor, Eyal Shnarch, and Ido Dagan. Instance-based evaluation of entailment
rule acquisition. In *Proceedings of the Annual Meeting of the Association for Computational
Linguistics*, pages 456–463, Prague, Czech Republic, June 2007. Association for Computational Linguistics. 138

[237] Idan Szpektor, Hristo Tanev, Ido Dagan, and Bonaventura Coppola. Scaling web-based
acquisition of entailment relations. In *Proceedings of the Conference on Empirical Methods
for Natural Language Processing (EMNLP)*, Barcellona, Spain, 2004. 136, 137, 138

[238] Marta Tatu, Brandon Iles, John Slavick, Adrian Novischi, and Dan Moldovan. Cogex at
the second recognizing textual entailment challenge. In *Proceedings of the Second PASCAL
Challenges Workshop on Recognizing Textual Entailment*, 2006. 115

[239] Lucien Tesnière. *Éleménts de syntaxe structurale*. Klincksieck, Paris, France, 1959. 64

[240] Assaf Toledo, Sophia Katrenko, Stavroula Alexandropoulou, Heidi Klockmann, Asher
Stern, Ido Dagan, and Yoad Winter. Semantic annotation for textual entailment recognition. In *Mexican International Conference on Artificial Intelligence*. Springer-Verlag,
2012. To appear in Proceedings of the 11th Mexican International Conference on Artificial Intelligence, Lecture Notes in Artificial Inteligence, Springer-Verlag, 2012. DOI:
10.1007/978-3-642-37798-3_2. 121, 165

[241] Galina Tremper. Weakly supervised learning of presupposition relations between verbs.
In *Proceedings of the Association for Computational Linguistics, Student Research Workshop*,
pages 97–102, 2010. 141

[242] Tim Van de Cruys, Thierry Poibeau, and Anna Korhonen. Latent vector weighting for
word meaning in context. In *Proceedings of the Conference on Empirical Methods for Natural
Language Processing (EMNLP)*, pages 1012–1022, 2011. 150

[243] Lucy Vanderwende and William B. Dolan. What syntax can contribute in the entailment task. In Joaquin Quiñonero Candela, Ido Dagan, Bernardo Magnini, and Florence
d'Alché Buc, editors, *Machine Learning Challenges Workshop*, volume 3944 of *Lecture Notes
in Computer Science*, pages 205–216. Springer, 2006. 10

[244] Lucy Vanderwende, Arul Menezes, and Rion Snow. Syntactic contributions in the entailment task: an implementation. In *Proceedings of the Second PASCAL Challenges Workshop
on Recognizing Textual Entailment*, 2006. 165

[245] Vladimir N. Vapnik. *The Nature of Statistical Learning Theory*. Springer-Verlag, New York, 1995. DOI: 10.1007/978-1-4757-2440-0. 71

[246] Ellen M. Voorhees and Donna Harman. Overview of the seventh text retrieval conference trec-7. In *Proceedings of the Seventh Text REtrieval Conference (TREC-7*, pages 1–24, 1998. 19

[247] Rui Wang and Günter Neumann. Recognizing textual entailment using a subsequence kernel method. In *Proceedings of the National Conference on Artificial Intelligence (AAAI)*, Vancouver, Canada, 2007. 113

[248] Rui Wang and Günter Neumann. An accuracy-oriented divide-and-conquer strategy for recognizing textual entailment. In *Proceedings of the Second Text Analysis Conference (TAC 2009)*, 2009. 117

[249] Rui Wang and Yajing Zhang. Recognizing textual entailment with temporal expressions in natural language texts. In *IEEE International Workshop on Semantic Computing and Applications*, pages 109–116, Incheon, South Korea, 2008. DOI: 10.1109/IWSCA.2008.25. 117

[250] Rui Wang and Yi Zhang. Recognizing textual relatedness with predicate-argument structures. In *Proceedings of the Conference on Empirical Methods for Natural Language Processing (EMNLP)*, pages 784–792, Singapore, August 2009. Association for Computational Linguistics. 9

[251] Rui Wang, Yi Zhang, and Günter Neumann. A joint syntactic-semantic representation for recognizing textual relatedness. In *Proceedings of the Second Text Analysis Conference (TAC 2009)*, pages 133–139, 2009. 121

[252] Julie Weeds and David Weir. A general framework for distributional similarity. In *Proceedings of the Conference on Empirical Methods for Natural Language Processing (EMNLP)*, pages 81–88, 2003. DOI: 10.3115/1119355.1119366. 134

[253] Hila Weisman, Jonathan Berant, Idan Szpektor, and Ido Dagan. Learning verb entailment from diverse linguistic evidence. In *Proceedings of the Conference on Empirical Methods for Natural Language Processing (EMNLP)*, 2012. 142, 145

[254] Dominic Widdows and Scott Cederberg. Monolingual and bilingual concept visualization from corpora. In *Proceedings of the Human Language Technology Conference of the North American Chapter of the Association for Computational Linguistics (HLT-NAACL)*, 2003. DOI: 10.3115/1073427.1073443. 139

[255] Yorick Wilks, Brian M. Slator, and Louise M. Guthrie. *Electric Words: Dictionaries, Computers and Meanings*. MIT Press, 1996. 129

[256] Ichiro Yamada, Jong-Hoon Oh, Chikara Hashimoto, Kentaro Torisawa, Jun'ichi Kazama, Stijn De Saeger, and Takuya Kawada. Extending WordNet with hypernyms and siblings acquired from Wikipedia. In *Proceedings of the International Joint Conference on Natural Language Processing (IJCNLP)*, pages 874–882, Chiang Mai, Thailand, November 2011. Asian Federation of Natural Language Processing. 130

[257] Alexander Yates and Oren Etzioni. Unsupervised methods for determining object and relation synonyms on the web. *Journal of Artificial Intelligence Research*, 34:255–296, 2009. DOI: 10.1613/jair.2772. 145, 148

[258] Deniz Yuret, Aydin Han, and Zehra Turgut. Semeval-2010 task 12: Parser evaluation using textual entailments. In *Proceedings of the 5th International Workshop on Semantic Evaluation*, pages 51–56, Uppsala, Sweden, July 2010. Association for Computational Linguistics. 15

[259] Annie Zaenen, Lauri Karttunen, and Richard Crouch. Local textual inference: Can it be defined or circumscribed? In *Proceedings of the ACL Workshop on Empirical Modeling of Semantic Equivalence and Entailment*, pages 31–36, Ann Arbor, Michigan, June 2005. Association for Computational Linguistics. DOI: 10.3115/1631862.1631868. 8, 165

[260] Fabio Massimo Zanzotto and Lorenzo Dell'Arciprete. Efficient kernels for sentence pair classification. In *Proceedings of the Conference on Empirical Methods for Natural Language Processing (EMNLP)*, pages 91–100, 6-7 August 2009. 75

[261] Fabio Massimo Zanzotto, Lorenzo Dell'arciprete, and Alessandro Moschitti. Efficient graph kernels for textual entailment recognition. *Fundamenta Informaticae*, 107 (2-3):199–222, 2011. DOI: 10.3233/FI-2011-400. 75

[262] Fabio Massimo Zanzotto and Alessandro Moschitti. Automatic learning of textual entailments with cross-pair similarities. In *Proceedings the International Conference on Computational Linguistics and Annual Meeting of the Association for Computational Linguistics (COLING-ACL)*, pages 401–408. Association for Computational Linguistics, 2006. DOI: 10.3115/1220175.1220226. 43, 61, 75, 112

[263] Fabio Massimo Zanzotto and Marco Pennacchiotti. Expanding textual entailment corpora from Wikipedia using co-training. In *Proceedings of the 2nd Workshop on The People's Web Meets NLP: Collaboratively Constructed Semantic Resources*, pages 28–36, Beijing, China, August 2010. Coling 2010 Organizing Committee. 155

[264] Fabio Massimo Zanzotto, Marco Pennacchiotti, and Alessandro Moschitti. A machine learning approach to textual entailment recognition. *Natural Language Engineering*, 15-04:551–582, 2009. DOI: 10.1017/S1351324909990143. 67

[265] Fabio Massimo Zanzotto, Marco Pennacchiotti, and Maria Teresa Pazienza. Discovering asymmetric entailment relations between verbs using selectional preferences. In *Proceedings the International Conference on Computational Linguistics and Annual Meeting of the Association for Computational Linguistics (COLING-ACL)*, pages 849–856. Association for Computational Linguistics, Sydney, Australia, July 2006. DOI: 10.3115/1220175.1220282. 142

[266] Naomi Zeichner, Jonathan Berant, and Ido Dagan. Crowdsourcing inference-rule evaluation. In *Proceedings of the Annual Meeting of the Association for Computational Linguistics*, 2012. 153

[267] Shiqi Zhao, Haifeng Wang, Ting Liu, and Sheng Li. Pivot approach for extracting paraphrase patterns from bilingual corpora. In *Proceedings of the Annual Meeting of the Association for Computational Linguistics*, pages 780–788, 2008. 144

[268] Shiqi Zhao, Haifeng Wang, Ting Liu, and Sheng Li. Extracting paraphrase patterns from bilingual parallel corpora. *Natural Language Engineering*, 15(4):503–526, October 2009. DOI: 10.1017/S1351324909990155. 144

[269] Maayan Zhitomirsky-Geffet and Ido Dagan. Bootstrapping distributional feature vector quality. *Computational Linguistics*, 35(3):435–461, 2009. DOI: 10.1162/coli.08-032-R1-06-96. 126, 151

[270] Zhi Zhong and Hwee Tou Ng. It makes sense: a wide-coverage word sense disambiguation system for free text. In *Proceedings of the Association for Computational Linguistics, System Demonstrations*, ACLDemos '10, pages 78–83, Stroudsburg, PA, USA, 2010. Association for Computational Linguistics. 2

Authors' Biographies

IDO DAGAN

Ido Dagan is an Associate Professor in the Department of Computer Science at Bar-Ilan University, Israel. His interests are in applied semantic processing, focusing on the development of generic textual inference models, knowledge acquisition methods, and novel application schemes that are based on them. Dagan and colleagues defined the textual entailment recognition task and organized the series of Recognizing Textual Entailment Challenges. He was the President of the Association for Computational Linguistics (ACL) in 2010 and served on its Executive Committee during 2008-2011. In that capacity, he led the establishment of the Transactions of the Association for Computational Linguistics journal. Dagan received his B.A. summa cum laude and his Ph.D. (1992) in Computer Science from the Technion. He was a research fellow at the IBM Haifa Scientific Center (1991) and a Member of Technical Staff at AT&T Bell Laboratories (1992-1994). During 1998-2003 he was co-founder and CTO of FocusEngine and VP of Technology of LingoMotors.

DAN ROTH

Dan Roth is a Professor in the Department of Computer Science at the University of Illinois at Urbana-Champaign and the Beckman Institute of Advanced Science and Technology, and a University of Illinois Scholar. He is a fellow of AAAI, the ACL, and the ACM, for his contributions to the foundations of machine learning and inference and for developing learning centered solutions for natural language processing problems. Roth was the program chair of AAAI'11, ACL'03, and CoNLL'02 and has been on the editorial board of several journals in his research areas; he is currently the Associate Editor-in-Chief of the *Journal of Artificial Intelligence Research (JAIR)* and will serve as Editor-in-Chief for a two-year term beginning in 2015. Roth has published broadly in machine learning, natural language processing, knowledge representation, and reasoning and received several paper, teaching, and research awards. Prof. Roth got his B.A Summa cum laude in Mathematics from the Technion, Israel, and his Ph.D. in Computer Science from Harvard University in 1995.

MARK SAMMONS

Mark Sammons is a Principal Research Scientist working with the Cognitive Computation Group at the University of Illinois. His primary interests are in Natural Language Processing and Machine Learning, with a focus on Textual Entailment and Information Extraction. He has led teams that participated in research projects and shared tasks involving the design and implementation of large end-to-end NLP systems. He has given a tutorial on textual entailment at NAACL in 2010, and written chapters surveying textual entailment research in two books. Mark received his MSC in Computer Science from the University of Illinois in 2004, and his Ph.D. in Mechanical Engineering from the University of Leeds, England, in 2000.

FABIO MASSIMO ZANZOTTO

Fabio Massimo Zanzotto is an Associate Professor in the Department of Enterprise Engineering of the University of Rome "Tor Vergata." Since 1996, he has been interested in the research endeavor of Artificial Intelligence. He is active in the area of Natural Language Processing, mainly working in three areas: recognizing textual entailment, syntactic parsing for Italian, and, recently, distributed/distributional models for NLP. He is a member of ACL and of the Italian Association on Artificial Intelligence (AIIA). He chaired Brain Informatics 2012 and he reviews for the major conferences and for journals in the areas of NLP and AI.

Printed in the United States
by Baker & Taylor Publisher Services

Printed in the United States
by Baker & Taylor Publisher Services